DENBIGHSHIRE VILLAGES

Geoffrey Davies

© Geoffrey Davies, 2017

All Rights Reserved. No part of this publication may be reproduced, stored in a retrieval system, or transmitted in any form or by any means – electronic, mechanical, photocopying, recording, or otherwise – without prior written permission from the publisher or a licence permitting restricted copying issued by the Copyright Licensing Agency, 90 Tottenham Court Road, London W1P 0LA. This book may not be lent, resold, hired out or otherwise disposed of by trade in any form of binding or cover other than that in which it is published, without the prior consent of the publisher.

Moral Rights: The author has asserted his moral right to be identified as the Author of this Work.

Published by Sigma Leisure – an imprint of
Sigma Press, Stobart House, Pontyclerc, Penybanc Road, Ammanford, Carmarthenshire SA18 3HP.

British Library Cataloguing in Publication Data
A CIP record for this book is available from the British Library.

ISBN: 978-1-91075-824-3

Typesetting and Design by: Sigma Press, Ammanford.

Cover photograph: Mill at Bontuchel © Geoffrey Davies

Drawings: © Geoffrey Davies

Printed by: TJ International Ltd

Disclaimer: The information in this book is given in good faith and is believed to be correct at the time of publication. No responsibility is accepted by either the author or publisher for errors or omissions.

Contents

Introduction   5

Villages of Denbighshire   11
(in alphabetical order)

Bibliography   175

Introduction

This book is one of a series on the villages of Wales and covers the county of Denbighshire as established by the Laws in Wales Acts of 1535-42 and abolished in 1974. The new county of Denbighshire which reappeared in 1996 as a unitary authority has much altered borders. Denbighshire was one of the younger counties of Wales with Caernarvonshire, Flintshire and Merionethshire dating from the 1283 Statute of Rhuddlan.

The name Denbighshire is taken from the county town of Denbigh. The original Welsh name was *Castell Caled-Vryn yn Rhôs*, "the castle on the craggy hill in Rhôs," from the prominent situation of the castle in the ancient territory of that name. The later Welsh name of Dinbych is thought to be a corruption of Dinbach, meaning a small hill.

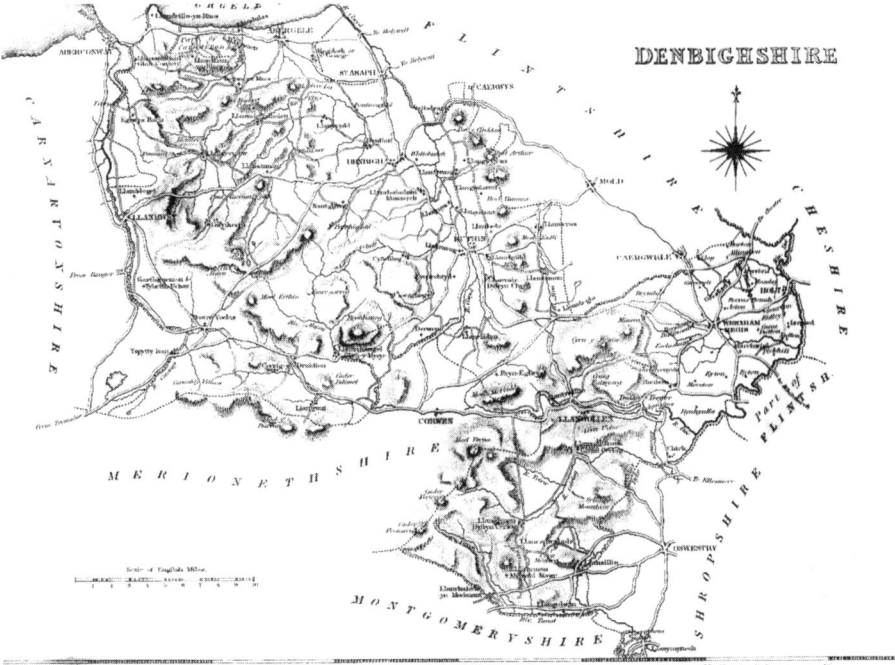

Denbighshire 1833

The population of the county is concentrated around the industrialized east and the seaside towns of the north coast. The remainder is largely rural and offers beautiful scenery admired by writers like Wordsworth and artists like Turner. There are some spectacular viaducts and aqueducts around Trevor and Chirk carrying the canals and railways across deep wide valleys, remnants of the industrial age now used for tourism.

Prior to the Roman occupation of Britain Denbighshire was the land of the Ordivices, a Celtic tribe which occupied much of the northern part of Wales, and the Deceangli who occupied the north-eastern corner and the coastal strip as far as Llandudno. According to Tacitus a rebellion by the Ordivices in the 70s resulted in Agricola wiping out the whole tribe. The Roman occupation seems to have had little physical effect on the county save for some mining activity and the roads. A branch of the Watling-street, crossed the northern parts, from the station *Varis*, at Bodvari (Caerwys), on the western confines of Flintshire, to *Conovium*, at Caerhên, near Conway, in Carnarvonshire, and the *Via Devana*, which, from the station *Deva* (Chester), passed southward within or near the eastern confines of Denbighshire towards *Nidus* (Neath), in Glamorganshire.

After the Romans left Britain in 410 we enter the era of the Celtic Saints. There was contact between the Celtic priesthoods of Wales, Cornwall, Ireland, Brittany (known as Armorica) and the area of the north-west of England and south-west of Scotland where the use of the Brythonic language continued. The Anglo-Saxon invasion of England saw the language and culture of the British confined to these areas and circa 616, at the Battle of Chester, the forces of Powys and other British kingdoms were defeated by the Northumbrians under Æthelfrith. This battle, probably fought at Bangor on Dee is thought to have cut the land links between Wales and the Brythonic tribes of the north west of England and south west Scotland. Wales was divided among a number of minor kingdoms, with Denbighshire divided between the kingdoms of Gwynedd and Powys. In the 7th century the Welsh kingdoms were concerned with the defence of their territories against the growing strength of the Kingdom of Mercia. The border was marked by King Offa of Mercia in the 8th century by Offa's Dyke which was built with a ditch on the Welsh side. The dating of the dyke is now disputed.

Another dyke, Wat's Dyke runs almost parallel to Offa's for 40 miles in North Wales. Both dykes pass through the old county of Denbighshire. Around 890 the remaining Britons of the Strachclyde region, an area stretching from

Lancaster to the Clyde, applied to the King Anarawd of Gwynedd for asylum from the Scots, Danes and Saxons. He acceded to the request on condition that they seize land from the Anglo Saxons and this they did, taking back lands between the Dee and Conway, establishing themselves in the areas of Flintshire and Denbighshire which was named Strath Clwyd.

For a brief period in the 9th century Wales was united under a King, Rhodri the Great, and again in the 10th century Wales was united under King Hywel, known as Hywel Dda (Hywel the Good) but by the time of the Norman Conquest the country was once more divided. The Welsh used the system of gavelkind or cyfran whereby property was divided among all the male issue, legitimate and illegitimate in equal shres. This led to the breakup of estates and numerous minor wars.

After initiual gains in North and South Wales the Normans were forced on to the defensive after concerted Welsh attacks across Wales in 1094. In 1157 Henry II led an army against Owain Gwynedd but Welsh rule continued while recognising the sovereignty of the English crown until the reign of Edward I. He established the castles in the north-west while granting the lordships of Holt, Chirk and Denbigh to John, Earl Warren, Roger Mortimer and Henry Lacy Earl of Lincoln respectively. Edward I granted the Lordship of Ruthin to Reginald Grey. Wales had traditionally been a rural society and the towns that grew up to support the castle garrisons were predominantly English, as shown in the charter for Holt where the officials of the borough could not be Welsh. However the Welsh language survived as the predominant tongue in the county until the influx of workers in the 19th century to the mining and iron, steel and chemical industries and later the emergence of the North Wales coast as a holiday and retirement destination for north-west England.

In 1400 the Welsh nobleman Owain Glyndŵr who had castles at Sycharth near Llansilin in Denbighshire and Glyndyfrdwy near Carrog in Merionethshire led a rebellion against Henry IV. Glyndŵr had trained as a lawyer and served in the English army and was married to the daughter of the prominent English lawyer, Sir David Hanmer. At first successful, the revolt petered out and Glyndŵr disappeared, apparently without trace.

The county of Denbighshire created under Henry VIII stretched from the River Conway in the west to Flintshire, Cheshire and Shropshire in the east and from the north coast to the counties of Merionethshire and Montgomeryshire in the south. The boundaries were not straightforward however with a small enclave of Caernarvonshire containing Colwyn Bay surrounded by Denbighshire and Llandudno, although east of the Conway estuary also in Caernarvonshire. In the east the area around Wrexham, Gresford and Holt separated two parts of Flintshire and also contained a small enclave of that county to the south-east of Marford.

The English Civil War saw leading families take opposite sides. Sir Thomas Myddelton took Parliament's side while the majority of the county sided with the King who stayed at Chirk Castle before the Battle of Rowton Moor in 1645, the castle having been taken for the King in 1643. After the battle Charles I retreated to Denbigh Castle and stayed again at Chirk before his return to England. By 1647 the last Royalist castles had fallen. In 1659 Sir Thomas Myddelton declared himself in favour of the restoration of the monarchy and Chirk Castle was taken by Cromwellian troops under Colonel Lambert, to be restored in 1660.

The county was rich in minerals with lead, iron ore, coal, limestone and clay deposits in the east giving rise to the industrialization of that part of the county in the 18th and 19th centuries. As old industries died out, Wrexham has become the centre for new industries.

The non-conformist movement was strong in the county and industrialization saw a marked increase in the number and size of chapels. The last 50 years have seen a marked decline in church and chapel attendance with the resulting closure of many chapels and churches.

Village shops and pubs have also suffered with increased car ownership allowing visits to supermarkets and changes in social habits. There are a small number of community run village shops and pubs in the county and while some pubs are re-opening the trend is for closure.

Many of the county families traced their ancestry to the Welsh princes and incomers like the Thelwalls and Myddletons married into prominent Welsh families. These families played an important role in the history of Denbighshire and in the life of the community, standing for Parliament or acting as High Sheriff. In the 19th century industrialists like Robertson, Beyer and Graesser established country seats as did a number of former Liverpool slave traders and their families, all adding to the cultural life of the county

Genealogy has always been strong in Wales. It has on occasion been ridiculed with some family trees being produced claiming direct descent from Adam. Nicholls gives the reason for this concentration on pedigree:

"A person past the ninth descent formed a new Pen Cenedyl, or head of a family. Every family was represented by its elder, and these elders from every family were delegated to the national council. Hence the appointment of public officials called anvydd-feirdd, "heraldic bards," whose duty it was to register arms and pedigrees. In later times the great houses had their family bards and genealogists, who on occasions of state and ceremonial recited the descent of the lord of the house, attended at births, marriages, &c., of persons of rank, to record the facts. A "gentleman" among the Welsh was called gwr bonheddig, "a man with ancestors", or with a pedigree, i. e., a man whose ancestry was duly recorded and of legal effect. On the death of a proprietor, the family bard pronounced his eulogium, detailing his honourable descent and worthy actions, and this document, duly registered, after a month from the day of the funeral was brought out and read before the assembled relations in the great hall of the mansion, who by their acquiescence in its accuracy gave it the requisite authority for preservation among the family archives."

It is worth pointing out the trend to the adoption of anglicized surnames by Welsh families. It had long been the tradition for the Welsh to be identified through their father's Christian name. Sion ap Rhys was Sion son of Rhys. In the 15th and 16th centuries the English system of surnames was adopted and for example ap Rhys became Price or Pryse or Rice, ap Sion became Jones and so on. The spelling of names also varied. For example the Salusbury name was variously spelt Salusbury, Salesbury, Salesberie and Salsbury.

Villages and hamlets covered are listed in alphabetical order with a location, a brief description, a note of important buildings and a history of industry and prominent people and families. A translation of Welsh placenames is given. Llan is translated as church, though strictly it refers to the circular site in which the church was situated. A brief description of Welsh saints associated with a church is given. Where old texts are quoted the original spelling is used.

Villages of the Denbighshire

Aberwheeler Welsh: Aberchwiler

Aberwheeler is a scattered community with the main population centre at Waen Aberwheeler, some three miles north-east of Denbigh near the confluence of the Rivers Wheeler and Clwyd.

Waen Welsh Calvinistic Methodist Chapel was built in 1822 and rebuilt in 1862. There was also the Oak Inn on the crossroads. There has been new building with bungalows on Bro Leweni. A quarter of a mile north-west of Waen is Geinas with its restored corn mill and leat running along side the River Wheeler. A mile and a half upstream is the Grade II* Listed Candy Mill, established in the late 18th or early 19th century. It contains a corn mill and what is thought to be the last surviving example of a clover mill in Wales. The mill was in operation until 1950 and the machinery remains intact with an undershot wheel with Anglesey mill stones for wheat and French stones for oats. The clover mill was used to collect and clean clover seed, using a form of threshing machine formed by a vertical wheel set with a series of spokes and beaters. The mill was fed by a 440 yard leat from the river and the mill had a house and stables attached. Adjacent to the mill is the old bakehouse and a set of three pigsties.

Aberwheeler House is thought to be late medieval in origin with a substantial 17th century north-south range. In the garden is a set of bee boles, holes set in the wall to act as beehives.

Castell Calvinistic Methodist Chapel was built in 1882 a mile south-east of Waen Aberwheeler. It closed in 1963 and is now a private dwelling.

On the hills east of the village are a number of cairns some dating from the Bronze Age but others formed from stone clearances in the 20th century. On Moel y parc there is evidence of an abandoned medieval farm with a longhouse and field system.

Acrefair Mary's Acres

Acrefair lies on the A539 midway between Wrexham and Llangollen. The oldest part of the village lies on Bethania Road near its junction with Chapel Street, though very few of the oldest buildings remain.

In 1817 Edward Lloyd Rowland established an ironworks at Acrefair on land to the north-east of Chapel Street. Following Rowland's bankruptcy in 1825 the works were taken over by British Iron Company, later the New British Iron Company which continued to operate until closure in 1887. George Borrow on his journey through the area gave the following description of the New British Iron Company works:

"the light of the Cefn furnaces before me which cast their red glow upon my path. I debauched upon the Llangollen road near to the tramway leading to the collieries. Two enormous sheets of flame shot up high into the air from ovens, illumining two spectral chimneys as high as steeples, also smoky buildings, and grimy figures moving about. There was a clanging of engines, a noise of shovels and a falling of coals truly horrible. The glare was so great that I could distinctly see the minutest lines upon my hand. Advancing along the tramway I obtained a nearer view of the hellish buildings, the chimneys, and the demoniac figures. It was just such a scene as one of those described by Ellis Wynn in his Vision of Hell. Feeling my eyes scorching I turned away, and proceeded towards Llangollen, sometimes on the muddy road, sometimes on the dangerous causeway."

Part of the site south of Llangollen Road was operated by Air Products until closure in 2009. Coal and clay were extracted in the area around Acrefair. The Penbedw Fireclay Works on Bowers Lane, manufacturing bricks, sanitary pipes and chimney pots from its seven kilns, was in operation in 1840. All trace of the works was wiped out by opencast mining. The Acre Brickworks operated between 1852 and 1868 on a site near Acre House. Established by Edwards and Williams the site included Brickworks Terrace but all had been demolished by 1874. The Delph Brick and Tile Works were located north of Bethania Road. Founded in 1860 the works produced salt-glazed sewage and drainpipes from up to ten kilns. The works eventually closed in 1966 and were then demolished. The Tref-y-nant brickworks to the west produced firebricks, chimney pots and ornamental terracotta goods. It was one of four local works owned by James Coster Edwards who purchased Tref-y-nant in the 1860s. They operated from 1852 to 1958 with up to 29 kilns. The works have been demolished and the area is now woodland save for the brick gate piers of the office entrance. Limekilns at Tref-y-nant were in operation from the 1830s until the end of the 19th century.

The village had a station on the main Wrexham to Barmouth rail line which closed to passengers in 1965. There was also a branch line connecting with the canal terminus at Trevor.

St Paul's, a chapel of ease to Rhosymedre had been established by 1874. It was rebuilt in 1894 and enlarged in 1908. Situated on King Street opposite the junction with Station Road it was a small church with a bellcote over the chancel arch. Sadly the church has been demolished.

Trinity English Presbyterian Chapel on Llangollen Road was built in 1840 and rebuilt in 1864 and 1880. A hall and vestry, which are now used as a bedroom sales store, were added in 1910. The chapel designed by Richard Owen of Liverpool is no longer in use. Acrefair Wesleyan Methodist Chapel, also on Llangollen Road, was built in 1887 and rebuilt in 1898. The chapel closed in 1975 and is now a kitchen and bedroom furniture showroom. Bethel Welsh Calvinistic Methodist Chapel off Chapel Street was built in 1840, rebuilt in 1864 and 1880. It has now been converted to residential use. Salem Welsh Wesleyan Methodist Chapel on Bethania Road was built in 1899 and closed in 1978. Salem became a Roman Catholic Church for a time before being converted for residential use. Bethania Welsh Baptist Chapel was built in 1895 in the Vernacular style. Bethania gave its name to the road which had previously been known as Black Lion Road.

A Board School was built in 1877 but demolished when Acrefair Primary School was built on the site in 1934. Tref-y-nant Park adjacent to the school was the site of Tref-y-nant Colliery which was shown as an old shaft in 1874.

Acrefair has a number of pubs including the Duke of Wellington, Eagles Inn, Oddfellows Arms and the Hampden Arms. There has been a large amount of building but the few amenities include a newsagent, petrol station, post office, a chemist and two Chinese takeaway restaurants. The Plas Madoc estate north-east of the village has a leisure centre.

Berse Drelincourt (see Caego)

Bersham Welsh: Y Bers
The quiet, rural village of Bersham, a mile and a half south-west of Wrexham on the River Clywedog hides its past as a centre of the industrial revolution.

The name derives from the Anglo Saxon, "Bers" being a personal name and "ham" denoting a settlement or manor.

According to Alfred Neobard Palmer in his article *John Wilkinson and the Old Bersham Iron Works*, 1899 Berse or Bersham *"is a large township which stretches westward from the borough of Wrexham, between the rivers Gwenfro and Clywedog, to the mountain township of Minera or Mwnglawdd. It is bounded on the north by Broughton-in-Bromfield and Brymbo, and on the south by Esclusham Above, Esclusham Below, and Erddig – all, but the last-named, townships in the old parish of Wrexham. The name "Bersham" was formerly applied to the township only, and not to the village now so-called."*

Iron was produced in the area from the mid 17th century and around 1717 Charles Lloyd of Dolobran operated a blast furnace at Bersham on a site just west of the A483. In 1721 it became the first furnace in Wales to use coke. In the 1750s it was leased by Isaac Wilkinson and later operated by his sons John and William as the New Bersham Company. John Wilkinson patented a machine for the precision boring of cannon and the works became a major producer of cannon for the American War of Independence and the Napoleonic wars. John also patented a machine for boring out the cylinders of the Boulton and Watt steam engines. The works were partially destroyed in 1795 following a dispute between the Wilkinson brothers, though John had already started new ironworks at Brymbo. The works continued to operate until their sale in 1812. Bersham Mill was originally built as a foundry but in 1828 was converted into a corn mill and continued in operation until 1947. It is now the site of the Bersham Iron Works Museum which contains a number of interesting artefacts including part of a wooden railway. The octagonal building nearby dates from 1775 and was used for the manufacture of cannon with four furnaces and chimney stacks. The site was excavated 1987-91 and foundations of other furnaces and buildings on the site exposed.

Huw Davies had established a forge at Groes Foel in the 17th century and was renowned for the quality of his wrought ironwork, among which are handrail of exquisite design in the choir of Wrexham church and a small gate in Malpas churchyard. Huw died in 1702 and his trade was carried on by his sons John and Robert. Among other works they produced the gates at Chirk Castle, Eaton Hall and Erddig. Perhaps their finest work are the White Gates at Leeswood Hall in Flintshire which have been praised as being the finest of their type in Britain. Nicholas Pevsner described their work as miraculous.

After the demise of the iron industry paper mills were built, harnessing the local water power. Esclusham Mill was built in 1801 to the east of the village by Edward Bozeley who also built and resided at Laurel Grove. Esclusham had a reputation for high quality paper. Bersham Paper Mill was built on the site of the old East Ironworks. It was sold to Thomas Fitzhugh in 1829 and after being used for a number of purposes it was demolished in 1869 and redeveloped to build Bersham Boys National School in 1876. East of the A483, the old school has been converted into a heritage centre.

A plaque over the doorway of St Mary's Church records "This chapel was built by T.L. Fitzhugh for the use of his household and dependants. It was opened for divine service on the 6th January 1876 and it was consecrated with the vault as a private chapel by the Bishop of Saint Asaph on the 13th October 1883". The architect was John Gibson of Warwickshire. The upper stage of the tower was added in 1892-3 and following the death of Captain Godfrey FitzHugh on active service in Palestine in 1917 his widow Ethel had the bells installed in his memory. They consist of a carillon of eight bells operated by hand. The church is cruciform with north and south transepts and an apsed chancel. The tower is situated to the north-west, forming the entrance porch. It is topped by a short spire with pinnacles at each corner.

Plas Power Park lies to the west of the village. In the 15th century the estate was owned by Robert Bellot. The Bellot or Billott family were prominent in the Wrexham area in the 15th and 16th centuries. Hugh Billott or Bellot, D.D. was Bishop of Bangor in 1585, translated to Chester in 1595 and was buried in the chancel of Wrexham Church. In the 17th century the Power family inherited the estate and named it Plas Power. The estate was sold to William Fownes of Dublin in 1702-1704 for £1,800 and in 1732 Mary Myddleton of Croes Newydd, daughter of Sir Richard Myddleton, 3rd Baronet, of Chirk Castle, purchased the estate from the Fownes family. William Lloyd, son of the Rev. Thomas Lloyd, Mary Myddleton's chaplain, inherited the estate when she died in 1747. Under the ownership of William Lloyd the old house was demolished and replaced by a red brick square Georgian mansion. Lloyd also constructed the wall around the park which still stands. William died in 1793 and was succeeded by his second son, also William, who died without issue in 1816. The estate then passed to William's nephew, Thomas FitzHugh, son of Thomas FitzHugh of Portland Place, Marylebone, London, and Mary Fitzhugh, the sister of William Lloyd (junior). Their son Thomas Lloyd Fitzhugh enlarged and remodelled the house under the direction of the architect John Gibson in 1858.

The house was demolished after 1945 and Plas Power Park is now operated as an adventure centre. It remains in the Fitzhugh family.

The village retains much of the character of an estate village and is a conservation area. It is enhanced by the river with its numerous bridges and weirs set in the wooded valley.

Robert Waithman, the son of a joiner at Bersham Ironworks born in 1764 worked at a London linen drapers shop until acquiring his own drapery business on Fleet Street in 1786. He made a fortune and entered politics. Described as "An energetic and combative man, he was proud, touchy, honest and brave, but often self-righteous and tiresome". He was elected to Parliament for the City of London in 1818-20 and from 1826 until his death in 1833. He served as High Sheriff of London and Middlesex in 1820 and Lord Mayor of London in 1823.

Betws yn Rhos

Three and a half miles south-west of Abergele, Betws yn Rhos is an attractive village in a small valley. The centre of the village is a conservation area. It was recorded as Ecclesia de Bettws in the Lincoln *Taxatio* of 1291. The name Betws is thought to derive from the Anglo Saxon *Bedehus*, a form of almshouse built to accommodate travellers to an abbey. Yn Rhos signifies that it was built on a meadow. Over the centuries it has also been known as Bettws Abegele and Bettws Wyrion Wgan. The latter translates as the grandchildren of Gwgan though there is some disagreement as to the identity of Gwgan with some believing he was involved in the Battle of Chester in 610 while others identify him as Gwgan Gleddyfrudd a 9th century leader in Ceredigion.

The striking twin towered church of St Michael was rebuilt in 1838-9 by John Welch of Overton. This is a small church but retains its western gallery. The chancel is very short with 19th century Commandment boards in Welsh and the east windows of 1844 depicting scenes from the Passion in memory of the Wynnes of Coed Coch (see Dolwen). The furnishings are Victorian though there is a 1790 tablet to Gabriel Lloyd of Peniarth, relocated from the old church. The nave has five lancet windows on each side and the exterior has been limewashed. Entrance is through the base of the tower on the south side. The tower contains a clock of 1877 by Joyce of Whitchurch. Above the oblong base of the tower rise a pair of octagonal towers with the bellcote between them. The towers are topped by cemented spires with ball finials. The shape of the original raised circular churchyard is evident from the road. There are Grade II Listed tombs of the Foulkes and Wynne families.

Hyfrydle Welsh Calvinistic Methodist Chapel on Ffordd Abergele was built in 1819 as Sion and rebuilt in 1857 and again in 1898, to the design of architect Thomas Parry of Colwyn Bay, in the Romanesque style. It is still in use. Salem Wesleyan Methodist Chapel dates from 1825. Seion Welsh Independent Chapel at Trefonnen west of the village was built in 1872, to the design of architect J.W. Vaughan of Colwyn Bay. It closed in the 1980s and has now been converted for domestic use.

Opposite the church is The Wheatsheaf Inn. The Bee Hive Inn which was opposite the village store has closed. The village school was built in 1861 as a National School. There is a small industrial estate as well as playing fields and the Silver Birch Golf Club with its two nine hole courses.

Set in two acres of garden Ffarm is today run as a country house hotel offering bed and breakfast and dining as well as acting as a wedding and function venue. The house, built in a castellated style, dates from 1706 but was enlarged in the early 19th century by John Oldfield, a solicitor and Deputy Lieutenant of the county. The house was further remodelled in what has been described as Venetian Gothic style in 1881 by the architects Richard Lloyd Williams and Martin Underwood.

Bontuchel High Bridge

Bontuchel is an attractive small hamlet standing on the Afon Clywedog at its confluence with the Nant Melin Dwr, two and a half miles west of Ruthin. Below the 18th century bridge is the substantial mid 19th century saw mill which operated until 1912 but is now a private dwelling. Bridge House was formerly the Bridge Inn. Bontuchel Welsh Calvinistic Methodist Chapel was built in 1771 and rebuilt in 1896. It stands above Pont Uchel Bach which crosses the Nant Melin Dwr. (The Ordnance Survey map shows the village as Bontuchel but the bridges as Pont Uchel and Pont Uchel Bach.)

Bradley

Bradley lies two and a half miles north-west of Wrexham. The name derives from Old English meaning "broad wood" Until the 20th century the tiny hamlet of Bradley was located half a mile north of the modern village on the other side of the River Alun. The first houses in the modern village were on the eastern side of Barretts Hill. The major development occurred between the wars with the council estate. New private estates have been developed to the south and east with a small development replacing the Queens Head pub.

There is a Chinese takeaway, village shop and village hall. The Bradley English Congregational chapel on Glan Llyn Road has been replaced by housing.

There were a number of mills on the River Alun. Bradley Mill was a corn mill just north of the village. Operating from the 16th century it had two undershot wooden wheels powered by a leat running from a weir to the north. It was in operation until after World War II but was gutted by fire in 1966. Downstream there was a wire mill and fulling mill but both had ceased functioning by 1870.

To the east of the village the River Alun makes a 'U' turn as it skirts Bryn Alun with its hillfort. The river provided defence on the west while there is a line of three banks and a ditch to the north and double ramparts guarded the east.

Bradley was the childhood home of Welsh footballer Robbie Savage.

Brymbo

Brymbo is a former industrial village three and a half miles north-west of Wrexham. The village was known as Brinbaw in 1339, translated as Hill of Dirt. Offa's Dyke passes to the west of the village.

Thomas, Earl of Arundel granted a charter to the villagers of Holt to dig for coal and turf here in 1410. Brymbo was best known for its iron and steel works, active between 1796 and 1990. In 1792 John Wilkinson purchased Brymbo Hall Estate where the land was rich in coal and ironstone. John Wilkinson was the son of Isaac Wilkinson, a Cumbrian Iron Master who in 1753 had taken a lease on the Bersham furnace. John, born in 1728 had by this time acquired interests in iron making plants in the Midlands. Isaac's business failed in 1761 and John took control of the New Bersham Company, producing munitions and, between 1775 and 1795, the cylinders for Boulton and Watt steam engines. By 1796 he had built blast furnaces at Brymbo and was extracting coal. As well as his industrial interests he farmed at Brymbo, using the first steam threshing machine in North Wales. On his death in 1808 his fortune was dissipated by disputes between the children of his mistress and his nephew Thomas Jones (Wilkinson). The works closed to be reopened in 1841 by Robert Roy, one of Wilkinson's trustees, to be taken on in 1842 by Henry Robertson who appointed William Henry and Charles Edward Darby, grandsons of Abraham Darby of Coalbrookdale to help develop the works. In 1854 Robertson acquired Roy's interest in Brymbo and the plant developed rapidly. The Darbys died in 1882 and 1884 and the business became the Brymbo Steel Company Ltd. Robertson appointed John Henry Darby and Peter Williams to run the works and persuaded them to develop the first open hearth process for steel making in Britain. The works went into liquidation in 1931 to be saved by Robertson's son Sir Henry Beyer Robertson. The new company supplied the steel for Rolls Royce aero engines and in 1946 became part of Guest Keen and Nettlefolds.

The works saw a major expansion with new electric furnaces and in 1970 a new rolling mill. Nationalized in 1967 the automated blast furnace was taken out of production in 1978, switching to producing steel from scrap metal. Steel production ended in 1990 with the loss of 1,100 jobs. The site is now being developed for housing. There were a number of coal mines associated with the iron and steel works, including the Bye pit on the site and the Smelt Colliery established by John Wilkinson around 1790. The Bye pit was opened in 1842 and employed up to 185 men before its closure in 1914. Smelt Colliery was to the west of Brymbo but much smaller employing fewer than 30 men and in later years produced only clay for the Cae-llo brickworks which closed in 1975. Smelt closed in 1967.

Wilkinson also established a lead smelting works to the west of the village, between Brymbo Pool and Minera Road. It continued in production from 1792 to 1880 though in later years was used for carbon production. The only remnant is the 18ft Bottle Chimney. Originally reaching a height of 100ft it was partially demolished in 1962 but is now Grae II Listed, being the only example of this type of structure in Wales. South-west of the lead smelting works was Pentre Saeson Foundry, established by Wilkinson around 1792 and in operation until 1981. The foundry building and chimney remain and are visble from Brymbo Road to the west of Minera Road. To the north was another colliery while to the east of Minera Road on Brymbo Road is the Penrhos Engine House. Again built by Wilkinson this is thought to be the oldest surviving colliery beam engine house in Wales. It was designed to house a Hornblower double cylinder engine to pump water from the coal mine. The building was converted into a three storey cottage in the 1820s but later abandoned. The site is open to the public. Other works in the village included a phosphate works and the Cambrian Safety Fuse Works.

The original church in Brymbo was built in 1837 on a site opposite the Coop Pharmacy on High Street. By 1869 it was structurally unstable and a new church, St Mary's, was built to the north of the village. A Welsh language church was built on the original site and opened as St John's in 1892. It was demolished in the 1970s though the outline can be seen in the Garden of Remembrance which contains the village war memorial. St Mary's church was designed by Thomas Henry Wyatt who donated the central window in the chancel. The foundation stone was laid by the Marquis of Westminster in 1871 and the church was consecrated on 10th September 1782. Its building was in large part funded by the Marquis of Westminster, Robert Roy and Henry Robertson of the Brymbo Iron Works, the Westminster Company, and the Great Western Railway Company. The church is cruciform in shape with an apsed chancel. There is a double sanctus bellcote. Apart from the nave seating which is contemporary with the building, the fittings including a fine chancel screen date from 1916. The panelled and glazed entrance doors were installed in 1950 and were originally designed by Alfred Waterhouse for Eaton Hall.

Tabernacl Welsh Baptist Chapel opposite the site of St John's church was built in 1817, rebuilt in 1847-8 to the design of Samuel Jones of Brymbo, enlarged in 1850, and rebuilt once more in 1865. The main door has been blocked and the chapel has been converted to residential accommodation known as Valley View. Engedi Welsh Calvinistic Methodist Chapel on the High Street was built in 1820, and rebuilt in 1840, 1861 and 1895. It is no longer in use. The first Brymbo English Wesleyan Methodist Chapel was built in 1804, rebuilt in 1837 and 1864, on a site on Mount Hill. In 1892 the present red brick chapel was built on High Street, adjacent to Engedi to the design of architect William Lloyd Jones of Bangor. Another Welsh Wesleyan Methodist Chapel, Bethel was built on New Road in 1890 but closed in 1972 and later demolished. Bryn Seion Welsh Independent Chapel on Clayton Road was established in 1802 when it was converted from a house. A formal chapel was built in 1840 and rebuilt in 1851 and 1860. It closed in 1968 but is Grade II Listed as a good example of a neo Classical chapel enjoying a prominent hilltop position. The interior has been gutted by fire.

A church school was established alongside St John's Church but the village school is now the St Mary's Voluntary Aided Church in Wales Primary School off Ael-y-bryn.

The village was served by a number of railway lines including the Wrexham and Minera Railway branch of the Great Western Railway and the Vron branch of the Grand Central Railway but all the lines have now been removed.

Only the George and Dragon is left of the public houses in Brymbo, the Mount and the Miners' Arms having been demolished and closed. There is a Premier Store and the pharmacy and a number of small industrial units. The Enterprise Centre acts as a community centre with a business centre, conference suite, gym and nursery. There has been new housing in the village which now acts as a residential area for commuters.

Bryneglwys Church Hill

Bryneglwys is a rural village five miles north-west of Llangollen. The signs for the village start on the A5104 but the main part of Bryneglwys lies to the south.

The church is dedicated to St Tysilio, a cousin of St Asaph and son of Brochwel Ysgythrog (of the Tusks), the reigning prince of Old Powys who resided at Shrewsbury. Tysilio, also known as Suliau became Abbot of Meifod but was forced to flee to Brittany in the early 7th century where he founded St Suliac. He died there circa 650.

The present church dates from the 15th century with a restoration in 1570 following the building of the Yale Chapel, beneath which is the Yale family vault. The Yale or in Welsh Iâl family lived at Plas yn Iâl. There were perpetual curates until 1870 when the first vicar, the Revd Richard Owen employed the Kensington architect Arthur Baker to restore the church. A font donated by the Yale family was installed for the first time and new pews and choirstalls replaced. The west gallery was removed at this time. The east window depicting Faith Hope and Charity was donated in memory of Revd and Mrs J.P. Jones-Parry. The pulpit dates from the 17th century. The Yale chapel contains memorials to members of the family and is now home to the 14th century coffin slab of Tagwystyl, daughter of Ieuaf ap Mareded, inscribed in Lombardic letters. The nave and chancel are of equal width with steps leading up to the chancel. There is a south porch and western bellcote with a single bell recast in 1735.

Plas yn Iâl lies two miles to the east of the village, north of the A5104. It was the family home of the Yale family from the 15th to the mid 20th century. The best known member of the family was Elihu Yale who was born in the Newhaven colony in America where his father's stepfather was governor. Elihu worked for the East India Company and rose to become Governor of Fort St George, Madras from 1687 to 1692. He amassed a fortune largely through unofficial deals with Indian merchants and returning to Wales he lived at Plas Grono near Wrexham. In 1718 Yale sent 417 books, a portrait of King George, and nine bales of goods (value £800) to Cotton Mather to help with the building of the Collegiate School of Connecticut. In recognition the new building was named after its benefactor and eventually became Yale College. Plas yn Iâl was enlarged and remodelled in the 19th century and part is now available for self catering accommodation.

Seion Welsh Calvinistic Methodist Chapel stands to the west of the school. It was built in 1818, rebuilt in 1854 and 1874. Ebenezer Wesleyan Methodist Chapel on the A5104 was built in 1824 and rebuilt in 1887. It is no longer used as a chapel and converted to residential use. The old school with house attached has a rounded gable end. It was founded in 1714 with a rent charge of £6 per annum by Mrs Margaret Lloyd for a charity to teach the poorest children of Bryneglwys. Originally there were apsidal ends north and south, but two cottages were built, one for the schoolmaster and the other to provide an income adjoining the schoolroom. It remained in use as a school until 1873 when the National School opened.

On Llantysilio Mountain a mile and a half south-east of the village is the Iron Age Moel y Gaer hillfort. Defined by a single rampart up to 10 feet high it encloses an area of 1.1 hectares.

North of the church at Pont Bryneglwys was Melin y Llan corn mill which was powered by the Afon Morwynion. The mill buildings have been converted to residential use.

The village which once had two pubs, the New Inn and the Wild Boar has seen a fair amount of modern building and retains its school.

Brynteg Fair Hill

Situated some two miles north-west of Wrexham, Brynteg developed in the final years of the 19th century with the quarries and collieries of the Moss Valley. In 1873 there were just a few farms and Broughton Hall. Today Brynteg forms part of the built up area stretching from Caego and New Broughton in the south to Pentre Broughton in the north.

The church of St Peter was established in 1894 as a mission church, largely at the instigation of Revd Meredith Hamer, the former curate at Berse Drelincourt. The church was extended in 1916 with new furnishings of an exceptional quality by Cecil Hare, donated by Revd Hamer's widow Margaret. In 1918 it became a chapel of ease to St Paul's, Pentre Broughton. Sited on Church Road it is a dark stone faced building with chancel, north porch, western bellcote and two vestries. The interior fittings are the reason for its Grade II Listing which include an elaborate font and the chancel screen with the pulpit forming an integral part.

Zion Primitive Methodist chapel was built in 1892 with a Sunday School on the opposite side of Church Road facing Daisy Road. Both buildings have been converted for residential use. Bethesda Independent Chapel on Victoria Road was built in 1878 but was demolished in the 1990s for a housing development.

Broughton Hall is now a residential care home. The present building dates from around 1700 though there was a house on the site in 1661.

Today there are some local stores and the Brynteg Inn. Roberts Bakery gave its name to Roberts Road and Bakery Fields but the bakery has long gone. The modern Brynteg Memorial Centre combines a hall, library, training centre and crèche. There has been new housing but the late 19th century dark stone terraces of cottages interspersed with Victorian villas in narrow streets make this a popular commuting village.

Bryn y Maen Stone Hill

Two miles south of Colwyn Bay on Llanrwst Road is Bryn y Maen which until 1895 was a tiny hamlet consisting of a few farms and cottages. In 1895 Mrs Eleanor Frost commissioned the architects Douglas and Fordham to build a church at Bryn y Maen in memory of her husband Charles and a new house for her occupation. Eleanor had been born in Bryn y Maen but had married into the wealthy Frost family and lived at Min-y-don, Old Colwyn.

Christ Church, also called the Cathedral of the Hills, has a substantial crossing tower though the transepts are small as is the chancel. There is a broad nave with a narrow south aisle. The roof has ornate carvings. The church and furnishings are of a single period and Christ Church is Grade II* Listed. The exterior is dressed in Helsby sandstone with a green slate roof. The vicarage opposite the church was also designed by Douglas and Fordham and financed by Mrs Frost. Her house was Bryn Eglwys, standing on the cross roads to the north of the church. Built in the Elizabethan style, like the Vicarage it is Grade II Listed.

Bryn y Maen Farm stands to the south of the church.

Burton

The hamlet of Burton lies to the west of Rossett beyond the Wrexham by-pass and the railway. Station Road Rossett is now blocked and a footpath runs beneath the by-pass to Burton. The hamlet was not named on the 1873 Ordnance Survey map when there were just a few large houses and farms. It takes its name from Burton Hall, a house dating from 1632 although the site is known to have been occupied prior to that date with evidence of a moat. The name Burton derives from the Old English *Burh Tun* meaning a fortified house.

Burton Hall has been modified externally but retains some fine original 17th century features internally. Ball's Hall was built in 1650 for Captain Thomas Ball who married into the Santhey family, owners of Burton Hall. Captain Ball was High Sheriff of Denbighshire in 1651.

Burton English Presbyterian Chapel towards the north-western end of Burton Hall Road was built in 1830 but closed in 1918 and has been converted into residential accommodation. There was a Primitive Methodist Chapel in the small hamlet of Golley, north-west of Burton Green, but it too has closed and is now a private dwelling. Nearby on Cobblers Lane the house was originally a National School. Finds at East View Farm suggest that there was a Roman settlement there while in 2004 three metal detector enthusiasts discovered the Burton Hoard consisting of 14 artefacts of gold, bronze and ancient pottery believed to date from between 1300-1100 BC and now held at the National Museum of Wales.

Like Burton, Burton Green is a relatively modern development but to the east is the 17th century timber framed Golden Grove Inn, claimed to have been an inn on the site since the 13th century.

Housing at Burton is on three developments, separated by fields. There is a farm shop but no other amenities. Burton Green consists of a few cottages and four bungalows.

Bwlchgwyn White Pass

Five miles north-west of Wrexham, Bwlchgwyn ranks as one of the highest villages in Wales at an altitude of 1,090 feet above sea level. Two explanations are given for the name of White Pass. The local limestone is white but alternatively snow settles here ahead of the surrounding area.

Bwlchgwyn was the site of a Bronze Age settlement, since destroyed by quarrying, while half a mile to the north-east was a Roman mining settlement.

In the 19th century lead mining and quarrying saw an increase in population and the village grew with a National School established in 1867 in a combined school and chapel of ease on Brymbo Road. It was later extended with the addition of a chancel, vestry and porch and converted into Christ Church. The date above the porch is 1877 but the consecration took place on 1st October 1879. A Sunday School was built across the road. A council school was established in 1875 on Stryt Maelor but has now been demolished and replaced by housing.

Salem Welsh Calvinistic Methodist Chapel on Brymbo Road was built in 1868, rebuilt in 1879 and demolished during the 1980s though the foundations, surrounding wall and graveyard remain. The new primary school is opposite. Nebo Welsh Independent Chapel at the junction of Neboh with the A525 was built in 1852 and rebuilt in 1866 but has now been converted to a private dwelling. Bethesda Wesleyan Methodist Chapel on Ruthin Road was built in 1859 possibly to the west of the present graveyard, rebuilt in 1866 and again in 1876. A Sunday School was erected in 1896 and a manse in 1910. Bethesda closed during the 1980s and has been demolished. Peniel Welsh Calvinistic Methodist Chapel on Old Road was built in 1823 and rebuilt in 1831 and 1862. The chapel has closed and shows signs of vandalism.

The King's Head pub in the centre of the village is community run while at Four Crosses on Old Road is the Moors Inn, previously known as the Four Crosses. The Westminster Arms, Joiners' Arms, Red Lion, Hwntw Arms, The Gors, Mount Pleasant, Dog and Partridge, Travellers, Gegin, Hand and Three Jolly Miners have all closed. There is a community centre with tennis courts and open space to the south-west on old quarry sites. There has been new building taking advantage of the views of the surrounding countryside.

Bylchau Gaps

Five miles west of Denbigh at the junction of the A543 and A544 lies the tiny hamlet of Bylchau. The church district of Bylchau was created from the parishes of Henllan and Llansannan by an Order in Council in 1855. The church of St Thomas was built to the designs of Sir George Gilbert Scott and consecrated in 1857. A single cell building the nave and chancel are separated by a wooden chancel arch. The east windows are by William Wailes and depict the Crucixion, the Virgin Mary and St John. The church has a western bellcote, north porch and southern vestry.

When the church was built the only other building was the turnpike cottage and gate. The Rectory was the next house to be built and by 1900 there was a school and post office. Since 1900 just seven houses have been added to Bylchau.

Caego

Caego is a small village a mile and a half north-west of Wrexham town centre, across the A483 Wrexham by-pass. While building in the village had commenced in the 1930s adjoining the larger village of New Broughton, the name, does not appear on Ordnance Survey maps until 1963. The name can be translated as 'true field'.

On the south-eastern edge of the village Peter Drelincourt, Dean of Armagh built a Queen Anne house on land inherited by his wife Mary from the Maurice family. In his will of 1716 he gave £700 to endow an orphanage for 20 girls to be built in the grounds. It was some 30 years before the orphanage and school were built and it was managed before her death by the Drelincourts' only daughter Ann, Lady Primerose. Mary also founded the church, built in 1742. Until the 1960s the house was used as the vicarage with the orphanage run by the diocese of St Asaph. Vicarage and orphanage have now been converted to private houses. The old vicarage has formal gardens with a maze constructed in the shape of the Star of David. An avenue of beech trees leads to the Neo-classical church which appears to have had no dedication. It was enlarged in 1828 to accommodate family pews for local landowners. It was declared redundant in 2010 and has been converted to a private dwelling.

At the entrance to the village is a garden centre, a day nursery and the Arriva bus depot. There has been additional modern development in the village but services are provided at New Broughton.

Capel Garmon St Garmon's Chapel

Capel Garmon is a small village five miles south-east of Llanrwst. Situated high on a minor road there are fine views across the Conway valley to Snowdonia. Originally a chapel of ease to Llanrwst it became a parish in 1927. The church was rebuilt in 1862-3 to the designs of E.G. Paley of Lancaster. The church is a single cell building with a western bellcote, gabled south-west porch, and vestry with chimney to the north. The church has been declared redundant. The font bore the date 1695 and the communion table was reported as being 17th century. St Garman is identified as the 6th century St Germanus, a native of Brittany who became Bishop of Man although he is sometimes confused with St Germanus of Auxerre.

Bethania Welsh Wesleyan Methodist Chapel at the northern end of the village, was built in 1846 and rebuilt in 1878 but has been converted for agricultural use. Seion Welsh Calvinistic Methodist Chapel at the southern end of the village was built in 1798, rebuilt in the late 19th century and remains in use.

The 400 year old White Horse Inn re-opened in November 2015 after having been closed for five years. The pub was reputedly where former Tory leader William Hague was taught the Welsh National anthem by his future wife Ffion.

1,100 yards south-east of the village is the 5,500 year old Capel Garmon Burial Chamber. Dating from the Neolithic era it shows a marked similarity to similar tombs in the Severn area 100 miles to the south-east. The tomb was used as a stable before restoration in the 19th century.

Cefn Mawr Great Ridge

Cefn Mawr is a former industrial village a mile and a half south-west of Ruabon, set on the ridge north of the River Dee. Until the end of the 18th century the area was largely agricultural, the eastern section forming part of the Wynnstay estate, the northern part of the area was in the possession of the Lloyd family of Plas Madoc, the southern the Chirk Estate while the Owens who were descendants of the Kynastons owned the central area of the Plas Kynaston estate until 1813 when it was acquired by Wynnstay. The Kynastons were descended from Bleddyn ap Cynfyn, the last Prince of Powys, of the House of Mathrafal and were prominent in Shropshire and the Marches in the 15th century. The nature of the area changed dramatically with the building of the Pontcysyllte Aqueduct though coal had been mined on the Plas Kynaston estate since the early 18th century.

It is thought that William Hazeldine who was awarded the contract for the castings of the Pontcysyllte Aqueduct in 1802 produced at least some from the Kynaston Foundry which he established in 1800 at the north-western end of Cefn Mawr. The foundry later benefited from the extension to the canal built between 1825 and 1830 by the remarkably named Exuperius Pickering and Thomas Edward Ward. Pickering was the owner of the Cefn Colliery, limekilns and the Pontcysyllte Forge just west of Trevor Basin and the Plas Kynaston Canal extension connected all three as well as Hazeldines's Plas Kynaston Iron Foundry. Thomas Edward Ward was responsible for building part of the canal and also built a tram road to connect his Plas Kynaston Colliery to the canal extension which started in a north-easterly direction from Trevor Basin before turning south to end just north of the Queens Hotel on Queen Street. All trace of the canal disappeared when it was filled-in in 2004 save for a canal bridge in the middle of the chemical works complex. The Plas Kynaston Canal Group however have plans to restore the canal as a tourist attraction, bringing visitors into Cefn Mawr with a 60 berth marina behind the Queens Hotel.

The Plas Kynaston Pottery was established at the southern end of the Plas Kynaston Canal in 1856 producing small terracotta and earthenware products such as flowerpots and seed pans but it was the chemical industry which was to have the greatest impact on the area. In partnership with a Manchester lawyer, Timothy Crowther, the German chemist Robert Ferdinand Graesser from Obermosel in Saxony began producing paraffin from colliery shale but the market collapsed and the partnership ended. Graesser then started to produce phenol or carbolic acid and by 1910 was responsible for 50% of the world's production. Gradually the chemical works took over the sites of the foundry and pottery. Graesser died in 1911 and in 1920 the Monsanto Company acquired a half share and in 1928 took complete control switching production to saccharin, vanillin, salicylic acid and aspirin and from 1930 under the Flexsys name, rubber chemicals. The works closed in 2008.

Plas Kynaston on the lane which bears its name stands behind the modern library. It dates from the 18th century but was remodelled in the 19th century. In 1813 William Mostyn Owen sold the house to Sir Watkin Williams Wynn and it was leased to Exuperius Pickering and later to T.E. Ward. It subsequently came into the hands of the local authority and was used as a library but was left vacant after the building of a new library. There are now plans to convert the house into apartments.

There is no church in Cefn Mawr, it forms part of the parish of St John's Rhosymedre. Hyfrydle Welsh Calvinistic Methodist Chapel on Well Street was built in 1861 but closed in 1966. It is now a private dwelling. Tabernacl Welsh Baptist Chapel, also on Well Street, was built in 1859 but closed in 1974. A car park occupies the area in front of the old chapel. Cefn Mawr English Congregational Chapel later the United Reformed Church on Hill Street was built in 1866. Bethel English Baptist Chael was built on Hill Street in 1904 but has now been demolished and replaced with a red brick detached house. Bethel was originally built on Queens Road in 1805. Gorphwysfa Welsh Wesleyan Methodist Chapel was built on Hill Street in 1815 and rebuilt in 1828, 1838 and 1869 when the architect was Richard Owen. Gorphwysfa was demolished in 2000. Ebenezer English Baptist Chapel on Crane Street was built in 1874. This large Gothic chapel has a modern extension and is now known as the Ebenezer Centre and used as a community centre. Crane Street United Methodist Chapel was built by 1904 but has been demolished. Seion a'r Tabernacl Welsh Baptist Chapel on Rock Lane was built in 1795 and was rebuilt in 1817, 1821, 1867 and 1899. It has been replaced by a bungalow Hen Capel Seion though the graveyard remains along Zion Street to the rear. The Christian Baptist Chapel on King Street was built by 1899, replacing a chapel built in 1837 though on another site. After serving as a Salvation Army Hall it was taken over by Maelor Amateur Boxing Club.

The George Edwards Hall on Well Street was erected as a theatre in 1911. It operated as a cinema, changing its name to The People's Cinema in 1944. It has reverted to its original name and operates as a theatre, dance venue and community centre.

The Ellesmere Canal Company built a tramway known as the Ruabon Brook Railway from Trevor Basin to Acrefair and on to Ruabon Brook. It followed a circuitous route via the centre of Cefn Mawr where it took a very sharp hairpin bend. A crane was said to have been positioned here to tranship loads too long for the bend, giving Crane Street its name. An alternative explanation is that it is derived from the Welsh word for slope, *Y Graen*. Cefn Mawr has a range of shops as well as a new Tesco Superstore and two primary schools. It forms the centre of an urban area which includes Acrefair, Rhosymedre and Newbridge and it is difficult to know where one community starts and another ends. There was considerable house building in the Cefn Bychan area in the mid 20th century and infill building continues. There are parts, in Mill Lane and on the ridge, where the village has a rural feel though elements of its industrial past both in housing and evidence of tram roads, quarries and inclined planes remain.

Cefn Meiriadog Meiriadog's High Ridge

Lying a little over two miles south-west of St Asaph, Cefn Meiriadog is a small scattered village. Cynan Meiriadog was a legendary British leader said to have been the founder of Armorica (Brittany) and identified with St Cynon.

The church of St Mary was built on high ground as an estate church by Sir Watkin Williams Wynn in 1863-4 using the services of the architect Benjamin Ferrey who was also responsible for the rebuilding of Wynnstay Hall. The church has a polygonal apse with lancet windows and small north and south transepts. There is a south porch and western bellcote.

On the bank of the River Elwy are the remains of Ffynnon Fair and its Well Chapel. The spring was channelled into a polygonal basin within the chapel. In the 19th century there was a partial rebuild to enhance the picturesque value of the ruin. It was at one time a place of pilgrimage and there are records of clandestine marriages in the chapel into the 17th century. Cliffe reports of its water "*the beautiful features of which will not be readily forgotten by whoso has once tasted of its limpid waters*".

Plas yn Cefn was the ancestral home of the Lloyds of Cefn. The house which has parts dating back to 1611 is mainly 18th century and in the 19th century came under the ownership of the Williams-Wynn family. The limestone cliffs above the River Elwy contain a number of large caves. Excavations of Pontnewydd Cave discovered tools, flints, jaw fragments and teeth of Lower Paleolithic early Neanderthals dating back some 225,000 years. Cefn Caves were visited by Charles Darwin and the remains of bones of straight-tusked elephant, rhinoceros and hippopotamus of the last interglacial age (c. 125,000 years old), were discovered in 1832. In 1870 *The Times* reported that a strange amphibian had been reported living in the caves. In November 1870 the *Flintshire Observer* reported that a crocodile-like creature some four feet seven inches in length had emerged from the caves and had been slain by Thomas Hughes, chimney sweep of Rhyl. The creature had in fact escaped from a travelling circus but the shrewd Mr Hughes exhibited it as the "marvellous lizard of Cefn". Cliffe describes a natural arch 63ft deep and 36ft high at the base of the cliff which at one time straddled the Denbigh to Abergele road.

Cerrigydrudion Stones of the Warriors

Cerrigydrudion lies on the A5 some nine miles north-west of Corwen. Historically part of Denbighshire, it is now in the Conwy County Borough. The name is derived from a large heap of stones that stood a century or two ago, near the church in memory of some celebrated warriors.

The centre of an agricultural area with a preponderance of moorland, it was a stopping point for drovers en route from Anglesey. Lewis recorded in 1830 "*The breeding of cattle and sheep, the digging of peat for fuel, the spinning of woollen yarn, and the knitting of stockings form the principal occupations of the inhabitants*".

According to the *Life of St Ieuan Gwas Padrig*, a manuscript held at the National Library Aberystwyth, the saint was instructed by an angel to walk south until he saw a roebuck rising and there build his cell. The roebuck rising was at Cerrigydrudion and Ieuan established his cell there, according to tradition in 440. St Ieuan was a disciple of St Patrick and travelled with him to Ireland. Baring Gould gives the following account: "*But Ieuan was not destined to remain in Ireland long. One day S. Patrick, whilst preparing to say Mass, sent his Welsh disciple to fetch fire. Ieuan went to the cook, and returned with the glowing embers in his lap, without his garment having been even singed. S. Patrick, in compassion for the Welsh, that they should not be deprived of having so great a wonder-worker in their midst, requested him to return to his native country. Ieuan bade his master farewell and went down to the shore, but could find no means of embarking. In his perplexity he prayed, and saw a blue slab floating on the surface of the water towards him; and on this he safely landed on the coast of Anglesey. He now felt very thirsty; he thrust the point of his staff into the ground, and forthwith bubbled up a crystal spring."*

The church was once dedicated to St Ieuan and St Mary Magdalene, but only the latter dedication now remains. It was built on a circular Celtic llan but the present structure dates from the 13th century. The porch was added in the 14th century and the chantry, later the Geeler Chapel, in 1503. It was re-roofed and the windows replaced in 1874 with a further restoration in 1982. The open rafter roof is thought to be constructed of medieval timber. There is a single cell nave, chancel and sanctuary defined by steps, with the Geeler Chapel which has a sundial set in the gable, off the chancel. There is a south porch and western double bellcote. The 1918 octagonal stone font replaced a small 18th century bracket bowl font of red marble, which now serves as a stoup. The Geeler Chapel is named after Geeler or Gilar a 17th century house four miles to the west and covered under Rhydlydan.

The Hafan Prys Almshouses opposite the church were endowed and built in 1717 by the Honourable Robert Price Esq. of Gilar, a Sergeant at Law and Baron of His Majesty's Court of Exchequer in 1714. Originally built to accommodate six churchgoing men of the village aged over 60, the almshouses are now reduced to three. The Charity later supported ten men with payments of 3/6d a week, new stockings and shoes every year, and a new overcoat every two years. Robert Price's son was Sir Uvedale Price, the author of a treatise on the 'Picturesque'.

Moreia Welsh Independent Chapel on King Street was built in 1876. Originally known as Ty'n Ryhyd, Jerwsalem Welsh Calvinistic Methodist Chapel was built in 1805 and rebuilt in 1825, 1851 and again in 1900. Seion Wesleyan Methodist Chapel on Ruthin Road was built in 1840 and rebuilt in 1883. It closed in 2002 and has been converted to private accommodation, as has the 1868 National School north of the church.

The village by-pass was built by Thomas Telford because the road through the village was considered too steep. The whole route to Holyhead was completed in 1826.

Cerrigydrudion once had three hotels, The White Lion, the Saracen's Head and the Queens Head Inn. Only the White Lion, where Borrow stayed, remains open. The Queens Head is a cruck house reputedly built in 1417 though rebuilt in 1900. As well as Borrow, David Lloyd George stayed at the White

Lion. One of its landlords was Ronnie Williams, half of Welsh comedy duo Ryan and Ronnie.

The village has a range of shops, a café and a bank.

There is a legend that the devil once occupied the church. His face stared out from the window and the vicar having entered the church stumbled out confirming that Satan was indeed in occupation. The villagers sought advice and were told to tempt the devil out with a beautiful maiden. They captured two huge oxen on Waun Banawg, attached them to a sledge and dowsed chains with holy water. The maiden known as Eira Wyn (Snow White) was dressed in silks and lay flowers on the gravestones. The Devil was tempted out and immediately set upon by the villagers who chained him to the sledge. They drove the oxen to a lake on Hiraethog Mountain. The oxen entered the lake and disappeared beneath the waters together with the Devil, never to be seen again. The lake was named Llyn y Ddau Ychain (Lake of the Two Oxen) which has now disappeared under the waters of the Alwen Reservoir.

Borrow records that in the 18th century the vicar was the Revd Peter Lewis who wrote a beautiful song called *Cathl y Gair Mwys*, or the melody of the ambiguous word.

In the 1870s there were proposals to build a narrow gauge railway from Ruthin to Cerrigydrudion and an Act of Parliament was passed in 1876. Work started in 1879 but abandoned in 1884.

East of the village is Melin y Bwlch, formerly a corn mill with an internal overshot wheel fed from a pond, together with two corn drying kilns. Now a private residence.

North of the village, Alwen Reservoir was built to supply water to Birkenhead between 1911 and 1921. Today it is part of the River Dee regulation system and is operated by Dwr Cymru. Farther north is Llyn Brenig which was built in the 1970s. Both reservoirs are now used for leisure activities.

Chirk Welsh: Eglwys Y Waun meaning The Church on the Moor

Chirk lies to the west of the A5 eight miles south of Wrexham. The name Chirk is thought by some to be derived from 'church', as in the Scottish 'kirk', while others believe it to be a corruption of 'Ceiriog' the local river. Chirk has a town council but has been described as a village by current residents and by Samuel Lewis in his 1833 *Topographical Dictionary*, so has been included in this book.

At the southern entrance to Chirk is the motte of Castell y Waun, mentioned in 1165 and 1212. In the 19th century it formed part of an ornamental garden of The Mount. Chirk Castle, a mile and a half to the west was built by Roger Mortimer, starting in 1295. Its similarity to Beaumaris Castle suggests the work of Edward I's builder Master James of St George from Savoy. Mortimer was granted the area by Edward I following the defeat of Llewelyn the Last in 1282. With Mortimer's fall from favour in 1322, Chirk was granted to Edmund Fitzalan, Earl of Arundel but he was dispossessed in 1326 and it reverted to Mortimer's nephew in 1327 but he in turn was dispossessed in 1330. In 1337 it was granted to Richard Fitzalan, Earl of Arundel and remained in the family until 1415. In 1324 the Earl of Arundel granted Chirk a market charter and it became a free borough, with 23 burgage plots, but evidence of the original grid-iron street system has disappeared. Chirk passed through several families, including the Beauforts and in 1475 it was granted to Sir Henry Stanley until he was charged with treason in 1495. It was administered by the Tudors until granted by Elizabeth I to her favourite Robert Dudley Earl of Leicester in 1563. It was inherited by his brother Ambrose, Earl of Warwick whose widow sold it to John, Lord St John of Bletso who in turn sold it in 1595 to Thomas Myddelton. Myddelton was one of the four sons of Richard Myddelton, M.P. for Denbigh and Governor of Denbigh Castle.

Thomas had amassed a fortune as a London merchant, investing in the East India Company and the various buccaneering ventures of the age. He was knighted in 1603 and served as Lord Mayor of London in 1613 and represented the City of London in Parliament. His brother Sir Hugh Myddelton was goldsmith to James I and was responsible for the New River project which brought fresh water to London. Another brother Henry Middleton built Middleton Hall, now the home of the National Botanic Garden of Wales in Carmarthenshire. During the English Civil War Sir Thomas's son, also Thomas was a Parliamentarian and commanded the Roundhead forces in North Wales. Chirk castle however was held by Sir John Watts for the Royalists who successfully saw off a siege by Myddelton before eventually falling to Cromwell's forces. In 1659 Thomas Myddelton joined the Cheshire rising in favour of restoring Charles II. He was defeated and Chirk Castle damaged. On the Restoration Thomas was awarded £60,000 in compensation and his son, another Thomas became Sir Thomas Myddelton 1st Baronet of Chirk Castle. The hereditary title died out in 1718 when Sir William Myddelton died childless. The estates passed through other members of the family to

Chirk Castle

Charlotte Myddelton who married Robert Biddulph in 1801 who adopted the name Myddelton Biddulph. Work on the interior was carried out over the years by various owners and architects including A.W. Pugin and his son. During the early part of the 20th century the castle was home to Lord Howard de Walden, President of the Campaign for the Protection of Rural Wales who made further improvements.

Chirk Castle remained in the Myddelton family until acquired for the nation in 1978 and placed in the care of the National Trust in 1981 though the Myddelton family remained in residence until 2004. In addition to the castle there are formal gardens and 480 acres of parkland.

The mid 19th century village of Chirk consisted of Church Street with buildings extending from the Castell y Waun motte to the National Girls' School, now Chirk Furniture and Carpet Centre, with houses on what is now Ffordd Trevor as far as the vicarage. Chirk Green formed a separate hamlet.

The Grade I Listed church of St Mary dates from the 12th century. Originally it was dedicated to St Tysilio, suggesting that the church occupies the site of an earlier Celtic church. The north nave was added in 1519 with the tower inserted into the western end shortly after. The two parts of the nave are separated by a four bay arcade with octagonal pillars. There were refurbishments in the 17th,

18th and early 19th centuries with the gallery and seating altered by Benjamin Gummow of Ruabon in 1829 and the furnishings altered in 1877 by E. Griffiths of Chirk. There are monuments and memorials to members of the Myddelton and Trevor families, while the fine carvings of the medieval roofs are a particular feature. The tower contains a ring of six bells from the Gloucester foundry of Rudhall, installed in 1803. A 20th century stone built meeting hall is attached to the north nave. The sundial in the churchyard was erected in 1827 by the churchwardens. The small Trevor Mausoleum was erected in 1905 following the death of the child of Arthur William, 2nd Baron Trevor in 1904. It is one of a number of interesting monuments.

The Roman Catholic Church of the Sacred Heart on Castle Road is a 1928 mock Tudor building. Chirk Green Free United Methodist Church on Chapel Lane was built in 1875 with the Sunday School added 20 years later.

With the exception of the corner terrace at the junction of Castle Road and Church Street which once contained the Post Office, the shops and bank on the western side of Church Street are modern, replacing the Cross Keys public house. The Hand Hotel, takes its name from the hand depicting a knight's glove on the Myddelton crest. It was built in the 18th century and subsequently extended to serve travellers on what was until recently the A5, the main road to Holyhead. The building to the south is believed to be the 17th century precursor, later used as the town house for the Myddelton family. A brewery to the rear of the hotel was demolished to provide additional accommodation. The War Memorial opposite was designed and sculpted by Eric Gill, commissioned by Lord Howard de Walden in 1919.

Chirk Royal British Legion was founded by Dr Travis Hampson, a G.P. in Chirk for 40 years. Dr Hampson was awarded the Military Cross during the First World War for a long period of valuable service in forming the 20th Field Ambulance and in many acts of gallantry rather than one isolated incident, but especially in the action at L'Epinette on March 12, 1915, and also for conspicuous service in attending a large number of seriously wounded under heavy gunfire during the hours of darkness. Another Chirk man, Leading Aircraftman Robert Emrys Williams, Royal Air Force Volunteer Reserve was awarded the George Medal in 1943 for acts of bravery in saving crew from burning aircraft. Both men represented Chirk as councillors. The British Legion social club occupies the former British Boys School built in 1857. The earlier National Girls' School which took infants of both sexes was built in 1834 to a design by A.W.N. Pugin. As noted above it is now a furniture and carpet store. Hand Terrace was built in 1820-25 to house workers from the castle. The Council Hall was built in 1902 to house the newly created Chirk Parish Council. Richard Myddleton laid the foundation stone on the 2nd August, marking the coronation of Edward VII.

A little over a mile north-east of the church on a site now partly occupied by the A5 Chirk by-pass, was the Black Park Colliery, established in the early 19th century, employing up to 520 men before closure in 1949. It was reopened for a while to provide ventilation for the Ifton Colliery across the border before finally closing in 1968. Brynkinallt Colliery at Chirk Green was sunk in the 1860s and employed up to 1,675 men at its peak after the Great War. Chirk Green grew to accommodate the workforce. The colliery closed in 1968.

East of the by-pass is Brynkinallt Hall (originally Bryncunallt Hall) which was built in 1612 for Sir Edward Trevor. The Trevor family claimed descent from Tudor Trevor, son-in-law of Hywel Dda and in the 10th century ruler of the borders from the Maelors to Gloucester. Sir Edward, whose father John Trevor was Constable of Whittington Castle, gained lands at Rostrevor in Ireland fighting for Elizabeth I. During the English Civil War the family were staunch Royalists which brought them into conflict with their neighbours the Myddeltons, feuds which lasted until the 18th century. In 1681 Sir Thomas Myddelton challenged Sir John Trevor to a duel for calling his grandfather a traitor. Sir John was the grandson of Sir Edward and a cousin of Judge John Jeffreys. He was a lawyer and judge and was knighted in 1671. He entered Parliament in 1673 and in 1681 defeated the Myddelton candidate becoming Member for Denbighshire. Subsequently by agreement, he took the Denbigh Borough seat with the Myddeltons regaining the county seat. He became Speaker of the House of Commons in 1685 and Master of the Rolls and a Privy Councillor. In 1695 however he was expelled from the Commons for bribery. In 1688 he was appointed joint constableship of Flint castle and 'custos rotulorum' of Flintshire, offices which were returned to him in 1705.

It was said of him that "*if stratagem, duplicity and political charlatanry, are desirable excellencies, the royal distinctions had not been misplaced. What was said of Sir Robert Walpole was reported of Trevor, that he was first, who by purchasing or unduly influencing votes with money, or offices, obtained from the court, was able to manage a party in the house*". Apparently "*He had a very disagreeable cast on his eyes, which led the wits to observe, on the detection of his criminal conduct, that justice was blind but bribery only squinted*" (Beauties of England and Wales). He died in 1717 and his son died in 1762 without issue and the estates passed to Arthur Hill – Trevor 1st Viscount Dungannon of the 2nd creation. The Duke of Wellington was a frequent visitor to Brynkinallt as his mother was a daughter of Arthur Hill-Trevor. In 1862 the male line again failed and Brynkinallt passed to Arthur Edwin Hill-Trevor created 1st baron Trevor of Brynkynallt in 1880. The family continue to reside at Brynkinallt. The Hall is said to have been designed by Inigo Jones, but was extended in 1808 by the 2nd Viscount Dungannon. Much of this extension was removed in the mid 20th century. The gardens were laid out at the time of the 1808 extension. While still a family home the Hall is available for weddings and conferences. There are business premises in the estate buildings and residential estate properties to rent. Group tours of the Hall can be arranged and the gardens open under the National Gardens Scheme.

On the banks of the Ceiriog, south of the village is Chirk Mill. The first mill was recorded on the site in 1506 but the present three storey building dates from 1780. Originally a corn mill, in 1924 it was fitted with a turbine, supplying Chirk with electricity until 1930. It is now a tea room and bed centre. To the west was Castle Mill, said to have been the site of the 1165 Battle of Crogen when the forces of Owain Gwynedd defeated Henry II. A plaque on the Castle Mill Bridge commemorates the battle. Nearby are the pools and lakes of the Chirk Trout Farm and Fishery.

Chirk Aqueduct

The Ellesmere Canal, later known as the Llangollen Branch of the Shropshire Union Canal crosses the Ceiriog valley by means of the Chirk Aqueduct designed by Thomas Telford and built between 1796 and 1801. The 10 stone arches, each wth a span of 40 feet carry the cast iron canal trough 70 feet above the river. At the Chirk end the canal widens to form a basin before entering the 459 yard tunnel beneath the road to the castle. With the nearby Whitecross Tunnel it was the first in Britain to have a towpath. Adjacent to the aqueduct is the Chirk Railway Viaduct, built in in 1846-1848 to the design of Henry Robertson, chief engineer to the Shrewsbury to Chester Railway and owner of Brymbo Iron Works. The 283 yard structure carries the line 100 feet above the river over 16 arches. The three arches at either end were originally built of wood but replaced by stone in 1858. To the east the A5 crosses the valley on a 7 span pre-stressed concrete viaduct.

Chirk Viaducts

Chirk today has a small, busy shopping centre near the church and is served by two primary schools. In addition to the Hand Hotel there is the Stanton House Inn. The old village has seen expansion to the west and north with Chirk Green no longer a separate hamlet. Two major employers are Cadbury chocolate and Kronospan wood products.

Clawdd-newydd New Dyke
Five miles south-west of Ruthin Clawdd-newydd was until recently a small hamlet with two pubs, a chapel and a few houses. The second half of the 20th century saw new building both as infill and the Trem y Coed estate of bungalows.

Clawdd Newydd Welsh Calvinistic Methodist Chapel was built in 1827 and rebuilt in 1897. Of the two pubs, the Cymro Tavern in the centre of the village has closed but the Glan Llyn is now run by the community as is the village shop next to the community centre.

Clocaenog Mossy Knoll
This small rural village lies some four miles south-west of Ruthin with the church built on the side of a hill.

The dedication of the church is somewhat confused. St Trillo and St Foddhyd have been used. Baring-Gould suggests that the correct name is Meddwid or Medwida described as a virgin but otherwise unknown. In 1530 a cleric at Bangor Cathedral directed his body to be buried in *"ecclesia Sancte Medwide Virginis"*, Which with mutation would be St Feddwid, though Foddwid was used by Iolo Morganwg and is the current form. The earliest documentary mention of the church is the late 13th century and there are some late medieval features including the east window, the roof and the rood screen. There were renovations by Kennedy in 1856-7 and in 1882 when the porch was built and medieval frescoes were uncovered but not preserved. It is a single cell structure with a partitioned vestry in the nave. There is a western bellcote and the lych gate bears the date 1691. In the graveyard is a sundial made by Joyce of Ruthin. The dial is inscribed with its latitude. There is also the very elegant War Memorial erected after the First World War but also recording the sacrifices of World War II.

Bethesda Welsh Wesleyan Methodist Chapel near the school was built in 1836, though a Sunday School had been built in 1828. The chapel was rebuilt in 1864 and 1914 but is no longer in use. Gades Welsh Calvinistic Methodist Chapel to the north of the church was built in 1871 and a chapel house added seven years later. Closed in 1972 it has been converted to living accommodation. The school was established as a National School in 1824.

North of the church was the Cloion Tavern, now a private house, while the house south of the church was the old Post Office. The road which skirts the south of the churchyard leads to Plas Clocaenog, a late 16th/early 17th century farmhouse which was part of Lord Bagot's estate. The farm, barn and stables are Grade II Listed.

West of the village is the 25,000 acre Clocaenog Forest, an area rich in wildlife including, in an enclosed section of a former Iron Age settlement, rare wild Przewalski horses. There is also Lord Bagot's Monument at Pryncyn Llys which offers extensive views. Lord Bagot owned extensive estates locally, including Pool Park (see Efenechtyd).

The village while small has seen some modern housing.

Coedpoeth Burnt Wood

Located three miles west of Wrexham the village of Coedpoeth came into being in the 1860s, the combining of the four hamlets of The Smelt, The Nant (Stream), Talwrn (Cockpit) and Adwy'r Clawdd (Gap in the Dyke). The Nant in the south had mills on the River Clywedog, The Smelt was a centre for lead smelting while Talwrn had its coal mining. Gradually the village formed with the High Street running from Adwy'r Clawdd in the east to The Smelt in the north-west along the ridge between the valleys of the Clywedog and the Gwenfro. Today the village is a commuter centre for the industrial estates of Wrexham to the east and the small Minera industrial estate to the north-west.

In 1410 Thomas Earl of Arundel granted the villagers of Holt the right to dig for coal at Brymbo and Coedpoeth. The area around Coedpoeth had been wooded but much of the woodland disappeared to produce charcoal. Coal mining was on a small scale with shallow pits until the Coedpoeth or Earl Grosvenor's Colliery began production in 1790, reaching a depth of 120 feet. Two further collieries bore the Grosvenor name, the Jockey which closed in 1869 and the New Grosvenor Colliery north of Bethel Chapel on Gwernygaseg Road which operated between 1869 and 1890 and reached a depth of 300 feet. The Pentrefron or Old Talwrn Colliery closed after flooding in 1819. Two men died from drowning while a third, John Evans survived for 12 days in a cavity in the roofspace. The management had prepared three coffins but John Evans apparently used his as a piece of furniture until his death. The Talwrn Colliery north of the junction of Castle Road and Talwrn Road was operating in 1857 and employed up to 119 men. All coal mining in the village had ceased by 1914. The Wrexham and Minera Railway ran to the west of the village with Coedpoeth station in neighbouring Minera. The station buildings were destroyed by suffragettes in 1914 and passenger services ceased in 1930.

The church on the High Street is dedicated to St Tydfil, a daughter of King Brychan. She was martyred near Merthur Tydfil circa 480. The church was built in 1895, replacing the 1875 tin church which previously stood on the site. The architects were Middleteon, Prothero & Phillott of Cheltenham. The building has north and south aisles incorporated as lean-to structures. The chancel occupies the southern end of the church. The vestry in the north-east corner was intended to be the base of a tower which was never built. The chancel screen by Herbert L. North was erected in 1921 as a War Memorial. The church is a chapel of ease to St Mary's Minera.

Bethel Welsh Calvinistic Methodist Chapel is shown on the Ordnance Survey maps of 1873 and 1899 as being on Gwernygaseg Road while the now closed chapel on Ruthin Road also bears the name. It is assumed that the original Bethel built in 1859 was on Gwernygaseg Road but the 1878 rebuilding was on Ruthin Road. Opposite Bethel on Ruthin Road was a Primitive Methodist Chapel, shown on the 1873 map. Capel Salem, a Welsh Independent Chapel on High Street was built in 1858, and rebuilt in 1891-2 to the design of a local architect, John Harrison. The chapel and its railings are Grade II Listed as being a fine example of a late 19th century chapel enriched by ornate decorations including a central rose and painted organ pipes. It was put up for sale in 2013. Rehoboth Welsh Wesleyan Methodist Chapel on High Street was built in 1843 and rebuilt in 1858 and 1866. The site is now occupied by a Cooperative store. Tabernacl Welsh Baptist Chapel on Park Road was built in 1868 but is now a private dwelling. Dysgwylfa Welsh Calvinistic Methodist Chapel on Middle Road was built in 1866 and rebuilt 12 years later. An adjoining schoolroom predated the chapel having been built in 1859. The site is now occupied by private housing. Saron Welsh Independent Chapel on Middle Road was built in 1880 with a school room added in 1897. Horeb Wesleyan Methodist Chapel on Nant Road was built in 1889 but closed in 1973 and was subsequently demolished. Bethlehem English Congregational Chapel on Smithy Road was built in 1897. Adwy'r Clawdd Welsh Calvinistic Methodist Chapel on Heol Maelor was built in 1750, rebuilt in 1815 and 1860 but destroyed by fire in 1884 to be rebuilt again in 1885, by the Liverpool architect Richard Owen. A chapel house and school were added in 1888 but all have now been replaced by a small red brick terrace of houses. Offa English Wesleyan Methodist Chapel on Heol Offa was built in 1862, enlarged in 1864 and rebuilt in 1877. It has now been converted to residential use. Bathafarn Welsh Wesleyan Methodist Chapel on Talwrn Road was built in 1901. Seion Welsh Independent Chapel also on Talwrn Road was built in 1880 and rebuilt in 1899. It is now a private dwelling.

One of the oldest buildings in the village is Llidiart Fanny Farm on Llewelyn Road, parts of which date from 1616. A British School (Non-conformist) had been established by 1873 opposite what is now Bryn Tabor Welsh Medium Junior School. In 1904 the Carnegie Library was built on Park Road, a gift by the Scottish American steel magnate Andrew Carnegie. The building is now used by the Community Council with a new library housed in the Enterprise Centre on Castle Road. In addition to Bryn Tabor School there is Penygelli Infants and Primary School.

There were two corn mills at Nant. New Mills has disappeared but Nant Mill on Rhosberse Road is now a visitor centre. Originally a pandy or fulling mill, Nant became a corn mill around 1770 though the current building dates from 1832. It operated until World War II but fell into decay until given its new role as an information centre for the Clywedog Valley.

The village is well supplied with open spaces and sports grounds. High Street and Heol Maelor has a range of small shops, pubs, takeaways and restaurants.

On 6th October 1945, Mrs Evans, the teacher at Frondeg School was murdered in a quiet lane near the cemetery. She lived with her mother at the City Arms in Coedpoeth. Her murderer, Lionel Raymond Rusdell, also confessed at his 1950 trial to the murder of Mrs Dilys Myfanwy Scott. He was just 14 when he murdered Mrs Evans and proclaimed from the dock that the reason was "sex". Rusdell was condemned to death but was transferred to Broadmoor where he assaulted two guards with a knife. He subsequently committed suicide at Broadmoor in 1953, aged just 22.

William Low, a local man, an engineer and coal owner associated with the Vron Colliery developed a plan for a channel tunnel. Land was purchased in Kent and France by the Anglo Welsh Submarine Railway Company. The scheme was taken up in 1880 by Sir Edward Watkin who started the preliminary work, driving two shafts in readiness for tunnelling before the scheme was abandoned.

Cross Lanes

Cross Lanes as the name implies lies on a crossroads on the A525 Whitchurch to Wrexham road a little over a mile north-west of Bangor on Dee.

In 1873 there was a small hamlet on Kiln Lane to the south-west with its Methodist chapel though there was a police station on the crossroads. Maes-y-nant is a mid-Victorian country house, which since 1959 has been the Cross Lanes Hotel. The oak panelling in the hall dates from 1620, having been removed from Emral Hall in Worthenbury. The other major house is Bedwell

Hall, now found on Fern Close and surrounded by modern housing. It was built in the late 17th/early 18th century, a two storey plus attic brick built house. The modern estates north-east of the crossroads have meant a major increase in population and there is a Cooperative store though Cross Lanes lost its only pub, the Kiln Inn in 2009. Cross Lanes English Wesleyan Methodist Chapel was built in 1834 but closed in the 1980s. Pickhill Old Hall to the east of Cross Lanes dates from 1681 but was remodelled in the 1720s. Left to decay in the 20th century it was subject to a fire in 1985 and subsequently restored and divided into apartments. Pickhill Farmhouse dates from the 16th century and among its outbuildings was a chapel, used later as stables.

Set in rich agricultural land, Cross Lanes is just a mile from the Wrexham Industrial Estate and there is the Maelor Abattoir and the Maelor Creamery, producing cheese in the vicinity.

Cyffylliog Place of Pollarded Trees

Attractively situated on a hillside, Cyffylliog is a small village four miles west of Ruthin in the valley of the Clywedog where the river is joined by the Afon Corris and Nant Gladur. The village was first mentioned in 1259. On Saturday 27th September, 1645 the church register records a meeting locally between King Charles I and his local commanders on the eve of the sieges of Denbigh and Ruthin.

The church of St Mary dates from 1300 but is thought to be on the site of a Celtic llan. Until 1874 it was a chapel of ease to Llanynys. It was the subject of a major refurbishment in 1874-6 by Arthur Baker which lost much of its medieval character, though the chancel retains its late 15th century wagon vaulted roof and original pointed-arched east window east of 1300. The medieval octagonal font was retooled in 1904. A wall painting of the crowning of the Virgin was uncovered during the restoration in 1876 but was not preserved. The south porch was removed by Baker and the west porch incorporating a vestry was added in 1904. A single cell structure, the furnishings are largely 19th century, some re-using wood from the rood screen. There is a western bellcote bearing the date 1874. South of the church is the rare hearse house bearing the inscription "*This hearse-house was erected and given by Edward Owen Esq. of Fachlwyd for the use of this parish, 1823*". The lychgate dates from the 18th century but has been subject to repair.

Salem Welsh Calvinistic Methodist Chapel which was built in 1835 and rebuilt in 1905 remains in use.

A National School was built to the north-west of the church in 1855 and is now a private house. It was replaced by the 1905 Council School near the early 19th century Grade II Listed Cyffeilliog Bridge across the Clywedog. The Red Lion Hotel in the centre of the village was shown on the 1874 Ordnance Survey map and is still trading.

There has been limited development above the old village which is essentially early to mid 19th century in character.

Derwen Oak

The small rural village of Derwen stands some six miles south-west of Ruthin.

At the heart of the old village is the Grade I Listed St Mary's Church, recorded in the Norwich *Taxatio* of 1254 though the circular nature of the site suggests an earlier Celtic site. Closed for worship in 1999 the church is now in the care of the Friends of Friendless Churches charity. There was a restoration by Henry Kennedy the Bangor based church architect in 1857 when the west gallery was removed. Nave and chancel are contained in a single cell with the nave floor stone flagged, the chancel wood blocked and the sanctuary tiled. The rood screen and loft are of exceptional quality and unusually complete. The south porch contains a water stoup and the bellcote is dated 1688. The short north transept incorporates the chimney from the old heating system. Outside the late 15th century churchyard cross is Grade II* Listed. Standing nearly 15 foot high the shaft is highly decorated and while missing its apex there are depictions of the Crucifixion with the Virgin Mary and St. John, the Coronation of the Virgin, the Virgin and Child, and Archangel Michael holding scales and an upraised sword in preparation for Judgement Day. Church House which stands in the churchyard dates from the 17th century and it is thought originally incorporated a lychgate and bier storage with a vestry room, also used as a school above. The ground level has risen by about three feet from the date of building. There is a date of 1905 which refers to refurbishment. In the churchyard is a bronze sundial on a limestone pillar.

The National School south-east of the church was built in 1859 and is now a private house. Derwen Welsh Calvinistic Methodist Chapel was built in 1843, rebuilt in 1855 by the architect William Owen of Llanrwst and enlarged in 1908.

Derwen Hall, lies a mile and a half east of the church. Dating from the late 16th century it was the home of the Price family for eight generations ending with Revd John Price in the 18th century. The complex has a 19th century cartshed and granary.

Dolwen White Meadow
Dolwen is a scattered hamlet two and a half miles south-east of Old Colwyn and a mile west of Betws yn Rhos on the B5381. Dolwen Mill was a corn mill powered by the waters of the River Dulas diverted via a leat and small millpond. The machinery and wheel are said to be intact. To the east the river is crossed by the 1788 single span Dolwen Bridge near the early 19th century Dolwen Lodge, built for the Coed Coch estate.

Rhys ab Jenkyn was granted land at Trofarth by Robert Dudley Earl of Leicester in 1574. His grandson Richard adopted the surname Wynne. Coed Coch came into the hands of the Wynne family in the 18th century through marriage. John Lloyd Wynne (1776-1862) High Sheriff of Denbighshire in 1800 and of Flintshire in 1825, rebuilt Coed Coch in 1804 using Henry Hakewill as his architect. Hakewill was later appointed architect of Rugby School. Coed Coch was built in the Greek Revival style and had a Doric portico, removed in the 20th century. The house with its extensive landscaped park remained in the family until 1978 though the last of the male Wynne line, Edward Henry John Wynne a Lieutenant in the Grenadier Guards died in 1916 at the age of 23. His mother Ann had remarried in 1896 to Laurence Alan Broderick, 2nd son of the 8th Viscount Midleton (an Irish Peer) and their daughter inherited the estate. The house was used as a preparatory school between the 1940s and 1978 when the house reverted to being a private residence. Furniture commissioned by John Lloyd Wynne from Gillows is now in the library at the National Museum of Welsh Life St Fagans.

Dolywern and Llwynmawr Bog Meadow and Great Bush
The hamlets of Dolywern and Llwynmawr lie in the Ceiriog valley between Glyn Ceiriog and Pontfadog.

The main area of population lies to the south of the river and the most prominent building is the Leonard Cheshire Home. The Leonard Cheshire Foundation was established to administer the two homes Cheshire had founded in Hampshire and Cornwall looking after the severely disabled after World War II. In 1961 the Foundation purchased the Queens Hotel Dolywern on the banks of the River Ceiriog as its first home in North Wales and it opened in 1962, offering care to 34 residents under the age of 65 and suffering from a number of acute forms of physical disabilities.

On the road opposite the home is Ainon Welsh Baptist Chapel, built around 1860 and rebuilt in Gothic style with a gable-entry plan in 1887. The architect was Mr E. Evans of Llangollen. Gosen Welsh Calvinistic Methodist Chapel in Llwynmawr was built in 1853, when the congregation moved from Herber Chapel on the north bank of the Ceiriog midway between Dolywern and Pontfadog. It was rebuilt in 1886 and again in 1901.

Adjacent to the Cheshire Home is the small station waiting room which was served by the Glyn Valley Tramway. Opened in 1893 the waiting room still has its clock and postbox. The old tramway bridge across the Ceiriog can be seen to the east of the road bridge.

The two once distinct hamlets are now joined by 20th century housing with the Dolywern Memorial Hall serving the two communities. At the centre of Llwynmawr is the Mulbury Inn, formerly the Golden Pheasant, an 18th century inn offering accommodation.

Efenechtyd The Monks' Land

The small secluded village of Efenechtyd lies under two miles south-west of Ruthin, beautifully situated in a sequestered vale abounding with pleasing scenery. The name is a corruption of *y fynachdyd*.

The little church of St Michael and All Angels is at the centre of the village. It is thought to have been founded in the 8th century by monks from Llanynys but the church is 13th century. A single cell structure with a cluster truss roof of the 14th century the west porch was added around 1500. There was a restoration in 1714 and again in 1873 when the architect was the London based Arthur Baker, a pupil of George Gilbert Scott. Of particular note is the primitive late-medieval lead lined oak tub font. An article in the 1872 edition of Archaeologia Cambrensis gives a description while being somewhat disdainful of the font. "*It has been formed out of the trunk of an oak, and appears to have been roughly worked by an axe or adze: at any rate no modern carpenter would turn out such work. The only attempt at ornamental detail is the rude circle of knobs or beads, the date of which cannot easily be defined. Nor are the sides uniformly of the same size. There is an abundance of limestone close at hand, while within a little more than a mile is a small quarry of hard old red sandstone ; so that,even if the working of the limestone was not easy, the freestone was available. However, neither kind of stone was made use of; and oak, as probably the more economical material, was chosen.*" The bowl is mounted on a limestone plinth. Much of the furniture is formed from recycled wood from former box pews. The pulpit is 17th century while the oak reredos dates from 1962. There is a fragment of a post-Reformation wall painting, of the Ten Commandments in Welsh. The western bellcote is topped by a gable cross. The lychgate dates from the 18th century but re-used medieval sandstone blocks in its construction. Opposite the church is the 1898 Church Room.

Plas yn Llan was built in the early 18th century by Jacob Conway, a junior member of the Bodrhyddan family, with the gate pillars surmounted by busts of blackamoors, the family crest. The village pub was the Black Moor.

West of the village is Pool Park, once one of the five deer parks of Ruthin Castle. The Elizabethan styled house dates from the late 19th century but a substantial house was established in the 16th century. In 1617 Thomas Needham of Pool Park was High Sheriff of Denbighshire. The estate came into the possession of the Salesbury family and then through marriage to the Bagots of Blithfield in Staffordshire. The present house and its associated estate buildings were built between 1826 and 1829 for the second Lord Bagot by the architect John Buckler. In 1919 it was tenanted by Sir Ernest Tate, Bart., the sugar magnate, who served as High Sheriff of the county in that year. In 1937 the house became a convalescent home and subsequently a psychiatric hospital. During World War II a prisoner of war camp was established in the grounds for Italian prisoners.

Eglwysbach Small Church (also known as Eglwys-Fâch)

Situated in a pleasing and fertile vale watered by the River Conway, four and a half miles south of Llandudno Junction the village of Eglwysbach is now in the Conwy local authority area. The village was a ribbon development but since 1945 there have been developments to the east and west of the main street.

The church, dedicated to St Martin, was mentioned in the Norwich *Taxatio* of 1254 and was rebuilt in 1782, and restored in 1882 by the Denbigh architect Richard Lloyd Williams. The three aisled nave and chancel are of a uniform width. There is a fine 1816 tablet portraying the Coat of Arms of George III. Flanking the west tower are single storey structures, a former bier storage house to the south and boiler room to the north. The base of a sundial stands in the churchyard.

Bethania Welsh Calvinistic Methodist Chapel was built in 1884. Ebenezer Welsh Wesleyan Methodist Chapel was built in 1806 and rebuilt 1885 with a schoolroom added in 1894. Bryn Seion Welsh Baptist Chapel was built in 1839 in the hamlet of Brymbo north of the village. It is now a private house.

The school was built as a National School in 1835 and with additions remains the village school. The village retains the Bee Inn but the Hand Inn has been demolished.

The village holds a popular agricultural and horticultural show each August.

A mile north of the village is Bodnant House with its magnificent gardens. The house was built by Colonel John Forbes at the end of the 18th century. The late Georgian house, with its seven bay symmetrical southern façade was purchased in 1875 by Henry Davis Pochin, a wealthy industrial chemist who invented a process to produce white soap and subsequently a process for using china clay in the manufacture of paper. He acquired a number of china clay mines in Cornwall and was a director of the Tredegar Iron and Coal Company. Pochin remodelled the house and developed the gardens. His daughter and heiress, Laura married the Liberal politician Charles Benjamin Bright McLaren who was created Baron Aberconway in 1911. The Aberconways continued to develop the house and gardens and their son gifted the gardens to the National Trust in 1949, though the family still involve themselves in the gardens and retain the house and the rest of the estate.

Erbistock Welsh: Erbistog

The village of Erbistock lies within a bend of the River Dee, five and a half miles south of Wrexham. Palmer suggested that the name derives from 'Erbin's stoke' meaning 'Erbin's stockaded ford'. The church of St Hilary was originally dedicated to St Erbin, who according to Baring-Gould was King of Cornwall and according to legend was an uncle of King Arthur. The valley below the church was known as the Vale of Erbin. Other sources attribute the name to Old English terms meaning 'Erp's place'. The old county boundary ran through the village as a result of a change of course of the River Dee.

Erbistock was the site of a hand operated chain ferry across the Dee. Some remnants of the pull mechanism can be seen near the 17th century Boat Inn. The Inn was formerly known as the Erbistock Boat and was formed from two cottages.

St Hilary's Church was built in a Gothic Revival style in 1859-61 in memory of Henry Ellis Boates of Rose Hill, funded by his widow and daughter. This replaced a church of 1748 which in turn replaced a church recorded as dedicated to St Erbin in the Norwich *Taxatio* of 1254. Constructed of red sandstone, the church has a slate roof with red ridge tiles. The chancel has a polygonal apse while the nave and aisles are separated by arcades with polished granite columns, but the exposed timber scissor-braced roof is a single unit. There is a south porch, north vestry and a western bellcote containing three bells topped by a cross. Together with the Boat Inn and the River Dee the church provides an attractive scene.

Rose Hill lies to the north of the village and was bought by Henry Ellis Boates Senior in 1799. He was the son of Liverpool slave trader William Boates and was High Sheriff of Denbighshire in 1803. His son, also Henry Ellis, fought at Waterloo and attained the rank of Lt Colonel in the Grenadier Guards. He was High Sheriff in 1843. He died in December 1858 in a hunting accident while riding with Sir Watkin Williams Wynn's hounds at Stretton Hall. His wife did not long survive him and his daughter Gertrude, having lost her son and husband continued at Rose Hill until her death in 1914. She left the estate to her cousin Sir Frederick Kenyon, Director of the British Museum. It was inherited by his daughter Dame Kathleen Mary Kenyon, the noted archaeologist who resided at Rose Hill until her death in 1978. The house is late Georgian and surrounded by parkland and gardens. House barn and stables are Grade II Listed.

Erbistock Hall is an early Georgian brick mansion dating from 1720. Owned at one time by the Wynn family, in the 19th century it was in the possession of the Brancker family. From 1930 until his death in 1948 it was the home of Lieutenant-Colonel Sir Charles Bingham Lowther, Bt., D.S.O. Originally a three storey building it was reduced to two storeys in the 1950s by the present owner's father. It has a topiary garden and a large circular brick dovecote of 1737.

Erbistock Mill is a four storey corn mill at the northern end of a weir across the River Dee which provided its power without the need of a leat. A mill is said to have existed from Norman times but the present building has a stone fireplace dated 1602. The mill was still in operation in 1963. Mill House to the south is late 17th century though remodelled.

Manley Hall was originally a late 16th early 17th century 'H' plan house, substantially remodelled in the 19th century. According to Samuel Lewis it was in the possession of the Manley family for several hundred years prior to 1848.

The village had a school which is now the village hall. In addition to the Boat Inn there is the 18th century Cross Foxes built by the Wynnstay Estate for its workers. It stands at the end of Overton Bridge.

Eryrys

Eryrys is a small village four and a half miles south-west of Mold. It takes its name from Yr Hên Gyrys o Iâl, a collector of Welsh proverbs in the eleventh century and is a corruption of 'Erw Yrys' meaning 'Yrys' Acre'. It was formerly a chapelry in Llanarmon parish with the new parish of Eryrys formed by an Order in Council on 11 October 1861. At a height of 1,148 feet above sea level it is one of the highest villages in Wales.

The local limestone is rich in deposits of lead ore and the village was a centre of lead mining from the 13th century though it tended to be a summer activity due to water levels. In 1635 the Grosvenor Estate acquired the mineral rights in the area and began working mines in Eryrys from around 1735. The local seam is known as the Westminster Seam and shafts to it were drained by no less than six steam pumps in the 19th century. Lead mining reached a peak in the mid 19th century and ended in 1903. There are remains of the industry, with the engine house for the 1841 Cornish beam-engine that pumped the Nant lead-mine almost intact and the chimney still standing some 55 yards away. The Castell chimney is located some 160 yards south-west of Castell Farm to the south east of the village, the site of the Bog East Shaft. Water is still pumped for use at the nearby Graig Quarry.

The church of St David at the centre of the village was consecrated in 1863. Designed by T. H. Wyatt it has a polygonal apse, north vestry and porch and a western bellcote. It closed in the 1980s and has been converted for use as the village hall.

Salem Welsh Wesleyan Methodist Chapel was built in 1837, enlarged in 1845 and rebuilt in 1852. After being recorded as derelict, it was rebuilt for the second time in 1888 and is still in use.

This pleasant now rural village has the Sun Inn and is a mixture of old cottages and modern housing.

Eyton

Eyton is a scattered hamlet two and a half miles west of Bangor on Dee. The name derives from the Anglo Saxon meaning 'river settlement', Eyton gave its name to the Eyton family who lived at Eyton Hall from the 11th century. The family descended from Elidyr ap Rhys Sais, who in the eleventh century wrested a great part of the parish from the English. The Eytons played a role locally, with Sir John ap Ellis Eyton supporting Henry Tudor at Bosworth and Sir Kenrick Eyton sitting as M.P. for Flintshire in 1660 and later appointed a

Welsh judge. Sir Kenrick was the 11th great-grandfather of Lady Diana Spencer.

Eyton Hall, situated at the northern end of a meander of the River Dee was demolished in 1822 and Eyton Hall Farmhouse which dates from the 18th century was the servants' quarters.

Plassau was a moated house built in the 16th century but rebuilt in the Victorian era. Today it forms the centre of The Plassey, a holiday park with retail village adventure playground, golf course and even a brewery.

The main centre of population and indeed the village sign lies to the west around the former National School, now Eyton Primary School, and what was until 2014 the Fox and Hounds.

Fron Pointed or Breast Shaped Hill

Situated a mile south of Brymbo and to the west of Talyfron, the hamlet of Fron grew around the Vron Colliery, which took its name from Vron Farm.

The Vron Colliery was sunk by Rogers of Coedpoeth in 1806. Never a large colliery it employed a maximum of 358 men before closure in 1930. The colliery was sited to the south of the hamlet to the east of Llewelyn Road. New houses now occupy the site. To the west of Llewelyn Road was the Vron Brick Works and clay pit. The Vron brick was regarded as high quality and more expensive than Ruabon bricks. Production started in the 1850s with a new works built in 1873. Production continued until 1911. The brickworks were served by a railway siding which connected with the Vron Branch of the Wrexham Mold and Connah's Quay Railway and the Vron Branch of the G.W.R. A tramway connected connected Talwrn Colliery, Coedpoeth with Vron Colliery.

A Methodist Chapel on Heol Offa is shown on the 1873 map but not on the 1899 map. Offa's Dyke runs along Llewelyn Road past Vron.

Today Vron has a mix of houses with some of the terraced houses on Llewelyn Road having been demolished. Both the brickworks and colliery sites have been landscaped.

Froncysyllte Cysyllte Hillside

The village of Froncysyllte lies some four miles east of Llangollen on the A5 trunk road. The 1874 map shows the village as Fron, meaning hillside. Cysyllte was apparently an ancient township of the area with a meaning of link or connection. The village grew up in the early to mid 19th century to house quarry workers. The Ellesmere Canal constructed between 1795 and

1805, now known as the Llangollen Canal runs through the village with the remains of lime kilns along its banks. The River Dee flows below the village to the north.

The village is famed as the southern end of the Pontcysyllte Aqueduct which carries the canal across the River Dee. It is generally attributed to Thomas Telford, the General Agent for the project, but it is thought that the Chief Engineer, William Jessop was in large part responsible for the construction. At such a height weight was a problem and the 18 piers are hollow towards the top and taper inwards. The four piers in the Dee have cutwaters. The trough carrying the water is a series of cast iron sections, built and installed by William Hazledine, the Shrewsbury Ironmaster who also worked with Telford on the Menai Bridge. There are cast iron arches between the piers. It has a length of 1,007 feet and a height of 124 feet above the Dee. There is a towpath and handrail on the eastern side, but none on the western.

Pont Cysyllte

A plaque on the Froncysyllte side commemorates the laying of the first stone on 25th July 1795.

> *"The nobility and gentry of*
> *the adjacent counties*
> *having united their efforts with*

the great commercial interest of this country,
in creating an intercourse and union, between
England and North Wales
by a navigable communication of the three rivers,
Severn, Dee, and Mersey,
for the mutual benefit of agriculture aud trade,
caused the first stone of this aqueduct of
Pont Cysstllti.
to be laid, on the 15th day of July, MDCCXCV.
when Richard Middleton of Chirk, Esquire, M. P.
one of the original patrons of the
Ellesmere canal,
was lord of this manor,
and in the reign of our sovereign
George the third,
When the equity of the laws and
the security of property
promoted the general welfare of the nation,
while the arts and sciences flourished
by his patronage, and
the conduct of civil life, was improved
by his example."

It was the third cast iron canal bridge to be built but the most spectacular. It is a Grade I Listed site and was listed as a UNESCO World Heritage Site in 2009.

Pont Cysyllte or Cysylltau Bridge carrying the road over the Dee is also Grade I Listed and dates from 1697 though only the southern part survives from this time and is narrower than the rest. The three arched sandstone bridge has cutwaters which form triangular refuges for pedestrians on the narrow carriageway. To the west of the bridge the Dee forms a deep pool, known as Llyn y Meddwyn or the Drunkard's Pool after a drunk fell in and drowned.

St David's Church was built in 1871 as a school and chapel of ease to Llangollen. It originally had an apse but this was replaced by the chancel in 1914. There is a sanctus bellcote, west door and inside the font is of Cefn Stone. Outside the churchyard is the unusual War Memorial. It was erected in 1909 to the memory of two soldiers who died in the Boer War. The drinking fountain is now flanked by memorials to those who died in the First and Second World Wars.

The Primitive Methodist Chapel of 1914 opposite the church is now an auction house. It replaced Mount Zion Primitive Methodist Chapel which was built in 1858 and later used as a school, now a school refectory.

Froncysyllte Chapel on Methodist Hill was built in 1860 and rebuilt in 1871 as a Welsh Wesleyan Methodist Chapel to the design of architect Richard Owen of Liverpool. By 1911 however the congregation was Welsh Calvinistic Methodist. It is now converted as a private house. Carmel Welsh Baptist Chapel was erected in 1877 on Woodlands Road, replacing a chapel of 1844 on Alma Road. It has since been demolished.

Argoed Hall, a small country house in Tudorbethan style, was built in 1864 and was the home of the German born chemist Robert Ferdinand Graesser, founder of the chemical works at Plas Kynaston to extract paraffin oil and paraffin wax from the local shale which developed into the world's leading producer of Phenol before being taken over by Monsanto. Graesser was also associated with Wrexham Lager. The house was used as a local authority home for the elderly before returning to private ownership. The stable block behind the village community centre was built in the early 20th century and is now converted to a garage.

The village has a primary school and the Aqueduct Inn together with a number of cafés. In recent years its male voice choir, the Fron, has gained an international reputation.

Gellifor

Gellifor is a hamlet a little under three miles north of Ruthin. The name appears to derive from 'Gelli Ifor' meaning 'Ifor's Grove'.

Gellifor Welsh Calvinistic Methodist Chapel was built in 1814 and rebuilt in 1870 and 1907 with what appears to be a balcony over the gable end entry vestibule. The village school was built as a British School in 1868. The headmaster of the school from 1931 until his death in a cycling accident in 1938 was Edward Stanton Roberts. Roberts was a Welsh scholar, poet and an expert in medieval handwriting, working as a transcriber of manuscripts and editor for the Guild of Graduates at the National Library of Wales. A conscientious objector during the First World War he joined the Quakers in 1930, leaving the Calvinistic Methodists where he had been an elder, although he continued as a Sunday School teacher at Gellifor.

There has been considerable building in recent years within the triangle of roads that define the hamlet but other than the school there are no amenities.

Glyn Ceiriog Ceiriog Glen

More properly named Llansantffraid Glyn Ceiriog, the village is a former slate mining and flannel producing centre a little over two miles south-west of Llangollen. It was described by Samuel Lewis as occupying "*a low and very retired situation, entirely encompassed by lofty mountains*".

Slate and stone was quarried in the valley for centuries with records showing that in 1329 stone was taken for the repair of the roof of Chirk Castle. The Wynne quarry just above the village opened in 1750 but it was in 1858 with the opening of the Cambrian Slate Company that slate mining and quarrying reached an industrial scale. To transport the slate and stone the Glyn Valley Tramway was built to the canal at Chirk Bank in 1873. Freight and passengers were carried using a combination of gravity and horse power. The 2 foot 4½ inch narrow gauge railway was extended, to meet the main rail line at Chirk and reopened to freight in 1888 and passengers in 1891 with services operated by steam locomotives. The line closed in 1935 though the locomotive shed remains in the village and work is in hand to restore the railway. The Cambrian Slate Quarry had started underground mining in the 1890s and while the workforce rose to a peak of 118 in 1938 the quarry closed in 1947. The Wynne Quarry closed in 1928 though was used as a bomb shelter during World War II. It opened briefly as a museum but closed due to the requirements of Health and Safety legislation. The area of the Cambrian Quarry has now been forested.

The church of St Ffraid (St Bridget) stands high on the hillside north of the village occupying the site of a Celtic llan. The earliest written record of the church is 1291 and for many years it was a chapel of ease to Llangollen. The church was rebuilt in 1790 with a further restoration financed by Arthur Hill-Trevor, 3rd Viscount Dungannon in 1838-9 and another in 1887. (The Hill-Trevors owned the Brynkiallt estates near Chirk, inherited from the Trevor family.) St Ffraid or St Bridget, also known as Brigid and Bride, was an Irish Abbess associated with the establishment of numerous foundations in Wales, Brittany and Ireland. There are still some 17 churches dedicated to her in Wales and she was also associated with Glastonbury. She died 30 years after St Patrick. The nave and chancel form a single cell with the west gallery intact.

The Royal Coat of Arms is displayed at the front of the gallery. Doors at the rear of the gallery give access to the ground floor and via a ladder to the bell chamber in the tower. There are memorials to the Hill-Trevor family and the east window depicting the Last Supper is in memory of Sir Thomas Storey of Plas Nantyr who died in 1898. It was dedicated by Arthur Edwards, Archbishop of Wales. The Commandment Boards are Victorian.

Salem Welsh Baptist Chapel on the High Street was built in 1832 but is now closed. Seion Welsh Baptist Chapel on Ffordd Tyn-y-Cestyll was built in 1762 and rebuilt in 1875. Bethel Welsh Wesleyan Methodist Chapel was built in 1899. Tŷ Capel now stands on the site on Ffordd Tyn-y-Cestyll. On the same road, Soar Welsh Calvinistic Methodist Chapel was built in 1875.

Glyn Ceiriog once boasted four inns. The Sun Inn to the west of the church is now a private house, while the Hand Inn on the High Street has been demolished. The Royal Oak on High Street is now The Oak while the New Inn Hotel dating from 1835 was renamed the Glyn Valley Hotel in 1900.

On the High Street is the Ceiriog Memorial Institute, built in 1911 in celebration of the lyrical poet John 'Ceiriog' Hughes of Pen y bryn (1832-87), winner of the National Eisteddfod and other local literary figures, including the poet Huw Morris (1662-1709), and the Rev Robert 'Cynddelw' Ellis (1812-75). The hall was designed by the Liverpool based architect Thomas Taliesin Rees. It was extended in 1929 by the Cardiff architect Thomas Alwyn Lloyd, who was noted for garden villages. The Garden of Remembrance was added at this time. The Institute served as a village hall, library, museum, courthouse and district office. It contained a women's parlour and games room. Books, including early Welsh Bibles and memorabilia from across Wales and the Welsh community in Patagonia were donated, most of which are now in Wrexham Museum.

There were two flannel mills in the village. Berwyn Mill is now occupied by Theo Davies & Sons, manufacturers of the Oswestry Wooden Standing Frame, used in the rehabilitation of spinal injuries, multiple sclerosis and cerebral palsy. Felyn Newydd corn mill lay to the east of the village.

There has been expansion of the village in recent years with a new school and village centre. There are some local shops and Glyn Ceiriog is well blessed with sports pitches and tennis courts.

South of the village is the hamlet of Pandy with its Penuel Baptist Chapel, built in 1894, in the Gothic style. The Pandy or mill is now a craft centre though in 1899 it was shown as the Woolpack Inn. When Borrow visited Pandy in 1854 his companion was offered ale from the inn as it was better than that served at Llansantffraid and Borrow later visited the inn.

Four miles west of the village, but within the community, is Plas Nantyr, a house built in 1825 for the Storey family. It replaced Blaen Nantyr, a house which was the home of a sister of Owain Glyndŵr. Plas Nantyr originally had 23 bedrooms but was partly demolished in 1954. It is now used as a residential outdoor education centre.

Graianrhyd Gravel Ford

Graianrhyd is a small scattered hamlet centred on the B5430 six miles east of Ruthin. To the west is the Lafarge Graig Quarry (limestone) while immediately to the north-east of the village is the Maes y Droell Quarry (silicates). A planning application to turn the quarry into a recycling plant with landfill was rejected in 2013.

Tabernacl Welsh Independent Chapel behind houses on the main road was built in 1843 and rebuilt in 1859. It is closed and has been converted to residential use. North of the village, near the former Llanarmon lead mine was Moriah Welsh Calvinistic Methodist Chapel, built in 1859. It was replaced by a modern building in 1981 though this too has been demolished, leaving only the cemetery.

Graianrhyd had two pubs, the Miners' Arms which had closed by 1920 and the Rose and Crown which still trades. The village school closed in 2002 when there were just three pupils. It is now the community hall known as The Old Schoolroom. There was a post World War II development of 12 houses but no other new building in this hamlet. Between Graianrhyd and the Graig Quarry is Bryn Ffynnon, a rare three storey 18th century farmhouse

Graig-fechan Small Rock

Lying three miles south-east of Ruthin on the B5429, the hamlet of Graig-fechan saw considerable expansion in the latter half of the 20th century. In the 19th century this was a quarrying area with two quarries and two limekilns on the hill to the east of the Three Pigeons.

Capel Ebenezer in the centre of the village is Grade II Listed. Built in 1839 this Welsh Independent chapel retains its original interior. At the northern end of the village Bethel Welsh Wesleyan Methodist Chapel was built in 1802 and rebuilt in 1845 and again in 1884. In 2009 it was converted for residential accommodation.

The Three Pigeons Inn was rebuilt in 1777 though an alehouse and drovers' stead has stood on the site since the 12th century. The inn is said to be haunted with at least two ghosts in residence.

Gresford Welsh: Gressfordd

Gresford lies some three miles north of Wrexham town centre. The name is derived from Grass Ford though in the 15th century there was a belief that it was derived from Y Groesfford meaning ford of the cross. The Manor of Gretford is mentioned in the Domesday Book of 1086 as having a church, seven villagers, twelve smallholders, one priest and one Frenchman. It is unclear where the 11th century church was located, as the land on which Gresford church is built was given by local landowners, Trahaearn ap Ithel ap Eunydd and his five brothers, at the end of the 12th century. It may have been the chapel of St Leonard at Pont-y-Capel, south of Llay which was in use until the 16th century but the only evidence of it today is the name of the lane. The village grew up around the new church and by the 17th century Lhuyd recorded 20 houses.

Samuel Lewis in 1848 noted: *"The little Vale of Gresford is one of the most lovely valleys in the principality, abounding with interesting objects, enlivened by the meanderings of the River Alyn through its meadows, and finely varied with richly wooded eminences, on one of which stands conspicuously the beautiful church, remarkable for the elegance of its architecture and for its picturesque appearance. The plantations and pleasure-grounds attached to the elegant villas and rural mansions which are scattered throughout this small but romantic dell, combine, with the natural beauties of its scenery, to render it in every respect one of the most attractive spots in this part of the country."*

Grade I Listed All Saints Church was built in the 13th century though only the 14th century tower and parts of the west and east walls were retained when the church was rebuilt in the 15th century in the Perpendicular style, creating what has been called the perfect Cheshire church in Wales. Glass for the rebuilding was donated by Thomas Stanley, Earl of Derby whose brother William was Lord of the Manor of Holt within the parish. It is believed that the church once held a relic which drew pilgrims from across the country. In 1542 Bishop Parfrew wrote to Thomas Cromwell that of *"late time many and divers oblatlons, offerings ... profits ... and advantages were yearly from divers parts of this Realm brought, given and offered at and in the said church of Gresford"* and in 1535 Cromwell's inspectors recorded a congregation of 1,000. Whatever the reason for the pilgrimage disappeared with the Reformation.

The church has a central nave with north and south aisles ending in chapels, the north containing the Lady Chapel and the south the Trevor Chapel (see Trevalyn at Rossett). There is a seven bay arcade to each aisle with clerestory windows above the arcades. The arcades stop short of the east wall with solid walls pierced by arched openings above which are doorways which once led to a gallery above the reredos. The shallow camber beam roof of the nave and chancel is richly panelled. The fine 15th century chancel screen is thought to have been produced at Ludlow. There are less ornate screens to the aisle chapels. There is a vaulted crypt beneath the chancel. The medieval glass is to be found in the chapels with later windows, some containing medieval glass in the tracery by Lobin of Tours. Other glass is by Clayton & Bell, Heaton, Butler & Bayne and Kempe. In 1966 the parishioners set about cleaning the windows using detergent, causing damage to the stained and painted glass. Subsequent conservation has helped but fortunately the windows in the Trevor Chapel were not cleaned. The sanctuary is by Caröe in 1913 and the reredos by John Douglas in 1879. The north porch designed by Sir Thomas Jackson was added in 1921 as a War Memorial. There are a number of monuments and memorials in the church and in the Trevor Chapel is a painting commemorating the Gresford mine disaster of 1934 when 266 men died. Externally the parapets are embattled and the 14th century tower was raised after a donation by John Roden in 1512. The pinnacles were added in 1582 when John Leach bequeathed 10 shillings for their building. In 1851 Cliffe recorded that on one side of the Perpendicular tower was a statue of Henry VII, and there were also figures of the twelve apostles. In 1865-7 George Edmund Street partially rebuilt the tower which had collapsed.

The bells of All Saints were regarded as one of the Seven Wonders of Wales for their purity and tone. The bells have been recast over the years and currently there is a peal of eight bells weighing in total 4.7 tonnes with the oldest dating to 1775. A ninth bell, the Priest's Bell dates to 1615. In 1877 a device was added to allow one person to ring all eight bells if there were insufficient ringers before a church service.

In the churchyard fourteen of the graves are Grade II Listed. The yew tree dates from around 500AD. A Roman altar stone was discovered in 1908 suggesting that the site had religious significance long before the building of All Saints which now houses that altar stone.

Pinfold Calvinistic Methodist Chapel was built on the High Street in 1843 next to Chapel Cottages, but has long been demolished. Gresford Wesleyan Methodist Church on Chester Road was built in 1879 in the Gothic style. It replaced an 1822 chapel on Turnpike Lane, off Pant Lane.

On The Green, north of the church is Strode House and a set of almshouses. Strode House was built in 1725 as a school from a bequest by Margaret Strode, daughter of Col. John Roberts of Gwersyllt for the education of three poor boys and three poor girls. It was extended in 1838 but is now a private house. The three almshouses were also built in 1725 by Dr Robert Wynne chancellor of the diocese and vicar at Gresford for 53 years. The central house is now used for church meetings while the others are now private dwellings. At Green Farm there is a rare example of an early 19th century circular privy. This was designed with two doors to provide both for the family and farmworkers. Green Farm itself was rebuilt in the early 20th century. All Saints Primary School was built in 1873-4 from a donation by Archdeacon Wickham in memory of Thomas Vowler Short, Bishop of St. Asaph who had died in 1872. The architect was Edward Jones of Wrexham. The school was enlarged in the 20th century with the old schoolroom now serving as a dining hall. The Schoolhouse is now a private residence.

Situated on a traffic island at the junction of Chester Road and the B5373 is the base of a medieval cross.

The village of Gresford expanded in the 19th century with High Street and its attractive lake, an area which together with the church and its environs is now a conservation area.

In 1908 the United Westminster and Wrexham Collieries Ltd began the sinking of Gresford Colliery, a mile south-east of the church on a site on the western side of the Wrexham By-pass. The first coal was produced in 1911 and by 1933 the mine was employing 2,224 men. On Saturday 22nd of September 1934 at 2am a massive explosion caused the deaths of 265 men, including three rescuers. On 25th September a second explosion blew a seal resulting in the death of a further man, on the surface, hit by flying debris. Only 11 bodies were ever recovered, the shaft being sealed. Coal production resumed in 1936 and continued until closure in 1973.

There are three inns in the village. The Griffin near the church was built on land owned by the church until 1924 and in the church is a carving of a griffin dating from 1350 beneath the vicar's seat. The Plough Inn stands at the end of the largely 19th century High Street. Against the wall on the junction near the

Plough is the last remaining of four public water taps that provided water for the village in the 19th century by way of a hydraulic ram. Prior to 1861 apart from a few deep wells the only source of water was the lake, then a dirty pond. Miss Anne Townshend of Trevalyn inspired the building of a water supply, with a pump from St Catherine's Well in Bottom Lane feeding a tank which in turn fed the four taps. Each villager was given a key though the pressure was low. The four taps remained the principal source of water until 1916. The Yew Tree Inn on Pant Lane was built in the 1840s for a Liverpool merchant, Mr T F Bennett. It was split into cottages in the 1850s with one becoming Jackson's Beer House.

The Shrewsbury and Chester Railway opened in 1848 with a station serving Gresford and Llay. The line was along the steep Gresford Bank with a siding provided to allow wagons to be detached enabling the train to climb the bank. The station closed in 1962 and the line reduced to single track.

The major expansion of Gresford took place in the 1950s and 60s with housing estates to the east of the old village.

South of the village, east of Old Wrexham Road is Pant-yr-ochain Hotel. Known as Pant Iocyn it was owned in 1592 by William Almer. Almer was a descendant of Ithel ab Eunydd and was M.P. for Denbighshire in 1572 but was defeated by John Edwards of Chirkland in 1588. The house was built using stone from the previous family seat of Almer around 1530. Subsequent owners included George Lloyd, Bishop of Chester and in 1785 it was purchased by Sir Foster Cunliffe. Sir Foster lived the high life in Wrexham at the now demolished Acton Hall, once owned by Judge George Jeffreys. The Cunliffe wealth was inherited from his grandfather, also Foster Cunliffe, who at one time was the major slave trader in Liverpool and served as mayor on three occasions. Pant Iocyn was used as a residence by his two unmarried daughters (he had 11 children in total). They were known for their parties with guests including Charles Watkin Williams-Wynn, the Glynne family of Hawarden and a young William Gladstone. The house remained in the Cunliffe family into the 20th century. It was remodelled in the 19th century and again in the 20th century when it was converted into a hotel and is now a gastro pub. In the grounds is a ride on model railway while nearby is The Flash, a man made lake used by the Gresford Sailing Club.

Groes Cross

The hamlet of Groes lies on the A543, three miles south-west of Denbigh. In 1875 there was the smithy, Y Groes Chapel and Groes Hall. Since World War II there has been some development, including the Bronallt Estate.

Y Groes Welsh Calvinistic Methodist Chapel was originally founded as a Sunday School in 1801. The chapel was built in 1817 and enlarged to its present condition 1862. The manse was added in 1932. The chapel has an unusual design with its gable entry via two porches with the doors set at rightangles to the chapel. It is still in use with regular Sunday services.

Groes Hall was largely rebuilt in the 18th and 19th centuries and has now been divided to form two dwellings. A fireplace bears the date 1667 and it is thought that the original house took the form of a timber framed passage building. It was the home of the Vaughan family with John Vaughan Esq. acting as High Sheriff in 1641.

Gwersyllt Encampment

Gwersyllt today is a large village on the A541 Mold Road two and a half miles north-west of Wrexham. Prior to 1851 the area was farmland but in that year the parish of Gwersyllt was established and Holy Trinity Church was built to the designs of Denbighshire County Surveyor Thomas Penson junior. Penson lived in the parish and gave his services free of charge. Prior to 1851 there was a small hamlet known as Wheatsheaf around the inn of that name. The Wrexham historian A.N. Palmer suggested that the inn's car park was the site of St Leonard's Chapel (see Gresford).

Holy Trinity is a large church with a five bay nave, with a tower north of the chancel and a vestry to the south. There is a south porch. The furnishings are mainly original apart from the tracery in the reredos where wood panelling replaced a painted zinc decoration in 1970. The church occupies a prominent position on Mold Road just south of the Gwersyllt Colliery site. Penson also designed the National School built to the west of the church on Llys Alyn.

By 1875 the colliery had been established but apart from the Wheatsheaf Inn and the 1820 Wheatsheaf Independent Methodist Chapel on Wheatsheaf Lane there was little building though there was Gwersyllt Station on the Wrexham Mold and Connah's Quay Railway and the Wheatsheaf and Ffrwd Branch line of the Great Western Railway (originally the Brymbo and Minera Branch of the North Wales Mineral Railway) had been built. This line included a rope worked incline when it was built in 1847 to cope with the 1 in 17 slope of Gwersyllt Hill. The Wheatsheaf Chapel was replaced by a new Wheatsheaf English Congregational Chapel on Hope Street which is still active. The Wheatsheaf Presbyterian Chapel on High Street was founded in 1827, with the chapel built in 1881 but since demolished and replaced by the Tudor's

Avenue development. Bethel Welsh Independent Chapel on Rhosrobin Road was built in 1890 but after closing in the 1960s was used as a shop before being demolished for the Chapel Mews development. Rhosrobin Welsh Calvinistic Methodist Chapel on Rhosrobin Road was built in 1893 but is now a private dwelling.

Gwersyllt Colliery was sunk in the 1870s by Thomas Clayton who operated it in conjunction with the Westminster Colliery at Moss. In 1896 it was shown as being used for pumping and closed in 1925. The last owner of Gwersyllt Colliery was W.H. Kaye who opened a petrol station on the site. In 1931 Anne and Ben Kaye converted one of the colliery buildings to the Gwersyllt Working Mens Club which remains active.

By 1890 the village was still small with housing around the station and High Street. Major house building took place through the 20th century and the village now boasts a shopping area, a number of takeaway restaurants, the Wheatsheaf Inn and four schools.

Gwynfryn White Hill
Gwynfryn is a hamlet three quarters of a mile south-west of Bwlchgwyn, overlooking the Sychnant valley, the site of Ragman Lead Mine and Lester and Minera lime works which provided the impetus for the original village.

Gwynfryn Welsh Wesleyan Methodist Chapel on Allt-y-pentref was built in 1882, to the design of architect Thomas Williams of Glanrafon but is now a private house. There was also the mission chapel of St David's which was closed in 2010.

Today the hamlet offers fine views, taken advantage of by some large modern houses.

Gwytherin
Gwytherin is an attractive small village five miles east of Llanrwst. According to Morgan the name derives from St Gwytherin, though he also gives the literal translation as 'Vein of Gold'. The church today however is dedicated to St Winifred and the early history of the village is shrouded in legend. Baring Gould maintains that the name Gwytherin was an error and a misreading of the genealogies 'Eleri of Pennant Gwytherin in Rhufoniog'. Eleri was Abbot confessor of a joint monastery at Gwytherin where his mother was in charge of the nuns. Baring-Gould points out the in the 19th century the church was like those at Llanvetherine in Monmouthshire (where the original dedication

of the church was to St Gwytherin) and Holywell dedicated to St James the Apostle.

St Winifred who lived in the 7th century was of noble though not Royal Welsh blood but refused to marry a local prince, Caradoc, preferring the life of a nun. Caradoc was so infuriated by her refusal that he decapitated her with his sword and her head rolled down the hill and where it stopped a spring broke forth. Winifred's uncle St Bueno re-attached her head and Winifred came back to life. The spring where her head had come to rest became Holywell in Flintshire. St Bueno having witnessed the beheading called on the wrath of heaven and Caradoc was struck dead on the spot. According to the legend St Bueno decreed that anyone who made a request three times on the stone at the well pool, which was for the benefit of their soul, would have their request granted. St Winifred, who it is said bore a scar on her neck, established a convent at Holywell but after eight years left for Gwytherin.

She was buried at Gwytherin which like Holywell became a place of pilgrimage. Her life was told by Prior Robert of Shrewsbury Abbey. The abbey was dedicated to St Peter and St Paul but eager for a shrine to attract pilgrims Prior Robert sent a party of monks to bring the remains of St Winifred to the abbey. In 1138 her bones were removed from Gwytherin and taken to Shrewsbury. The story formed the basis of the first of Ellis Peters' Brother Cadfael chronicles, *A Morbid Taste for Bones*. The shrine at Shrewsbury Abbey was destroyed by Henry VIII, but recently a small bone was discovered in Rome and part sent to Holywell. St Winifred is recognized as a saint by the Roman Catholic Church where she is known as St Winefridae.

After the removal of her remains a chapel was built over the empty tomb. It later became a house before being demolished with the stone used to build a stable. By the mid 19th century the church was in a poor condition and was rebuilt by Lloyd Williams and Underwood in 1867-9, using the original single cell floor plan and incorporating the original foundations and some of the stone. Inside are two 14th century tomb slabs and a medieval dug out chest. The font bowl is medieval but mounted on a 19th century base. There is a lean-to vestry to the north with a southern porch. The small spired bellcote is aligned with the porch. In the graveyard are three ancient yew trees and, to north of the church, a line of four standing stones dating from the 5-6th century, one of which is inscribed *VINNEMAGLI FILI SENEMAGLI*. The church was declared redundant in 1982, but was rededicated in 1990 only to be declared redundant again in 2005. It is now a Historic Centre and Creative Arts Studio known as The Gwenfrewi Studio.

On the hillside to the north of the village is Siloh Welsh Calvinistic Methodist Chapel which was built in 1815 and rebuilt in 1855. Also built around 1855 was the Non-conformist British School which is now used as the Community Centre. There was a corn mill on the River Cledwyn which gave its name to Pont y Felin.

In the heart of the village is The Lion Inn, formed from a row of 17th century cottages. The Lion offers six bedrooms and enjoys a high reputation for its food and ales.

Henllan Old Church

Henllan lies two miles north-west of Denbigh. It was once the centre of a large parish of some 60 square miles between St Asaph and Llanrwst. While the parish has been reduced in size, the village has seen a large increase in population since 1945. The older part of the village is a conservation area and offers views to the west.

The church is dedicated to St Sadwrn who was mentioned in the Legend of St Winefred by Robert, Prior of Shrewsbury. According to the legend St Winefred sought advice from Sadwrn and the two passed the night in prayer before he informed her that he had been instructed from heaven to pass her on to St Elerius at Gwytherin. Sadwrn accompanied Winefred part of the way on her journey. This Sadwrn lived in the 6th-7th century, later than the saint associated with Llansadwrn in Carmarthenshire. The church is built on a hillside with the separate tower built on a rocky outcrop higher than the church. Recorded as 'Ecclesia de Henlan' in the *Taxatio* of 1291 the present building dates from the late 13th century although restorations have removed much of the medieval work except for the north doorway (now giving access to the vestry) and a small piscina. The church was largely rebuilt in 1807-8 when the Gothic windows were installed. In 1878-9 the Denbigh architect Richard Lloyd Williams added a south porch and north vestry. It is a single cell building with a barrel vaulted pine ceiling and bare stone walls. The wood panelling of the west end is from Eaton Hall in Cheshire and was installed in 1965. Items of interest include a Jacobean altar table and a pair of 18th century chandeliers. There are a number of 18th and 19th century memorial tablets and stained glass windows. Of particular note are the 1935 Whitefriars Glass window commissioned by Sir Earnest Tate Bart., of Galltfaenan Hall, to commemorate King George V's jubilee and the small rectangular window in memory of Thomas Peake who died in 1837 designed by Charles Winston and made by Ward and Nixon. (For Gallfaenan Hall see Trefnant.)

Near the south porch is the sandstone shaft of a medieval cross standing seven foot high. The lychgate was another gift of Sir Earnest Tate to mark the 1935 Jubilee. The churchyard contains a group of four mausolea including the pyramidal mausoleum of the Heaton family of Plas Heaton and a number of 17th century chest tombs. The tower dates from the early 14th century and has always been detached. It is built on a rock outcrop and its position higher than the church allowed its bells to be heard over a wider area. Together with the church it is Grade II* Listed.

Henllan Welsh Wesleyan Methodist Chapel was built in 1810 but is no longer in use. Capel Salem, the Welsh Calvinistic Methodist Chapel off Denbigh Street is still in use.

The attractive thatched Lindir Inn is claimed to date from 1229 and one of the oldest inns in Wales. The Cadw Listing however suggests that the building dates from the late 16th century. The inn is alleged to be haunted by an 18th century ghost named Sylvia whose sailor husband returned home unexpectedly to discover his wife and her lover in bed. Sylvia was murdered by her husband and is said to haunt the first floor, appearing only to females on cold frosty nights. It seems that the ghost sightings coincided with the arrival of American servicemen stationed in Denbigh in World War II. Opposite the inn is a group of almshouses. School Street contains a number of older cottages with some dating to 1752. A National School was established on the site of the present primary school in the 1860s.

Henllan has a village store.

Grade II* Listed Plas Heaton, a little under a mile north-east of the church, was built in the late 17th century as a dower house for the Griffith family of Garn and originally known as Plas Newydd. It was enlarged in the 1760s and received a Georgian makeover in 1805 when the Heaton family took occupation, at first as tenants before purchasing and renaming the house in 1807. The Heatons had arrived in Denbighshire in 1280 with Henry de Lacy and were granted land at Lleweni Green by Edward I. Through marriage they were connected with the Myddelton, Wynne, Griffiths and Lloyd families. They lived at Plas Heaton near Denbigh before John Heaton moved to Plas Newydd and renamed it. The Heaton line ended in 1965 with the death of Wilfred John Heaton. The house is now the centre of a farm. Also Grade II* Listed is Garn, the home of the Griffiths family half a mile north-east of the church. The property was held by Thomas Griffith, a younger son of the poet and antiquary, Gruffydd ap Ieuan ap Llywelyn Vychan of Llannerch Hall, Lleweni in Elizabethan times. There is some fabric dating to the 17th century but the main building dates from 1738-9 when John and Mary Griffith employed Robert West to rebuild the house after a fire. The house was enlarged by the Denbigh architect Richard Lloyd Williams in 1889.

Another important house in the neighbourhood is Foxhall, three quarters of a mile south-east of the church. Originally known as Foulks Hall, Henry Rosingdale who accompanied de Lacy in 1288 married the heiress, their descendants assuming the Lloyd surname with its alternate spellings of Llwyd and Lhuyd. Members of the family were High Sheriffs in the 16th, 17th and 18th centuries, but the most celebrated member of the family was the physician and antiquarian Humphrey Lhuyd (1527-1568). Educated at Oxford he published a number of books including *An Almanack and Kalender containing the Day, Hour, and Minute of the Change of the Moon for ever,* a translation of Caradog of Llancarfan's *Chronicle of Wales* but probably his most impressive works were manuscript maps of Wales and England which he sent to Abraham Ortelius in Antwerp shortly before his death. Both appeared in 1573, in a supplement to the *Theatrum* first published by Ortelius in 1570, becoming the first printed maps of Wales. The house is thought to be one of the earliest non-military stone built houses in Wales with elements dating from the 14th century retained together with Tudor and later additions. 350 yards west of Foxhall stand the grand ruins of Foxhall Newydd. Started in 1592 by John Panton, Recorder of Denbigh and Chief Secretary to the Lord Keeper, with his office in the Strand, Foxhhall Newydd was designed to impress his neighbours. Only a third was ever built as Panton ran out of money but the three storey house was occupied until the end of the 18th century though it was in ruins, without a roof, by the 19th century. The house had three storeys plus a basement and attic rooms. In the grounds are remains of a substantial dovecote. The house is Grade I Listed.

Holt (from Old English meaning 'A Wood')
Situated on the banks of the River Dee five miles north-east of Wrexham, Holt was formerly a town. The parish of Holt was given to the Chester Diocese by Edward the Confessor, but it was also known by the Welsh name of 'Castell Lleon' meaning 'Castle of the Legions', referring to an outpost of Roman

Chester. The Welsh was mis-translated as Castle of Lions and the village was for some time known as Lyons.

At the time of Henry III the Lordship of Dinas Brân was held by Gruffydd ap Madoc, a supporter of the king. Gruffydd married Emma, daughter of Lord Andley and they had four sons. Gruffydd died in 1270 and there was a dispute between Emma and her late husband's relatives over custody of the children for fear she might raise them as Englishmen. Following his accession in 1272 Emma delivered the two eldest to Edward I who in turn entrusted Madoc to John Earl Warren and Llewellin to Roger de Mortimer. Warren built Holt Castle and Mortimer built Chirk Castle. The two boys died without issue and their guardians assumed ownership of their respective lands. This gave rise to the belief that the two boys had been murdered. In the 1810 book *Wales Illustrated in a Series of Views* there is an assertion that a document in the Bodleian Library evidenced the drowning of the boys beneath Holt Bridge and implicated their mother in the murders. Pennant however suggests that the murdered children were the grandsons of Gruffydd by his eldest son Madoc. Gruffydd's third son, also Gruffydd inherited Glandyfydwy and his grandson was Owain Glyndŵr. Holt castle and its lands passed by marriage

Holt

to Edward Earl of Arundel in 1347 and was in the hands of Thomas Earl of Arundel in 1410 when he granted the inhabitants of Holt a charter of incorporation, which precluded all but Englishmen from participating in the privileges and immunities which he then bestowed.

The Welsh Lordship of Dinas Brân was centred on the magnificent hilltop castle of Castell Dinas Brân situated to the north of Llangollen. The castle was damaged when torched by its own garrison in 1277 and abandoned in 1282 in favour of a new castle at Holt. Holt Castle was built between 1282 and 1311 to guard a ford across the River Dee. It was built in the form of a pentagon with four round towers and to the south a square tower containing the chapel. There was a gatehouse to the north and from Norden's survey circa 1620 a drawbridge and outer gatehouse. The castle occupies a quarry from which stone to build the castle was taken. In the 14th century it came into the hands of the Earls of Arundel.

In 1399 following the end of the Arundel line it reverted to the Crown and was granted to the Duke of Hertford who discovered jewels to the value of 200,000 marks and 100,000 marks in cash, the treasure of Richard II deposited before his expedition to Ireland. A planned town was built but destroyed by the Welsh under Glyndŵr in 1400 but the castle withstood the attack. Henry VII granted the castle to Sir William Stanley but on the latter's execution it reverted to the Crown complete with its treasure of 40,000 marks which Stanley had plundered after the Battle of Bosworth. It was held by the Royalists during the English Civil War, captured by the Parliamentarians in 1643 but retaken by the Royalists in 1644 when 13 of the Roundheads were put to the sword and their bodies tossed into the moat. Sir Richard Lloyd eventually surrendered in 1647 after which Parliament ordered the castle destroyed. The remains were denuded by Sir Thomas Grosvenor who used the stone from the castle to rebuild Eaton Hall. In recent years there has been work on the castle which was opened to the public in 2015.

Grade I Listed Holt Bridge was built in 1339 by Monks from St Werburgh's Abbey Chester. Originally it was a ten arched bridge across the River Dee connecting Holt and Farndon. According to tradition the bridge was fortified though all evidence of this was removed in the 19th century when the number of arches was reduced to eight, five over the river, two over the flood plain on the Holt side and one on the Farndon side. The date of the bridge disproves the theory that the sons of Griffith ap Madoc were drowned beneath the bridge. Beneath an arch known as the Lady's Arch it is said that on certain nights two fairies can be seen. A painting of Holt Bridge by Richard Wilson is on display in the National Gallery. Painted around 1762, it shows a crumbling tower above the central arch of the bridge.

By 1810 the town of Holt was described as 'an inconsiderable village', while Bingley in 1839 described it as 'obscure'. The original importance of Holt is witnessed by Grade I Listed St Chad's Church. Built at the same time as the castle it was rebuilt in the 14th century and then remodelled in the late 15th century under the patronage of Sir William Stanley. In the 18th century the parapet was added and there was a refurbishment in 1871-3 by Ewan Christian and John Douglas of Chester. Further restorations in the 20th century included the clock and re-roofing.

St Chad's is a large church with a five bay nave and north and south aisles continuous with the two bay chancel. The south aisle is wider than the north with chapels at the eastern end of each, separated from the chancel by wooden screens of 1871-3. Windows are plain glass save for south aisle windows of 1912 depicting Sts David, Asaph, Chad and Swithun in memory of G T Kenyon of Gredington Hall. The roof is of camberbeam construction. The font of 1493 is decorated with the fleur de lys of Henry VII and the stag's head of the Stanleys. There are various memorials through the church. The red sandstone building has a west door beneath the four storey tower of 1679 containing a peal of six bells by Rudhall of Gloucester which were installed in 1714 and rehung in 1896. The clock was installed in 1902 in celebration of the coronation of Edward VII, replacing a clock of 1720 presented by Thomas Grosvenor, a younger son of Sir Richard Grosvenor of Eaton Hall, when he was Mayor of Holt. During the siege of Holt Castle by the Parliamentarians the church was occupied by the besieging forces and holes in the church door are the result of musket shot. In the churchyard is the remnant of a sundial dated 1736.

The English Presbyterian Chapel on Castle Street was built in 1843 and rebuilt in 1865 at the instigation of Revd Ebenezer Powell who also inspired the Academy School opposite. Built in the Gothic style, to the design of architect Thomas Meak Lockwood of Chester it is Grade II Listed. The red brick Holt English Baptist Chapel on Chapel Street was built in 1827 and rebuilt in 1894. It closed in 1954. Bethesda New Connexion Methodist Chapel on Church Street was built in 1853. It has now been converted for residential use. The New Connexion Methodists broke away from the Wesleyan Methodists in 1797 eventually merging in 1907 with the Bible Christian

Church and the United Methodist Free Churches to form the United Methodist Church.

Although described as an 'inconsiderable village' in the early 19th century, Lewis reported that Holt was still *"governed by a mayor, two bailiffs, and a coroner, who are elected annually"* under the 1410 Borough Charter. It retained its mayor until 1884. Until 1897 there was a town hall situated on the Square near the White Lion. The Market Cross was positioned at its present location on the small green in 1896 but is of late medieval date. The village War Memorial nearby was designed by Mansley of Chester and unveiled on August 1st, 1920.

The village retains its two inns, The White Lion and The Peal of Bells. The Gredington Arms, formerly the Red Lion closed in 2010. There is a village primary school, various shops and takeaways and restaurants. On the outskirts is the Bellis Garden Centre and Farmers Market. The Kenyon Hall serves as the village hall. Built on land donated by Lord Kenyon in 1892 and opened by the Duchess of Westminster, the hall stands in the centre of the village opposite the market cross.

Holt saw considerable expansion in the 20th century and had a population of 1,521 in 2011. There are a number of older buildings giving character to this village with its long history. Among its famous visitors were Richard II, Henry VII and in 1603 Guy Fawkes while H G Wells addressed the Academy in 1883.

Johnstown

Lying three miles south-west of Wrexham, Johnstown is a former coal mining village which developed at the end of the 19th century. The village is named after John Bury, the landowner who sold the land for development and the Johnstown Estate Plan was drawn up by Jenkins and Jones. Prior to 1880 there were just a few buildings on the Wrexham to Ruabon Turnpike including the New Inn and Travellers Rest and the older Moreton Inn and houses around Moreton Street. By 1900 there was housing along High Street, Maelor Road and Merlin Street together with a range of churches, chapels and pubs. Industry in the village consisted of a gas works and timber yard, the former Ponkey Brick and Tile Works started in 1866 having closed by 1900. The main industry was carried on to the east with Hafod y Bwch Colliery and Hafod Red Brick Works. By 1900 The village had its railway station on the Shrewsbury and Chester branch of the G.W.R.

The Ruabon Coal and Coke Company opened the Hafod colliery in 1867. Initially it was known as the New Ruabon Colliery. It was connected underground with the Bersham Colliery and employed over 2,000 men at its peak. Production stopped in March 1968 and the surface buildings were removed. Five men died in an accident in 1873. The old coal tip has been landscaped and now forms Bonc Yr Hafod Community Park, a 90 acre park with lakes and trees on a hill known locally as Picnic Hill. The Hafod Red Brick Company was established by Henry Dennis in 1878. Now known as Dennis Ruabon Brickworks it is still in production.

St Mary's Church was built as an iron church in 1878, being replaced by the present red brick church in 1926-28 by the architect E Glyn Wooley. The chancel was not completed until 1957 and the planned tower has never been built. Nave and chancel are of a single cell with a south transept and north vestry and porch. The bellcote is located above the vestry in a pillar designed for the un-built tower.

The red brick Seilo Welsh Calvinistic Methodist Chapel had been built by 1900 on Merlin Street. Christchurch Congregational Chapel, also on Merlin Street, was built in 1899. It was later the United Reform Church but has been demolished and replaced by housing. Noddfa Welsh Baptist Chapel on Bangor Road was built in 1901 but has since been demolished and the site used for housing. Johnstown Welsh Wesleyan Methodist Chapel on the corner of High Street and Park Street was built by 1912.

Hafod House which gave its name to the colliery dates from the late 17th century. It is now an old people's home.

Johnstown now has a population in excess of 3,000, with two schools: Johnstown Infants School and Johnstown Junior School. There is a range of village shops, takeaways and services and Johnston is now left with three pubs, the New Inn, the Moreton Inn and the Grapes.

Kinmel Bay

Kinmel Bay, named after the Kinmel estate (See Llansant Sior) lies on the north coast between Rhyl and Towyn, immediately west of the estuary of the River Clwyd. It is a 20th century development. The 1877 Ordnance Survey map shows that what is now Foryd Harbour, with its yachts and pleasure boats, was a small commercial port with three cranes and a landing stage with a branch of the London and North Western Railway terminating alongside. The only buildings of note were a lifeboat station south of the bridge and Foryd

Lodge which remains. By 1899 there was a saw mill on the promontory and the Ferry Hotel.

The area was known as Foryd though the main centre of Foryd was across the river and county boundary. A toll bridge which opened to allow shipping through was built in 1861 by Middlesborough's Messrs McClune and McKenzie but proved inadequate for the motoring age with bus passengers having to walk across. The Foryd Bridge, known locally as the blue bridge was designed by the Flintshire County Surveyor, R.G. Whitley and built by Dorman Long and Company, also of Middlesborough. It opened in 1932. In October 2013 the Pont-y-Ddraig (Dragon's Bridge) for pedestrians and cyclists opened. It can be raised for the passage of yachts and forms part of the Wales Coastal Path. It was designed by Ramboll UK Ltd and built by the Swansea based Dawnus Construction. The promontory was the site of a telegraph station built in 1828 as part of the Liverpool and Holyhead Telegraph. It was replaced in 1836 by a station further south but in anticipation of the building of the railway a further station was built in 1848 to the north of the caravan park. In 1906 the *City of Ottawa*, a three masted square rigged ship, built in 1860, was brought to the estuary after being damaged in a storm and left to rot. The timbers are visible at low tide on the Rhyl side of the harbour between the road and foot bridges.

The Chester and Holyhead Railway opened in 1848. The holiday camp opened in the 1930s and now incorporates some of the buildings of the old saw mill. While there was some development of Kinmel Bay in the 1930s the major expansion was post 1945. Today there is a range of shops, pubs and takeaways as well as an Asda superstore and primary school. In addition to the holiday camp near the harbour there is the Oakfield Caravan Camp and Palins Holiday Camp to the south-west. It is a mainly residential area with a leisure centre and bowling green though there are some small industrial units. The sandy beach is backed by a promenade and offers swimming, canoeing, wind surfing and kite surfing. There is also the Kinmel Dunes Nature Reserve.

Lavister and Darland

Situated to the north of Rossett are the hamlets of Lavister and Darland. Lavister stretches along Chester Road towards the English border. There are some attractive cottages as well as some large modern houses. There was once a flour mill and two pubs, the Nags Head and the George and Dragon. Only the Nags Head remains.

Lavister English Congregational Chapel on Chester Road was built in 1890 but has now been converted to a private dwelling.

On Llyndir Lane is the Llyndir Hall Hotel, originally built in the early 19th century for Richard Barker, Gentleman, of Chester. It remained in the Barker family into the 20th century but has since been converted into a hotel.

Darland lies to the east of the Chester Road and has developed in the 20th century with Darland High School and small developments on and off Darland Lane.

Darland Hall developed over a long period. The Hall is said to be late 16th century, built for a Chester silversmith. It was extended to incorporate a cottage of 1636 and was developed by the Topham family who were the owners between 1786 and 1918. The Tophams were the developers and owners of Aintree, the home of the Grand National. The western end of the building was divided into flats in the 1950s but the main part of the hall remains as a single dwelling. A Roman Catholic chapel attached to the Hall has now been converted to living accommodation.

Llanarmon Dyffryn Ceiriog
The Church of St Garmon in the Vale of Ceiriog

Llanarmon Dyffryn Ceiriog lies in the valley of the Ceiriog at a point where several drove tracks met and the river was crossed by a ford. Some seven miles south-west of Llangollen it stands at an altitude of 900 feet. It is an attractive village with its two hotels at the wide cross roads and flower bedecked cottages.

The church of St Garmon stands on an ancient site with ancient yews and the Tomen Garmon, a mound alleged to have been a preaching mound with possibly the base of a preaching cross set at the top though some have conjectured that the mound has Bronze Age associations. (For details of St Garmon see Llanarmon-yn-Iâl.) An inscription in the church records that it was rebuilt in 1846 to accommodate 212 worshippers. The architect was Thomas Jones and there was a further restoration in 1986-7. A single cell building, it retains its box pews and west gallery. An unusual feature is the set of two wooden pulpits, flanking the altar rail. There is a memorial plaque to the 19th century Welsh poet John Ceiriog Hughes. The west tower rises from a square base containing the west door with an octagonal third storey topped by a short spire. In this beautiful rural setting it is a fine example of an early Victorian church.

Tabernacl Welsh Wesleyan Methodist Chapel to the rear of the West Hotel was built in 1835 and rebuilt in 1878 and 1911 in the Arts and Crafts style. At the southern end of the village, set back from the road is Salem Calvinistic Methodist Chapel which was built in 1843. Salem had a British School (non conformist) attached while across the road there was an Anglican National School. Ysgol Gynradd Llanarmon replaced both.

The West Arms Hotel was formerly known as the Eagle Inn and derives its present name from the West family of Ruthin, cousins of the Myddelton family of Chirk Castle whose family crest of a hand provides the name of the Hand Hotel opposite. The West Arms Hotel was opened in 1670 by the Watkin Williams Wynn family whose crest was the Eagle. It subsequently was owned by the Myddelton family and passed to the West family as part of a family settlement in the 19th century. The present building is largely 18th century. The Hand Hotel was formerly known as the Hand Inn and formed part of a farm offering accommodation to drovers and their animals. The farm finally closed in the 1960s and the old farmhouse became part of what is now the Hand Hotel with accommodation in the old farmhouse and converted stables and barns. There is also a spa and the restaurant is Michelin listed.

The three storey building across the road from Tabernacl was a flannel mill built in the 18th century. It is one of the few such buildings to survive although it had ceased to function by 1870. It was converted into a shop in the 1990s.

Llanarmon Mynydd Mawr
The Church of St Garmon on the Great Mountain

A tiny hill village a mile and a third north-east of Llanrhaeadr ym Mochnant with a few scattered houses and the church of St Garmon perched at 977 feet. (For details of St Garmon see Llanarmon-yn-Iâl.) The present church dates from 1886 and is a single cell building with south porch, north vestry and a western bellcote by W.H. Spaull of Oswestry. Formerly a chapel of ease to Llanrhaeadr it was mentioned as Capella de Llangarnayaun in the Norwich *Taxatio* of 1254 and as Lanarmavn in the Lincoln *Taxatio* of 1291. It became a parish in its own right before being joined with Llanrhaeadr. It was declared a 'pilgrimage church' in 2014.

A mile north-east of the church is Hermon Welsh Calvinistic Methodist Chapel, built in 1827 but rebuilt slightly to the west in the Art Nouveau style with a very elaborate window in 1906.

Llanarmon-yn-Iâl
The Church of St Garmon in the Commote of Iâl (Open Space)

Llanarmon lies in the Clwydian Hills four miles south-east of Ruthin. Garmon is the Welsh form of Germanus, commonly thought to be St Germanus, Bishop of Auxerre 378-448, but Baring-Gould suggests that there may be confusion with St Germanus, Bishop of Man. According to legend, Benlli Gawr was king of Powys and lived in the area of Iâl. Benlli was a brutal tyrant who refused to meet Germanus. In one version a fire sent by God destroyed Benlli and his city, in another: "*Germanus thrust him from his throne with his staff, and bade him surrender his seat to one more worthy to fill it. The king obeyed, and fled along with his wife and children. After that Germanus raised the subulcus to the vacant throne, and thenceforth to this day the descendants of the pig-driver gave kings to the Britons.*" (Baring-Gould). The new king, Cadell Ddyrnllug who ruled from 447 to 460 granted lands in Denbighshire to Germanus, including that at Iâl. (Subulcus is Latin for swineherd.)

The church of St Garmon is Grade I Listed and largely dates from the 15th century rebuilding when the south aisle was added to this double naved church. It once contained a shrine to St Garmon with an image of the saint said to have miraculous properties, making the village a place of pilgrimage. The arcade was replaced in 1733 by octagonal timber columns formed and installed by the Wrexham carpenter Edward Wettnall. About this time the windows were altered and the south porch was added. A restoration of 1870 by John Douglas saw the double bellcote added. There are the effigies of the owners of Bodidris, Gruffydd ap Llywelyn ab Ynyr, circa 1320, and Evan Llwyd, 1639 which retains much of its colour and has an inscription in Welsh recording his services to "*Brenin Siarls yn Ywerddon*" (King Charles in Ireland). The early 16th century 18 branch brass chandelier is a particular treasure and regarded as finer than that at Llandegla. The marble bowl font is 18th century while the pulpit dates from the 1870 restoration. On the south wall is a painting of the Royal Coat of Arms by David Davies dated 1740. The roof is late medieval. At the entrance to the churchyard is a bier house, for the storage of coffin carrying biers.

The church room south of St Garmon's was built as a church school in 1777 with the schoolroom over a basement residence for the teacher. It was replaced by a Board School in 1871.

At the end of Fford Rhiw Iâl is Bethel Welsh Calvinistic Methodist Chapel which was built in 1786 and rebuilt in 1812 and 1867 with Tŷ Capel built in similar style alongside. In front of the chapel is an obelisk in memory of John Parry (1835-97). Parry was the eldest son of Revd Hugh Parry of Llanarmon. He trained as a carpenter, but at the age of 20 lost a hand in an accident. At the age of 25 he was elected an elder of the Calvinistic Methodist church at Gwespyr, and, later at Llanarmon. He was a campaigner against tithes and refused to pay from 1886 until his death in 1897. In 1888 he was elected to the newly formed Denbighshire County Council but he is chiefly remembered for his extensive library of 4,000 books which were purchased by Sir John Williams and formed part of his donation to the National Library of Wales in 1909. The Obelisk, of polished red granite was made by Bowen & Florence of Aberdeen and unveiled in 1899.

Philadelphia Welsh Congregational Chapel was built in 1823 and rebuilt in 1850 with a decorated brick façade. It closed in the 1970s and is now a private dwelling.

The Raven Inn is now a community run pub. Dating from 1722 it was previously known as the Butcher's Arms. East of the village, across the River Alun is the 22 feet high natural rock outcrop of Tomen-y-faerdre, which formed the motte of an 11th century castle. The ditch away from the river appears to have been dug in 1212 when King John strengthened the castle and in the accounts is an entry *"For iron mallets for breaking the rocks in the ditch of the castle of Yale"*.

The village has expanded in recent years but the centre remains attractive with its church, pub and local store.

Llanbedr-Dyffryn-Clwyd
Church of St Peter in the Vale of Clwyd

Llanbedr Dyffryn Clwyd is a small rural village one and a half miles north-east of Ruthin. Most of the housing in the village is from the latter half of the 20th century.

The old church of St Peter is now in ruins in the grounds of Llanbedr Hall. It was first mentioned in the Norwich *Taxatio* of 1254 and dates from the 13th century. The walls are now reduced to six feet save for the early 19th century bellcote. The oldest part of the church was of red sandstone while later sections are of limestone. The graveyard offers extensive views over the Vale of Clwyd. It fell into ruin after 1863 when John Jesse F.R.S., J.P. and High Sheriff of Denbighshire in 1856 financed the building of the new St Peter's church after he witnessed that bodies in the old churchyard had to be disinterred to allow new burials. Ironically John Jesse died in September 1863 and is buried in the old graveyard. Among other tombs is the 1616 grave of Margaret Lloyd, heiress of Llanbedr Hall who married Richard Thelwall of Bathafarn Hall. The Thelwalls held Llanbedr Hall until 1804 when it was purchased by Joseph Ablett, a Manchester cotton cloth manufacturer, who also purchased Bathafarn Hall in 1831. Ablett largely rebuilt Llanbedr Hall and took an active role in the county, being a J.P. and High Sheriff in 1809. In 1826 he stood for Parliament, in lieu of Robert Myddelton-Biddulph who had not yet come of age, against Frederick West of Ruthin Castle. West had deliberately set the date of the election to prevent his cousin standing against him. Both candidates received 273 votes and a double return was declared. On petition West was declared elected though it was said to have cost him £40,000. Ablett died in 1848 and following his widow's death in 1854 it passed to his cousin, the Manchester surgeon John Jesse. Ablett is buried in the old graveyard but there is a memorial in the new church which reads *"At the northeast end in the old churchyard lie entombed the remains of Joseph Ablett, esq., of Llanbedr Hall, Dyffryn Clwyd. A pious and just man, of cultivated manners and refined taste and great benevolence. He went about doing good, offering consolation to the weary, and relieving the sufferings of his fellow men. To want and misery his purse was always open, and he ever strove to keep secret his acts of mercy. He died 9 Jany. 1848, aged 75 years. Ann, his wife, died 23 March 1854, aged 80."* Amongst his charitable gifts were land for the North Wales Asylum and the almshouses at Ruthin. Fire damaged the Hall in 1865 and it was remodelled by Poundley and Walker who were also responsible for the new St Peter's church. Llanbedr Hall is a two storey unlisted building and the present owner has plans for its demolition and replacement.

St Peter's Church is in the Early English style with an aisless nave, chancel, south porch, vestry and a square turret on which is an hexagonal bell opening, topped by a spire with small gabled openings or locarnes on each face and ostentatious crockets or leaf shapes protruding from the upper levels, all topped with a wheel cross. The roofs are of purple slate with grey slate bandings. A number of memorials from the old church have been placed in the new church. While in the porch is a 14th century tomb fragment. The east windows are by the noted London manufacturer Clayton and Bell. Furnishings date from the building of the church which is Grade II* Listed.

The Griffin Inn dates from the mid 19th century as does the former National School across the road.

To the south of the village is the 19th century Bathafarn Hall. Originally known as Bathafarn Park it was part of the deer park of Ruthin Castle. It was in the hands of the Thelwall family between the 16th and 18th century before passing to the Price family of Rhiwlas by marriage and then sale to Joseph Ablett. Since 1952 the Hall has been in the hands of the Smith family and has been divided into apartments. There is a small caravan and camping park and fishery.

A mile south-west of St Peter's Church is the Grade I Listed church of St Meugan. Meugant, Meugan, or Meigan, was the son of Gwyndaf Hen ab Emyr Llydaw, by Gwenonwy, daughter of Meurig ab Tewdrig, King of Morganwg. Built on a Celtic llan St Meugan's was established in the 6th century and was the mother church to Ruthin and indeed the parish church of Ruthin until 1310. A single cell building with a western double bellcote and south porch, the church retains its 1721 oak gallery and a late 15th century rood screen decorated with carvings which include a wyvern and Green Man. The 17th century altar table is supported by four rampant lions. There are a number of memorials including the late 16th century stone and marble funerary monument to John and Jane Thelwall of Bathafarn Park depicting the couple and their 14 children. Next to this is a life sized bust of their ninth son, Ambrose Thelwall (1570-1653), Yeoman of the Robes to King James 1st, King Charles 1st and Prince Charles. The seven bay arched-braced collar trussed roof is a good 15th century example. There was a restoration in 1852 by Henry Kennedy and the east window was donated in 1857 in memory of John Williams, M.P. Depicting scenes from Christ's life it is by Clayton and Bell with elaborate borders by the Whitefriars Glass firm of Powell and Sons. Outside there is a 1736 sundial with its original brass fitting. South of the church are the remains of a late medieval churchyard cross. The head is missing but the base and shaft is over 10 feet tall.

Opposite the church is the early 19th century Llanrhydd Hall. It was the home of the barrister turned novelist Stanley John Weyman who in 1900 was responsible for acquiring and installing the 18th century wrought iron gates by the noted ironsmith Robert Bakewell. South of the church is the old Llanrhydd flour mill.

Llanddoged

Llanddoged is a small rural village a mile north of Llanrwst. The upper part of the village enjoys views across the Conway valley to Snowdonia.

At the centre of the village is the late medieval double naved church of St Doged. Doged Frenin (the King) was son of Cedig ab Ceredig ab Cunedda Wledig and was mentioned in the Arthurian romance of Culhwch. and Olwen in which Culhwch's father murdered Doged to take his wife. The church at Llanddoged is the only church dedicated to him and Baring-Gould suggests that it was established as a martyrium. The church is built in the centre of a raised circular churchyard or llan and was renovated in 1838-9 by the then vicar, the Revd Thomas Davies. At this time the level of the roof was raised. The interior is particularly interesting with its arrangement of box pews. The two naves are divided by a six bay wooden column arcade. At the western end is a vestry and boiler room together with tiered box pews for boys and girls. The octagonal font is medieval while the 19th century wooden pulpit with arched frames to the side which contain an image of Christ and the Royal Coat of Arms. The monogram VR appears on the arms which are Hanoverian and in Welsh have the inscription 'Honour the King'. There is a simple western bellcote and a south porch. 90 yards north of the church, at the entrance to the road marked Ffynnon Ddoged is St Doged's Well, now covered. The water was said to have miraculous healing power and the village was a point of pilgrimage with a statue in the church to St Doged.

The village has a junior school which also serves as a village hall. The first school was built in 1827 as a National School for boys and girls. Soar Welsh Baptist Chapel was built in 1817 and rebuilt in 1863. It occupies an elevated position in the village offering superb views. It is Grade II Listed as a good example of a mid-Victorian Welsh chapel.

Llanddulas

The former limestone quarrying village of Llanddulas lies on the coast midway between Abergele and Old Colwyn. It has seen considerable expansion in the 20th century and has caravan and chalet parks. It is thought that the original name for the village was Llangynbryd after the dedication of the church, but the name of the local river, the Dulais was taken and appears in the Norwich *Taxatio* of 1254. St Cynbryd was said to have been one of the many children of Brychan Brycheiniog, the early king of Brecon, though he is not listed as a son. The church in the adjoining parish of Llysfaen is dedicated to his brother Cynfran. Cynbryd was martyred by unbelieving Saxons at Bwlch Cynbryd, a pass no longer identified.

On the eastern approach to the village are Tan yr Ogo Lodge and the boundary walls of Gwrych Castle estate. Either side of the arched gateway are four stone tablets recording historical events which occurred at this narrow strip between the mountains and the sea. In 1063 there was a battle here between the forces of Harold and Gruffydd ap Llewelyn. During the time of William the Conqueror Welsh forces attacked a Norman army led by Hugh d'Avranches, 1st Earl of Chester, leaving 1,100 men dead. Owain Gwynedd gave battle to the forces of Henry II and in 1399 Richard II, on his return from Ireland, was captured here by the forces of the Earl of Northumberland and handed over to Henry Bolingbroke a week later at Flint Castle.

Gwrych Castle occupies a prominent position on the hillside a little over a mile east of Llanddulas. Gwrych was the seat of the Lloyd family which traced its ancestry back to the 5th century ruler Cunedda Wledig. The Normans built a stronghold here which was captured by Rhys ap Gruffydd of Deheubarth

Gwrych Castle

in 1170 who rebuilt the castle in stone. This was destroyed by the Parliamentary army during the English Civil War. In 1785 Frances Lloyd, heiress of the Gwrych estate married Robert Bamford-Hesketh and their son Lloyd built the castle with the foundation stone laid in 1819. The architect was Thomas Rickman. This large 128 room castellated mansion with its 100 foot towers is impressive at a distance and as a fine example of the early 19th century Romantic movement and the 'picturesque', is Grade I Listed. On Lloyd's death the estate passed to his son Robert who with his wife Ellen employed George Edmund Street to design the chapel. Their daughter Winifred inherited the estate in 1894. Winifred married the Earl of Dundonald and they divided their family's time between Wales and Scotland. At her death in 1924 she bequeathed the castle to King George V to provide a Welsh Royal residence but the bequest was refused and the castle became the property of the Order of St John of Jerusalem. It was purchased by The Earl of Dundonald in 1928 but he sold many of the contents to finance the purchase. During World War II it was requisitioned and became home to 200 Jewish refugees. In 1948 it was bought by Leslie Salts who opened the castle to the public until 1968. It then passed through a number of hands being used as a restaurant and medieval centre. There are plans to restore the castle as a five star hotel and work began in 2014. A preservation Trust was established in 2001 and organises open weekends. Visible from the coastal road is Eleanor's Tower, a folly said to have been built in 1915 by the Countess of Dundonald in memory of her son who died at sea. Within Castle Wood are a cave and the shafts of a lead mine.

The Grade II* Listed church of St Cynbryd was rebuilt after the great storm of 1732 but by the mid 19th century was declared unsafe and was demolished and rebuilt in 1868-9. The building was financed by Robert Bamford Hesketh of nearby Gwrych Castle, with George Edmund Street employed as architect. Street was noted for his churches but his most celebrated design was for the Royal Courts of Justice in The Strand. The double naved church with its octagonal bell tower is in the Decorated style. The north nave is shorter than the south to accommodate the bell tower. There is a four bay arcade between the naves. The white marble font by Cecil Thomas is of a life-sized kneeling angel and installed in 1928. The medieval font is retained as is the stoup. The graveyard has been extended but the original circular llan is still discernible to the south. The Arts and Crafts style timber framed lychgate of 1899 was designed by Harold Hughes of Bangor for Alfred L. Jones, in memory of his mother. Hughes also designed the church hall, the foundation stone for which was laid by he Countess Dundonald of Gwrych Castle in 1910.

Beulah Calvinistic Methodist Chapel on Beulah Avenue was built in 1844 and rebuilt in 1905. It is now a private dwelling, as is the 1836 Bethesda Baptist Chapel on Minffordd Road. The New Hall English Wesleyan Chapel moved to its present site on Minffordd Road in 1951. Bryn-y-Felin Independent Chapel was built in 1838 and closed in 1858. Caersalem Welsh Independent Chapel was built on the site in 1868 and rebuilt in 1890 as part of a terrace on the A547. It is now a private house. On the eastern edge of the village is the New Life Revival Church a large stone built church with tower which doubles as the village hall.

Behind the terrace opposite the church on Mill Street was the mill pond, feeding the corn mill which was still in operation in 1939. The village has seen considerable expansion since 1939 and has a junior school. There are two pubs in the village, the Valentine and the Fair View with the Royal British Legion social club and bars in the Beach Holiday Park. The Dulas Arms has closed. There are takeaway restaurants and a service station with shop. The beach is a mixture of pebbles, rocks and sand while to the west a coastal defence scheme has seen the introduction of concrete dolos.

Llandegla

Llandegla, five and a half miles south-east of Ruthin, takes its name from the dedication of the church to St Tecla. This saint is thought to be an obscure Welsh saint and there are just two churches in Wales dedicated to her, the other being at Llandegley in Radnorshire. Tecla was a popular name in the early years of Christianity after the virgin-martyr companion of St Paul associated with *The Acts of Paul and Thecla*, the book in the *Apocrypha*.

The village which was on the main drovers' route was once celebrated for its October fair and for its Welsh Black Cattle. It was home to a number of inns though by 1872 only the Hand Inn survived and even this has now closed.

Baring-Gould records that "*Llandegla was formerly celebrated for its Holy Well, Ffynnon Degla, a small spring which lies in a quillet of the glebe-land, called Gwern Degla. Its water was considered highly efficacious in cases of epilepsy, so much so, that one of the names for that complaint in the Welsh dictionaries is Clwyf Tegla, Tegla's Disease or Sickness*". Bishop Maddox in the early 18th century gave the following account of the ritual "*In this Well the people that are troubled with convulsion fits or falling sickness call'd St Teccla's evil do use to wash their hands & feet, going about the well 3 times, saying the Lords prayer thrice, carrying in a handbasket a cock, if a Man; & a hen, if a Woman offering 4 pence in the said well. All this is done after sunset. Then going to the Churchyard after the same manner go about the Church, saying the Lords Prayer thrice, getting into the Church sleep under the Communion table with the Church bible under their heads, & the carpet to cover them all night till break of day. Then offering a piece of silver in the poor's box, leaving the Cock or Hen in the Church. They again repair to the Well & perform as above — if the cock dyed in the Church, the Patient was himself curd*". In 1749 the Rural Dean instructed the parish clerk to discourage this 'superstitious practice' and to admit no-one to the church after dusk. In 1813 however Evan Edwards, son of the sexton of the parish is recorded as having been through the ritual. Baring-Gould also records that it was customary "*to prick the fowl with a pin, which was afterwards thrown into the well; and that in church the epileptic was to put the bird's beak into his mouth and blow into it before letting the bird go*". The effects of the fits were thus transferred to the bird.

St Tecla's church, which in the 13th century belonged to Valle Crucis Abbey, was rebuilt in 1866 by John Gibson, the architect of Bodelwyddan church. It was paid for by Margaret, Lady Willoughby de Broke, sister of Sir Hugh Williams of Bodelwyddan Castle who had by this time acquired the local Bodidris estate. It is a single cell structure with north vestry, south porch and western bellcote. Inside there is a fine late-medieval font and a very fine late-medieval brass chandelier. The east window dates from 1800 by Francis Eginton and was part of a larger window brought from St Asaph's Cathedral.

Bethania Welsh Calvinistic Methodist Chapel was built in 1827 and rebuilt in 1903. It was closed and put up for sale in 2009. Seion Welsh Wesleyan Methodist Chapel was built in 1812 and rebuilt in 1842. It now forms the Llandegla Memorial Hall.

East of the church are the remains of Llandegla Flour Mill which was fed by a half mile leat from the River Alyn. There are a number of attractive cottages in the village including the Post Office, Church Terrace and the village school which was the gift of Sir Hugh Williams of Bodelwyddan . There has been new building and the village has expanded to merge with Pen-y-stryt. It is said that the old Rectory at Llandegla was haunted by a very troublesome spirit and a man named Griffiths of Graianrhyd was sent for to lay the Ghost. The Spirit appeared to him in various forms, but he was unable to master it until it came in the form of a fly, which Griffiths captured, and placed in a small box which he buried under a large stone in the river, just below Llandegla Bridge. The Spirit was trapped until a certain tree, near the bridge, reached the height of the parapet. To prevent this tree from growing, the school children nipped the upper branches, to retard its growth.

Bodidris Hall a mile north-east of the village is a late Elizabethan mansion, built by the Lloyd family who rose to eminence under the Tudors. Evan Lloyd fought alongside the Earl of Leicester in the Low Countries and was knighted by him. The Earl of Leicester is said to have used Bodidris as a hunting lodge, possibly using what is now Bodidris Cottage but was originally an impressive building in its own right. The bear and ragged staff, the emblem of the Leicesters appears on the south gable. Evan's son Sir John Lloyd was a supporter of the Earl of Essex and fought with him in Ireland. The Lloyds continued to own Bodidris until the mid 19th century when it came into the possession of Sir Hugh Williams. In the 1980s the hall was converted for use as a hotel but in 2014 it closed with plans submitted to revert to a private dwelling. It was said to have been the most haunted hotel in Wales.

Llandrillo yn Rhos The Church of St Trillo on the Heath

Llandrillo yn Rhos has been swallowed up by the urban conglomeration of Rhos on Sea, but in 1875 it consisted of church, vicarage, the Ship Hotel and a few farms though the parish covered Eirias, Colwyn, Rhiw, Cilgwyn, Llwyd Coed, Mochdre, and Dinerth. Rhos on Sea at that time was known as Glan-y-mor and consisted of a few houses together with the 15th century Rhos Fynach, thought to have been a monastic grange, the Blue Bell inn and Rhos Abbey Hotel (now a block of flats).

Trillo or Terillo was the son of Ithel Hael of Llydaw, and brother of Saints Tegai and Llechid. The family came to Wales from Brittany with St Cadfan. On the shore at Rhos is St Trillo's Cell, though the building dates from the 16th century. According to Baring Gould all the parish baptisms were carried out here using the water of the perpetual spring situated at its east end. There are the remains of a number of fish traps on the shoreline and Samuel Lewis in 1849 reports vast quantities of mackerel and salmon were caught.

The present church of St Trillo stands in an elevated position and dates from the 13th century. It is double naved with a four bay arcade. The roof is 16th century. The font is 13th century but other furnishings are 19th century save for the reredos which is a War Memorial. There was a restoration in 1857 by Henry Kennedy of Bangor. The west tower was added in 1552 and the lychgate in 1667. The graveyard has been extended and contains a number of fine 18th century chest tombs and a sundial from the same era. A replacement vicarage was built in 1902.

Llandyrnog

Llandyrnog is an expanding village three miles east of Denbigh. To the north of the village the Llandyrnog Creamery is the fourth largest cheese factory in Britain, producing Double Gloucester, Red Leicester and Cheddar cheese. It was opened in the 1920s and has a turnover of £60m a year, employing around 160 staff.

The Grade II* Listed church is dedicated to St Tyrnog, brother of St Carannog, and son of Corun ab Ceredig and a kinsman of St David. The church however was, according to Baring-Gould established by St Teyrnog, brother to Sts Tyfrydog, Tudur, Diefer and Marchell. Teyrnog is also identified with the Irish St Tighernach. The foundation of the church in its raised and once circular graveyard was Celtic but the first written evidence of the church was in the *Taxatio* of 1254. The building dates from the 15th century but was renovated in 1877-8 by the Eton educated architect William Eden Nesfield. Nesfield was better known for his domestic architecture including Kinmel Hall which he rebuilt for Hugh Robert Hughes, one of the donors for the church restoration along with P.S. Humberston of Glan-y-wern. The western gallery was removed and the organ loft installed in 1864. The church has a double nave with a western double bellcote over the northern nave. Prior to 1877 there were north and south porches, but the northern entrance has closed and the south porch is a half timbered structure. The naves are separated by a five arched arcade and have impressive medieval roofs. The chancel leads from the north nave while the vestry is at the eastern end of the south nave. Fittings are 19th century and there are a number of memorial tablets in brass and marble. The stained glass in the east window is medieval, restored in the 19th century. The other windows are 19th century as is the Nesfield designed lychgate.

Llandyrnog Wesleyan Methodist Chapel was built in 1810 and rebuilt in 1836 and again in 1874. It has now been converted to a private house. North of the village, Capel-y-Dyffryn Welsh Calvinistic Methodist Chapel was built in 1777 and rebuilt in 1836. The Baptist Chapel south-west of the village, near the Felin Isa corn mill was built in 1836 and rebuilt in 1868 but has been converted to private accommodation. Nearby, Plas Bennet is a house dating from 1710 but an earlier house on the site is said to have been the birthplace in 1585 of William Roberts, Bishop of Bangor who died at the rectory in the village in 1665.

The village continues to support its two pubs, the Golden Lion and the White Horse, both shown on the 1875 map, together with the Kinmel Arms Tavern to the north of the village. There is a general store and post office and a butcher's shop opposite the Golden Lion. The National School on the cross roads has been replaced by semi-detached houses and there is a new primary school.

Llanegwestl

According to Morgan, Llanegwestl refers to the the original dedication of a church on the site of Valle Crucis Abbey, the magnificent ruins of which are situated a mile and a quarter north of Llangollen. The Cistercian abbey was founded in 1201 by Madog ap Gruffydd Maelor, Prince of Powys Fadog and its building required the dispersal of the previous residents of the area. Valle Crucis takes its name, Valley of the Cross from Eliseg's Pillar, the remaining portion of a 9th century stone cross set on a mound by Cyngen, King of Powys

Valle Crucis Abbey

to commemorate his great-grandfather, Eliseg, who had reunited the kingdom by taking back land from the English. The first monks came from the abbey at Strata Marcella on the banks of the Severn near Welshpool. It had up to 60 monks and lay brethren and while it suffered damage in the wars of Edward I and the Glyndŵr rebellion, it became renowned as a seat of learning. A number of celebrated bards resided at the abbey, including Guto'r Glyn, Lewis Mon and Gutun Owain with the latter writing in praise of the architecture and hospitality of Valle Crucis. With the Dissolution of the Monasteries in 1536 the monks were evicted in 1537 and the estates were granted to Sir William Pickering, eventually forming part of the Coed Helen Estate. The abbey was reported to be in ruins as early as the end of the 16th century though parts were used as a manor house and later a farmhouse. In the late 18th century it became a focus of attention for the 'picturesque' movement and was painted by numerous artists including J.W.M. Turner whose watercolour and graphite painting is in the Tate Gallery. In 1872 there was a partial restoration by Sir George Gilbert Scott. Today the Grade I Listed abbey is in the care of Cadw and open to the public.

450 yards north-west of the abbey is Eliseg's Pillar, now standing at 7 foot 11 inches on a mound which contains a burial cist but it is not known whether this is Eliseg's burial chamber or a prehistoric tumulus. Between the pillar and the abbey was a fulling mill or pandy and the 1875 map shows lines of tenters where the cloth would be stretched out to dry. In addition to the road, a tramway ran past the abbey transporting slate from the quarries to the north.

On a conical hill to the south-east are the ruins of Castell Dinas Brân, the 13th century castle of the princes of Powys Fadog. This once impressive castle was besieged by Henry de Lacy in 1277 and set on fire by its defenders. Subsequently the seat of power moved to Holt. The castle was built on the site of an Iron Age hillfort.

Llanelian yn Rhôs Church of St Elian on the Moor
Perched on a hilltop a mile and a half south-east of Colwyn Bay the small village of Llanelian has views across to the Irish Sea and the Isle of Man.

St Elian or Eilian (Latin Elianus) has been mistakenly identified with St Hilary of Poitiers who lived 100 years before Elian. Elian landed on Anglesey near his other foundation at Llaneilian around 450.

The Grate II* Listed St Elian's church is doubled naved with a western bellcote over the north gable and a south porch approached through the cast

Castell Dinas Bran

iron lychgate next to the White Lion Inn. First mentioned as 'Ecclesia de Bodwelennyn' in the Lincoln *Taxatio* of 1291 much of the church is of a late medieval date. Of particular interest are the wagon roofs with the paintings over the chancel. There were sympathetic restorations in 1859 and 1903 and much of the furniture dates from this time though the font is early. The lower part of the rood screen remains in situ while nine richly painted panels of the screen depicting the Weighing of the Souls, the risen Christ and the legend of the Conversion of St Hubert are now on the north wall. There is a Commandments board in Welsh along with a number of memorials. The naves are separated by a five bay arcade with the chancel leading from the south nave and the organ in the north. The east windows are of 1862 by Ballantine and sons and were in memory of John Lloyd Wynne of Coed Coch and Teyrdan and his wife. That in the chancel depicts the crucifixion while that in the north nave portrays Sts Matthew, Mark, Luke and John.

Parts of the White Lion Inn date from the 17th century though as an inn it is early 19th century with modern additions. Yr Efail opposite was the village smithy.

Ebenezer Welsh Baptist Chapel on Llanelian Road was built in 1831. Nant-y-Ffynnon Welsh Calvinistic Methodist Chapel on Croes Road was built in 1833 and rebuilt in 1907

630 yards to the north-west of the village, beyond the chapel, along Groes Road is the 'cursing well' of Ffynnon Elian. It was mentioned by Edward Lluyd as a place where papists and old folk still offered a groat or bread to the value of a groat to heal a young child in 1699, though by 1723 its nature had changed due, it was said, to the greed of its visitors.

Baring-Gould offered the following legend of its origins: "*A saintly hermit passing through, fell ill at this spot, and sat down by the roadside. He prayed for a drink of water, and a copious spring burst forth at his side; he drank, and got well. He thereupon prayed that the spring might be the medium to grant to all who asked in faith anything that they might wish. Another tradition attributes its origin to S. Elian thrusting his sword into the ground.*"

Wirt Sikes in 1880 wrote: "*It is at the head of the cursing wells, of which there are but few in the Principality, and holds still a strong influence over the ignorant mind. The popular belief is that you can 'put' your enemy 'into' this well, i.e., render him subject to its evil influence, so that he will pine away and perhaps die unless the curse be removed. The degree and nature of the curse can be modified as the 'offerer' desires, so that the obnoxious person will suffer aches and pains in his body, or troubles in his pocket—the slings and arrows of outrageous fortune. The minister of the well appears to be some heartless wretch residing in the neighbourhood, whose services are enlisted for a small fee. The name of the person to be 'put into' the well is registered in a book kept by the wretch aforesaid, and a pin is cast into the well in his name, together with a pebble inscribed with its initials. The person so cursed soon hears of it, and the fact preys on his mind; he imagines for himself every conceivable ill, and if gifted with a lively faith soon finds himself reduced to a condition where he cannot rest till he has secured the removal of the curse. This is effected by a reversal of the above ceremonies—erasing the name, taking out the pebble, and otherwise appeasing the spirit of the well. It is asserted that death has in many instances resulted from the curse of this wickedly malicious well.*"

As late as 1912 Archdeacon Thomas wrote "*I have known a poor woman pine away to death under the dread impression that she had been so cursed and nothing that I could say was able to remove that conviction.*" (*Collections Historical & Archaeological relating to Montgomeryshire Vol 36*) A Methodist minister had the well destroyed in 1829 but a local man, John Evans, known as Jac Ffynnon Elian diverted the waters on to his own land and became the 'minister of the well'. He was sent to jail for fraud, having been found guilty of charging people to remove a curse that had never been cast. It was finally destroyed in 1850 and all that remains is covered but a path still leads to its site which was the subject of a BBC Wales *Hidden Histories* programme in 2010.

Llanelidan

The attractive estate village of Llanelidan lies five miles south of Ruthin. The church, Leyland Arms, village hall and cricket ground lie some 250 yards north-east of the village houses which was established as the estate village for Nantclwyd Hall.

The church is dedicated to St Elidan but little is known of him. He has been variously described as a knight, a king in Snowdonia, and a bishop and there is a depiction of him in the church at Llangurig holding a spear. Baring-Gould however suggests that Elidan is actually one of the two Welsh forms (the other is Hid) of the name of Julitta, the mother of the child-martyr St Cyriacus. Recorded in the Norwich *Taxatio* of 1254 as Ecclesia de Lanelidem the church building dates from the 14th century. The double naved church has the chancel off the north nave which is extended to the west with a vestry beneath the western bellcote. The naves are divided by a five bay arcade. Some box pews remain in the south nave. The roofs are collar beam trussed, that in the north being the original 14th century roof. There was a major restoration in 1889-90 with John Douglas of Chester the architect. Further work was carried out by G.R. Griffiths of Denbigh in the 1930s. The furnishings are mainly 19th and 20th century but the font is medieval and the reredos is Jacobean though reconstructed in 1890. A panel with the Lord's Prayer, the Ten Commandments and the Apostles' Creed in Welsh dates from the 19th century. There are memorials on the walls to members of the families of Nantclwyd Hall. On the north wall is a painting of the Blessed Edward Jones, who was born in the parish and baptized an Anglican but converted to Roman Catholicism at Reims in 1587. He was ordained a priest in 1588 and sent to England where he was arrested in Fleet Street in 1590, convicted of treason and hanged, drawn and quartered on 6 May 1590 in Fleet Street. The north porch is 14th century. There is a double bellcote at the western end of the north nave.

The Leyland Arms next to the church was built in 1844 as part of the Nantclwyd estate by the then owner Richard Christopher Leyland. Built in Tudor Gothic style. Minor alterations were carried out in 1966 by Sir Clough Williams-Ellis the creator of Port Meirion. The old National School to the north of the church was established by Revd Roberts in 1846 is now the village hall. The schoolmaster's house was joined to the school.

Brynbanadl Welsh Calvinistic Methodist Chapel in the village was built in 1804 and rebuilt in 1876 but is no longer in use as a chapel. Carmel Welsh Baptist Chapel was built in 1846 and rebuilt in 1906. Zion Methodist Chapel to the east of the village was built in 1804, and rebuilt in 1852 and 1894 with two cottages attached.

Three quarters of a mile north of the church is Nantclwyd Hall. The original estate was purchased in 1571 by Thomas Wynn ap John ap Harry. His son Simon adopted the anglicized surname of Parry and his granddaughter and heiress to the estate married Eubule Thelwall, a lawyer who in the late 17th century built Nantclwyd Hall. It remained the home of the Thelwall family, passing by marriage to the Kenrick family until purchased in 1843 by Richard Christopher Leyland. Leyland was a partner in Leyland and Bullins Bank founded by his great uncle Thomas Leyland, a Liverpool merchant and slave trader. In 1857 the house was enlarged by the architect J.K. Colling, in a style matching the original house. Further enlargement was carried out by David Walker for Tom Naylor-Leyland again in the style of the original 17th century building. In the 1960s work was undertaken by Sir Clough Williams-Ellis, redesigning the façade and gardens for Sir Vivyan Naylor-Leyland. It remains in the family. In 1873 a friend of the family, Major Walter Clopton Wingfield invented a game he called sphairistikè to amuse guests at Nantclwyd. This has claims to be the forerunner of lawn tennis. Wingfield went on to patent the game and produced a boxed set which included a net, poles, racquets, balls and a set of rules for playing the game which he marketed across the world.

Hendre Cottages in the village of Llanelidan were built as estate houses in 1877. The village remains small although there has been some 20th century development.

Llanfair Dyffryn Clwyd Mary's Church in the Vale of Clwyd

Llanfair Dyffryn Clwyd lies on the A525 a mile and a half south of Ruthin. The pre-Norman church was dedicated to St Cynfarch, a north of England Brythonic chieftain who married St Nyfain a daughter of Brychan Brycheiniog. Their son Urien Rheged features in the Arthurian legends. After the Norman Conquest the church took the dedication to St Mary but in recent years it has been combined as the church of St Cynfarch and St Mary.

The church was recorded as ecclesia de Lanweyr in the 1254 Norwich *Taxatio*, but was rebuilt in the 15th century as a double naved church. In 1870-72 the Bristol architect John D. Sebbing undertook a major refurbishment, raising the height of the walls by 20 inches, though retaining the original roof timbers. The west gallery was removed and new furnishings were installed. The chancels are defined by a low screen, that in the south nave formed from the original rood screen. The naves are divided by a six arch arcade. There are a number of memorials including a 14th century sepulchral slab. The tower is off the north nave and the bells date from 1631. The stump of the churchyard cross has been topped by a bronze sundial made in 1800 by Edward Tavo of Chester.

According to a legend not uncommon in Wales it was intended to erect the church close to where Jesus Chapel now stands, a mile to the south on the A525. Apparently a phantom in the shape of a sow's head, each night destroyed the previous day's work and the church was re-sited. The farm house built on the intended site is Llanbenwch, the church of the Sow's Head.

Jesus Chapel was established as a chapel of ease in 1619 by Rice Williams of Eyarth Hall who endowed it with a rentcharge on his land to provide "*a curate to read prayers and teach school in*". It was rebuilt in 1787 and at the time of a visit by members of Archaeologia Cambrensis in 1854 it was used solely as a schoolroom and they recorded that: "*It contains no detail of any importance, but presents a curious appearance at present, the result of a combination of its former with its present use. A font, pulpit, and gallery, associate rather strangely with the National Society's maps, and instruments of corporal chastisement.*" The school was closed when the National School opened in the village in 1859 and following the 1870-72 refurbishment of the church at Llanfair the Jacobean altar and font were brought to the chapel. It is Grade II* Listed but was put up for sale in May 2011.

The red and yellow brick Salem Welsh Calvinistic Methodist Chapel half a mile north-east of the village on the B5429 was built in 1886 and remains in use. The unusually designed Seion Welsh Baptist Chapel, 240 yards south of Salem, was built in 1840 but converted to a private house known as Tŷ Capel Seion in 1983.

Opposite the White Horse is the Order of Malta Homes Trust, Elizabeth Owen Terrace of eight almshouses, built in the 1830s and still used as pensioner accommodation. There are seven houses facing the road though there are eight chimneys for symmetry. The village War Memorial stands in front of the terrace. The White Horse is thought to date from the early 19th century.

Garthgynan farm house to the east of the village on the B5429 is thought to have been built in the mid 17th century by William Wynne, High Sheriff of Denbighshire in 1651. The nearby Garthgynan Mill was a corn mill later used to provide electricity to Garthgynan. The 19th century machinery was in operation until 1948. The mill stones and overshot wheel are intact.

The beautiful timber framed Eyarth Hall, a mile south-west of the village is in part possibly early 16th century but mainly dates from around 1600 and further enlarged in later centuries. The land was said to have been the property of the Lords of Chirk but by 1606 was in the hands of the Wynne family and later by James Goodrich, High Sheriff in 1878.

There are a number of substantial houses in the area, including Eyarth House, built for Major R.M. Wynne in 1812, the 17th century Plas Einion, the early 17th century Ffynogion of the Pryce family, Pentrcelyn Hall built for the Lewis family who owned lead mines, the 17th century Plas-Newydd Hall and the circa 1500 hall house of Plas Uchaf.

The village has expanded to the east and west in recent years but the heart of the village is largely unchanged. It retains its 1859 school, now enlarged, but apart from the White Horse there are no other amenities.

Llanfair-Talhaiarn

The church is dedicated to St. Mary, listed as Lanveyrdalhaern in the *taxatio* of 1274. Talhaiarn, was a native of Caerleon and a celebrated bard and saint of the 5th century. He was confessor to Emrys Wledig (otherwise known as Ambrosius Aurelianus said to have been the uncle of King Arthur); but after the latter was killed, he became a hermit, founding the church.

Situated on the River Elwy, five miles south of Abergele the attractive old village of Llanfair Talhaiarn with its narrow streets is built on a hillside with the church high above the village square.

The twin naved church is built on the site of the original llan but work in the 17th and the extensive renovation carried out by John Oldrid Scott, son of Sir George Gilbert Scott, in 1876 removed most of the medieval fabric. The original arched-braced collar truss roofs were retained but with replacement timber. The six bay arcade dates from 1876. There is a 13th century font next to the 19th century replacement. In 1849 a baptismal immersion tank was constructed at the western end of the north nave, accessed by trap doors. There are a number of fine memorials, principally to members of the Lloyd and Wynne families. There is a south porch and western bellcote. The graveyard has been extended and there is a bierhouse for the storage of the funeral bier.

The village is approached from the north over the late 17th century three arched Llanfair Bridge which was rebuilt in 1766. Water Street leads past the

Black Lion Inn to Swan Square with the Swan Inn, village store and the mid 19th century Neuadd Elwy, the former village hall. The plaque commemorating Richard Wynne of Garthewin was placed in 1933. In addition to the Swan and Black Lion the village once also had the Crown and the Harp Inn.

Salem Welsh Baptist Chapel behind Water Street was built in 1862 but has been converted to a private residence. Soar Welsh Calvinistic Methodist chapel which faces down Water Street was built in 1833 and has an attached manse. The Welsh Wesleyan Methodist chapel on Allt y Powls was built in 1812 and rebuilt in 1839 and 1897.

To the east of the village Melin Dolhaiarn dates from the 18th century and milled corn until 1950. The machinery complete with breast shot waterwheel was intact at the time of conversion to a private dwelling in 1978.

Two miles south-west of the village lies Melai, the ancestral home of the Wynnes of Melai and Maenan Abbey. The family were prominent in the Royalist cause during the English Civil War and Colonel William Wynne raised forces at his own expense prior to his death in 1643 at the Battle of Wem. Their descendants were the Wynnes of Garthewin and the Lords Newborough of Rug. The present house dates from the mid 19th century and was built by Lord Newborough, replacing the earlier 16th century house. There is a good example of an early 19th century stable block with a weathervane depicting the Boar's Head crest of the Wynne family.

Robert Wynne, a nephew of Colonel William Wynne, married Margaret Price, heiress of Garthewin. In the early years of the 18th century Dr Robert Wynne, Chancellor of St Asaph and Vicar of Gresford rebuilt Garthewin Hall which was further altered around 1770 by the Chester architect Joseph Turner. After years of neglect Sir Clough Williams-Ellis carried out a restoration in 1930 for Robert Oliver Francis Wynne. In the 19th century Colonel Robert William Wynne while serving in Arabia entered a harem for a bet. Unfortunately he was caught and suffered the penalty of castration. Not surprisingly he died without issue and the estate passed to his cousin, Brownlow Wynne Wynne. The last member of the family to own Garthewin was Menna MacBain who sold the house in 1995. This large country mansion with its three storey, nine bay white stuccoed façade is impressive and group visits can be made by appointment. The extensive gardens are opened under the National Gardens Scheme. The Bookroom on the estate was a lodge used for shooting parties and later as a library for the family. Also in the grounds is the Roman Catholic chapel, converted by Robert Wynne in 1932 from a former carpenter's workshop. In 1938 the 18th century main barn was converted by R.O.F. Wynne, using the modernist Scottish architect Thomas Smith Tait whose works include the Selfridges store and the pylons of Sydney Harbour Bridge, into a theatre for Welsh performances. The Garthewin Players commissioned works by Saunders Lewis and Kate Roberts for performances here.

Llanfair Talhaiarn has seen development in recent years but apart from a small amount of infill it is to the east of the village on both sides of the A544 with its new bridge over the Elwy. There is a primary school and doctor's surgery.

Llanferres

Llanferres is a small village four miles south-west of Mold, with the A494 acting as a by-pass. The village takes its name from the dedication of the church to St Berres, otherwise known as Brice or Britius. The church was recorded as Lanverreys in the *Taxatio* of 1291, and Llanferrys and Llanferreis in two late sixteenth century parish lists. Berres was a 4th century follower of St Martin of Tours.

St Berres church was substantially rebuilt in 1722 by Joseph Turner of Chester. The south transept and west tower were added in 1843 by Thomas Jones architect of Chester while there was a major refurbishment of the interior in 1891-2 by John Douglas, yet another Chester architect. Prior to 1843 it was a single cell building and nave and chancel are of equal width. The tower is square at the base with an octagonal stage above and topped by an octagonal bell turret and weather vane. Inside the chancel is separated from the nave by an oak screen and most of the furnishings are of 1892. The font is dated 1684 and there are a number of memorials. There is a gallery and the entrance is through the base of the tower. In the churchyard is a shed classed as a bier or hearse house. The original churchyard wall defining a llan has been altered in places and in 2001 the local council erected a drinking fountain near the entrance gates. There is a stile and mounting block incorporated into the wall.

The village in 1873 was tiny with Ty'n-llan farm, the Rectory, the Druid and Red Lion public houses and scattered cottages and houses. The Druid Inn remains open but there has been a comparatively large amount of housing built in the village which now has a primary school.

Llanfihangel Glyn Myfyr
Church of St Michael in the Valley of Myfyr

The parish of Llanfihangel Glyn Myfyr lay partly in the old county of Denbighshire and partly in Merionethshire. Situated on the beautiful Afon

Alwen, it lies seven miles north-west of Corwen. Samuel Lewis reported that the village had just four houses in 1849. The parish then had a population of 428 which by 2011 had fallen to 189. The village is first recorded in the Norwich *Taxatio* of 1254. In 1388 it was documented as Llanvyhangel Llenmyvyr and in 1614 as Llanvihangell llyn Myver. The 'llyn' was a pool formed downstream of the bridge. 'Llyn' changed to 'Glyn' sometime after 1700. Myfyr is a Welsh name, but can also mean meditation or contemplation and Wordsworth called it The Vale of Meditation.

The main area of housing lies to the west of the river in what was Merionethshire and is known locally as Bro Alwen. The old border between Denbighshire and Merionethshire deviates from the Afon Alwen in the area around the church suggesting that the course of the river has been altered and originally flowed on a meandering course to the west of its present line which at this point is straighter than its course upstream to the dam at Llyn Brenig and downstream from the bridge towards the River Dee. This would explain the semi-circular nature of the churchyard.

The present church of St Michael dates from around 1500 with the chancel walls and roof trusses the oldest parts as there was a rebuilding in the 18th century possibly after flooding in 1781. It is a single cell building though the chancel walls are thicker than those of the nave. There was further work in the 19th century and by Harold Hughes in 1900-02 when the church was re-roofed and new seating installed. The fine late medieval arch braced collar trussed roof of the nave gives way to a barrel vaulted roof over the chancel. The west gallery remains and there are various memorials on the walls and an early 18th century oak parish chest. There is a tall western bellcote and a south porch. In the churchyard is the gravestone of the antiquary Owen Jones who was born in the parish but died in London in 1814. He was buried at All Hallows the Less which was bombed during World War II and his gravestone was removed to Llanfihangel Glyn Myfyr.

250 yards east of the church is Llanfihangel Bridge, built in 1797 by the County Architect and Surveyor Thomas Penson. It replaced an earlier bridge to the south. It has a span of 53 feet and the arch is 25 feet above the river.

Next to the bridge stands the Crown Inn with its stable block. Originally a drovers' inn it claims Wordsworth was a visitor. To the south-east was a water powered woollen factory fed by a mill race which began near the inn.

Llanfwrog

Llanfwrog lies immediately to the west of Ruthin and it is difficult to determine a boundary between the two. For the purposes of this book it is taken as the junction of the A494 and the B5105.

St Mwrog is an obscure 7th century saint who is not mentioned in any of the Welsh saintly pedigrees. He does have two churches dedicated to him and the poet Lewis Glyn Cothi invokes his protection for Henry VII in an ode. In the Norwich *Taxatio* of 1254 Llanfwrog was recorded as Lammitant. The earliest part of the church dates from the 14th century, with a second nave added in the 15th century, incorporating the chancel. The original north nave was rebuilt in 1869-70 when the church underwent a large refurbishment by the Bristol architect John Dando Sedding. It is thought that the original four bay arcade between the naves was reduced to three by Sedding, reusing the original material. The seven bay roof of the south nave is medieval and the substantial west tower which dates from the 14th century has a fine tower arch and formed the original west entrance. It has a saddleback roof. The 1869 restoration included new windows, a low screen separating nave and chancel, removal of the box pews and gallery and repairs to the nave roof which was raised by 18 inches. The tower was restored in 1906. The font is a medieval octagonal bowl of red sandstone though the base is later. The south porch is Victorian. The churchyard walls show signs of an early circular llan and there are two lychgates.

The village has a Roman Catholic chapel, Our Lady Help of Christians, built in the latter decades of the 19th century.

The Cross Keys Hotel opposite the church dates from the 17th century. There are some attractive cottages and houses along the road into Ruthin.

Llangadwaladr

Now in the county of Powys, Llangadwaladr lies seven and a half miles southwest of Llangollen and seven miles west of Oswestry. Set in the upland valley of Afon Ysgwennant, there are just a few scattered houses and the church with telephone box and post box alongside.

The church is dedicated to Cadwaladr, son of Cadwallon ab Cadfan, the last of the Welsh princes who assumed the title of Gwledig or chief sovereign of Britain and died in 682. In the Lincoln *Taxatio* of 1291 it was described as *bettws Kadwaladr* a bedehouse or almshouse where the occupants prayed for their benefactor. Llangadwaladr did not become a parish until 1877. The foundation is Celtic as typified by the circular raised churchyard, traces of which are visible, and the ancient yew trees. The church was rebuilt in 1883 by William Henry Spaull of Oswestry, an architect better known for his non-conformist chapels. The collar beam truss roof is of 1883 but the medieval tie and collar beam truss against the west wall survives. Spaull removed the gallery and installed new furniture and windows. He also designed the apse and vestry. There is a south porch and western bellcote.

900 yards east of the church is the Bronze Age Ysgwennant Barrow. Excavations in the 1950s and 60s uncovered two burial pits adapted to receive a later cremation urn.

Llangedwyn

Seven miles south-west of Oswestry the small village of Llangedwyn lies in the Tanat valley. There is a small 20th century housing estate, village hall and Church in Wales primary school.

Llangedwyn Hall has its origins in the late Elizabethan period when it was known as Plas Newydd. The estate was acquired by Owen Vaughan through his marriage to Catherine, daughter of Morrice ap Robert. Their son, Sir Robert Vaughan died without male heir and his daughter Eleanor married John Purcell of Nantcribba. In turn their daughter Mary carried the estate to Edward Vaughan, M.P. for Montgomeryshire at various times from 1679 to 1718. On his death his not inconsiderable estates, including Llangedwyn, passed through his daughter Ann to her husband Sir Watkin Williams-Wynn of Wynnstay. Llangedwyn Hall remains in the Wynn family.

Sir Watkin inherited a three wing red brick mansion which was used as a secondary home to Wynnstay in the 19th century. In the 1950s the east wing was demolished and the house is now rendered. It is a substantial two storey house with two protruding wings to the south with attic windows and a sundial on the east wing. The east facia is now the front of the building, looking out over the lawn and terraced garden. There is a large west service wing angled to the north-west and sizeable outbuildings. Beyond the gardens in a field to the east there is an unusual octagonal stallion stable. The 1875 map shows it at the centre of four paddocks and the stable had an entrance to each paddock. The field between the hall and church was in the 19th century a formal garden.

The church is dedicated to St Cedwyn, the son of Gwgon Gwron ab Peredur ab Eliffer Gos-gorddfawr, mentioned in Arthurian legends, by Madrun, daughter of Gwrthefyr Fendigaid. Scrwgan, an area south of the river, is believed to stand for Esgair Wgan, the Ridge or Hill of Gwgan, embodying his father's name. The old church was taken down in 1869 and replaced with the present estate church by Benjamin Ferrey, though the Romanesque porch is attributed to Thomas Penson the Younger with a date in the 1840s. A number of features from the earlier church are retained, including an octagonal medieval font and a poor box of 1741, both in the west porch. The wood panelling of the pulpit is 17th century and there is an effigy of a 14th century cleric. Parts of the medieval masonry are incorporated in the west and east walls. The rebuilding was financed by Sir Watkin Williams-Wynn. Further work was undertaken in 1907 by Herbert Luck North who added the dormer windows. The War Memorial was designed by John Houghton Maurice Bonnor and completed after his death by his Chiswick studio. Bonnor who is buried in the family tomb at Llangedwyn was a noted sculptor whose work included *Kitchener's War Babies*. He died in Canada in 1916 where he was working on the mural decorations of the parliament buildings In Ottawa. The communion rail in the church was to his design. There are numerous monuments in the church including those to Edward Vaughan and members of the Bonnor and Williams Wynn families. There is a vestry to the south and a single bell in the western bellcote. Against the wall of the church is a 10th century Celtic gravestone, discovered in the 1869 rebuilding. A memorial, in the form of a preaching cross, to Sir Watkin Williams Wynn who died in 1885 is in the south-eastern area of the churchyard.

Bryn-y-gwalia, the home of the Bonnor family lies to the east of Llangedwyn Hall, near the late Regency Green Inn which formed part of the Bonnor estate. Plas Uchaf to the west of Llangedwyn Hall is a Grade II* Listed Regency house which was the old rectory and part of the Wynnstay estate.

On the road to Bwlchyddar was the Bridge Inn and the corn mill, now used as the Llangedwyn Craft centre. Llangedwyn Bridge was built by the Wynnstay estate in the 18th century as part of improvements to the River Tanat which was canalized downstream. The decorations on the bridge are more pronounced facing downstream.

Llangernyw

Llangernyw lies on the A548 a little over seven miles south of Colwyn Bay. The name means Church of the Cornishman, St Digain's church having been founded by the grandson of Cadwr, prince of Cernyw (Cornwall). Digain lived in the 5th century and his father Cystenyn Gorneu a British king founded the church at Llangystennin in Caernarvonshire. It is an attractive village with a number of old cottages, two inns and a Grade II* Listed church. In the churchyard is the Llangeryw Yew listed as one of the ten oldest trees in the world.

The white washed church stands at the centre of an oval churchyard which contains the 4,000-5,000 year old Llangernyw Yew. The cruciform church is unusual in the area and the transepts were added to an early medieval single cell building in the later medieval period. Substantial work was carried out in 1849 by R.K. Penson. The south door which now leads to the vestry is 15th century and the nearby stoup is earlier. The roof is 16th century and the font medieval. Entrance is now via the 19th century north porch. There are a number of monuments in the church to members of the Lloyd and Salusbury families while outside can be found two 5th-6th century incised cross pillar stones. A memorial window in the south transept is to the poetess Margaret Sandbach of Hafodunos Hall who died in 1852. The tall western bellcote has a single bell. The churchyard was used for markets until 1749 when the vicar, John Kenrick nailed the gate shut and stationed men at the other entrances to stop the market taking place. The lychgate was built in 1745 and re-roofed with the addition of a weathervane in 1867. In the extended part of the graveyard is a bier house.

There is a legend connected with the churchyard recorded by the Revd Elias Owen in 1896:

Angelystor – the Recording Angel – manifested itself in the church every Hallowe'en. Here, at dead of night, it would intone in a deep and solemn voice the names of all those in the parish who were to die in the following year.

One fateful Hallowe-en night, after a few too many pints, the village tailor, a know-all named Shôn ap Robert, laughingly derided the existence of the Recording Angel. Spurred on by his drinking pals, he barged out of the Stag hotel into the night and made his wobbly way to the church, to prove Angelystor a myth.

But when he arrived at the door he heard to his horror a deep voice booming from within. It was reciting names. And the first name he heard was – "Shôn ap Robert"!

"Hold, hold!" he cried. "I am not ready yet!" But, ready or not, he found his grave in Llangernyw churchyard that coming year."

Capel-y-Cwm Welsh Calvinstic Methodist Chapel on the A548 south of the church was built in 1836 and rebuilt in 1909. The small Bethabara Welsh Baptist Chapel north of Capel-y-Cwm was built in 1830 and rebuilt in 1871.

South of the church is the old National School, built in 1852 and now a private house. The Old Stag was built around 1650 as a farmhouse. By 1875 it was the Stag Inn, after the coat of arms of the Lloyd family of Hafodunos which is displayed on the wall of the inn. The Bridge Inn lies to the south.

Next to Capel y Cwm are the Sir Henry Jones Memorial Cottages, a pair of semi detached cottages now forming a museum. Sir Henry Jones was born in Y Cwm, one of the cottages in 1852, the son of a shoemaker. At the age of 12 he was apprenticed to his father, but persisted with his education and qualified as a teacher and taught at Brynaman, on the Glamorgan/Carmarthenshire border before deciding to enter the Calvinistic Methodist ministry. He won a Dr Williams Scholarship to study philosophy at Glasgow University and graduated in 1878, winning the Clark Fellowship allowing him to study at Oxford and in Germany. He lectured at Aberystwyth before being appointed professor of Philosophy at Bangor in 1884, at St Andrews in 1891 and succeeded his mentor Edward Caird as professor of Philosophy at Glasgow in 1894. He founded the Glasgow Civic Society in 1897 and was knighted in 1912. He promoted education in Wales and following his death in 1922 a memorial fund was established with Ramsey MacDonald as president and David Lloyd George vice president. The fund purchased the two cottages in 1934 and the museum was opened by David Lloyd George.

Half a mile south-west of the village is Hafodunos Hall. The name derives from the legend that St Winifred stayed here for one night on her journey from Holywell to Gwytherin, hence the name meaning a summer residence of one night. The estate was established in the early 13th century by the Lloyd family, which claimed descent from Tudwal the Lame, youngest son of Rhodri Mawr. The estate remained in the family until 1830 when it was acquired by Samuel Sandbach. Sandbach was the son of a yeoman farmer and innkeeper at Tarporley in Cheshire who made his fortune in the West Indies, returning to Liverpool as a West India merchant in 1801. A partner in the Sandbach Tinne company he was mayor of Liverpool in 1831-2. He was High Sheriff of Denbighshire in 1839, having retired in 1833. Following Samuel's death in 1851 Hafodunos passed to his son Henry Robertson Sandbach who in 1860 commissioned Sir George Gilbert Scott to build a new house replacing the 1674 manor house of the Lloyds. Hafodunos is the only domestic property designed by Scott in Wales and is Grade I Listed. Margaret Sandbach died in 1852 but she had been a patron of the Conway born sculptor John Gibson and a number of his marble reliefs were acquired for the house (now in the Walker Art Gallery

Liverpool). The Sandbach family sold Hafodunos in 1933 after which it was used as an accountancy college, a girls' school and a nursing home. Its last occupants were in 1993 and in 2004 it was badly damaged by fire. It was purchased by Dr Richard Wood in 2010 and is in course of restoration.

Llangwm Church in the Valley

Llangwm lies seven and a half miles west of Corwen in the valley of the Afon Medrad, a tributary of the River Dee. In the *Taxatio* of 1291 the village is recorded as Llandegoin.

There are three villages bearing the name of Llangwm in Wales, all three having a church dedicated to St Jerome. Writing in 1899 Frances Arnold Foster noted *"The only known English dedication to S. Jerome is at Llangwm in Monmouthshire, where he is commemorated under his Latin form of "Hierom". Across the Welsh border we find two other parishes similarly named Llangwm the one in Pembrokeshire (where the patron is again described as S. Hierom), and the other in Denbighshire, where he is anglicized into "S. Jerome". There can be little doubt that in all three cases the name of the parish contains the name of the saint, and of the same saint. The most natural supposition is that the intended patron was originally some national hero whose true name has in course of time been merged in that of the celebrated Latin Father; but since Mr. Pees, in his learned and exhaustive work, makes no such suggestion, we may well be content to take the name in its most obvious connexion, and with it all the noble associations that cling around the story of the recluse of Bethlehem; and if we choose we may please ourselves with the plausible fancy that the knowledge of S. Jerome was introduced into Britain by some Celtic pilgrim to the East, who had found in Jerome's guest-house at Bethlehem "the welcome which Mary and Joseph had missed"*. (Studies in Church Dedications 1899) Arnold Foster includes Monmouthshire in England and also fails to translate Llangwm. It is however of interest that three villages so far apart bearing the same name also have the same church dedication. One explanation is that the Normans made the assumption that 'Gwm' referred to a saint rather than a location and Jerome was an approximation.

The church is a long single cell structure with some medieval fabric surviving restorations of 1747 and 1873-4. It has a north porch and western bellcote. A wide arch separates nave and chancel but the church is no longer in use and the windows have been blocked and the furnishings removed. In the churchyard is an ancient yew and a number of early 19th century chest tombs.

Capel-y-Groes Welsh Independent chapel was built in 1821 and rebuilt in 1873. Pont y Capel at the northern entrance to the village was built in 1782. There was a chapel or possibly two chapels dedicated to St Gwnod and St Neithon but the 18th century antiquarian, Lewis Morris noted that the chapels had been converted to form part of a mill and a kiln. Edward Lhuyd in his *Parochialia* of 1698 recorded the mill as Melin y capel which later became Llangwm Mill. This was a corn mill with an enclosed waterwheel fed by a leat of some 650 yards with a weir on the Afon Medrad. The mill was operational until 1913.

There was a British School established in 1850, near the site of the later school for which a notice of closure was issued in July 2014. Tŷ Newydd, south of the church was formerly the New Inn. The small stone structure on the junction west of the church was the village smithy.

There has been some development in the village which remains small.

Llangwyfan

Llangwyfan lies some four and a half miles east of Denbigh. In 1918 it became the site of the North Wales Sanatorium, operated for tuberculosis sufferers by the King Edward VII Welsh National Memorial Association. Since 1981 it has been owned by Mental Health Care UK and is known as Alexander House, Highfield Park. It occupies the site of the Elizabethan Plas Llangwyfan, now demolished.

The church is dedicated to the 7th century St Cwyfan, a follower of St Bueno. It is first mentioned in the Norwich *Taxatio* of 1254 as Langeifin, but the present church dates from the early 15th century. Possibly the smallest church in the area, it retains its box pews but lost its gallery in the 19th century. There is a plastered barrel ceiling, Victorian font and a parish chest bearing the date 1734, south porch, north belfry and single western bellcote. It is Grade II* Listed.

Llangynhafal

Situated three and a half miles north of Ruthin, Llangynhafal is a small scattered rural village with the Golden Lion at its centre.

The Grade I Listed church is dedicated to St Cynhafal, the son of St Elgud ab Cadfarch ab Caradog Freichfras and his wife Tubrawst. According to legend Cynhafal used his miraculous powers to cause the death of the giant Benlli Gawr. Apparently "*he tortured the 'hoary giant','till he became like a 'frantic* lion', filling his body with agony and wild fire, which drove him to seek relief in the cooling waters of the Alun; but that river refused to allay his agony, and became dry three times, and the giant's bones were burnt upon its banks at Hesp Alun (the Dried-up Alun)." (Baring-Gould)

Foel Fenlli three miles south of the village is named after Benlli Gawr, King of Powis circa 450A.D. but it is thought that Cynhafal lived in the 7th century casting doubt on role of Cynhafal in the legend. Apparently Benlli Gawr was hostile to St Germanus and was burnt to death in the waters of the river. The church on its raised circular llan lies to the south-east of the Golden Lion. The double naved church dates from the 15th century with restoration carried out sensitively by Arthur Baker of Kensington in 1884 and further restoration work was carried out by Osborne Associates in 2007. Baker moved the chancel from the north to the south nave, repaired the roofs, installed the tiled floor and replaced most of the seating. The naves are separated by a five bay arcade with a Lady Chapel now occupying the former north chancel. At the west end of the north nave are two Jacobean box pews. The 17th century pulpit has been moved to the south wall. The carved reredos with the pelican above is also 17th century. The font is 19th century. The arched collar-braced roofs with pseudo hammer beams are impressive, with five angel terminals remaining while the minor trusses have painted carved faces at their base. The windows are 19th century although follow the medieval perpendicular designs. There are a number of wall monuments of the 18th and 19th centuries. The south porch is 19th century but the door masonry is medieval. There is a western bellcote on the south nave. A kitchenette was added in 2007 when the exterior was limewashed.

500 yards north of the church is Ffynnon Gynhafal, the waters of which were renowned for curing warts. The wart was pricked with a pin which was then thrown into the water and a prayer said to St Cynhafal. Steps leading into the water would indicate that the spring was used for baptisms. The large stone lined basin has a vaulted roof.

Plas Draw near the spring was the principal gentry house of the parish and dates from the medieval with alterations in 1700 and additions in the 19th century. Plas yn Llan to the east of the church has its origins in the 16th century. It was used as the rectory in the early 19th century and William Wordsworth stayed here 1791-93 with his college friend Revd Robert Jones. Jones and Wordsworth embarked on a walking tour of the continent in 1790, followed by a walking tour of North Wales in 1791 when they climbed

Snowdon. *Descriptive Sketches* is dedicated to Jones and he is mentioned in the sonnet *To a Friend* which begins: *"Jones! As from Calais southward you and I Travell'd on foot together".*

Llannefydd

Llannefydd is a small village five miles north-west of Denbigh. There is some confusion as to the identity of St Nefydd who founded the church here. Some have attributed the saint to being a son of Brychan, others that he was a grandson or great-grandson or even a daughter of Brychan. According to tradition Nefydd moved north after founding the church and became a bishop before being slain by Saxons and Picts.

For many centuries the church was dedicated to St Mary the Virgin and now is known as the church of St Nefydd and St Mary. Set on its raised Celtic llan the present building dates from the around 1500, when the second nave was added and it is believed that the dedication to St Mary was acquired at that time. In the Lincoln *Taxatio* of 1291 it was recorded as Ecclesia de Laundid est Capella Cathedral. The two naves are of equal size with a western double bellcote above the south nave and a south porch. There was a restoration in 1859 when the old bellcote was replaced. In 1908-9 Henry Harold Hughes of Bangor removed the gallery and box pews. In 1973 Anthony Clarke was the architect when the roof was repaired and the east windows re-glazed. There is a five bay arcade between the naves which both have an eight bay collar trussed roof. The font is dated 1688 while the pulpit was designed by Hughes. There is some medieval stained glass and a number of monuments and memorials, some dating from the 13th century. The Royal Coat of Arms is Hanoverian while the window depicting Saints Mary, David and Nefydd is from 1926. The church, a fine example of a well preserved late medieval church is Grade I Listed. Ffynnon Nefydd, St Nefydd's Spring lies in a field 300 yards north of the church.

Capel-y-Llan Welsh Calvinistic Methodist Chapel was built in 1867. The War Memorial stands on the small green to the side of the chapel.

At the heart of the old village with its narrow street is the Hawk and Buckle Inn, a 17th century building though not shown as an inn on 19th century maps, it boasts views across to the sea as far as Blackpool Tower. The village had both National and British Schools, serving the children of this farming area. There is a modern primary school but no shop. It remains an agricultural village with a large dairy farm on the edge of the village and the Llaeth y Llan yoghurt producer lies a mile to the east.

In 1740 at the time of the North Wales corn riots an armed mob of Denbigh shoemakers, approached the village *"with Drums beating before 'em"* with a view to stealing corn from the barns. They were confronted by the villagers one of whom, William Davies fell to the ground crying, *"O God I am shot in the heart"*. Soon afterwards he was dead, the only fatality of the riots. The Chirk Castle records give the following account of what ensued.,

"*Mad with rage ye Country gott ye Battle & Drove ye Denbigh Rabble as far as Henllan village ... as soon as ye Denbigh Burgomasters heard ye Event an Alarm was Rung & ye whole body of ye Corporation came as far as Henllan & ye Officers of ye Town. P'swaded men, women & Children to return to Denbigh. Sev'll of ye Denbigh folks have been much hurt ...*"

Llanrhaeadr ym Mochnant
Church of the Waterfall in the Commote of Mochnant

Llanrhaeadr ym Mochnant lies 11 miles south-west of Llangollen and is currently in the county of Powys. The parish of Llanrhaedr was divided between the counties of Montgomeryshire and Denbighshire with the Afon Rhaeadr forming the bundary. The parish church and the main part of the village was on the Denbighshire side. There are two interpretations of the name Mochnant according to Morgan. The first is 'swift water'. Others maintain that 'moch' means 'swine', and that the word nant is applied to the whole valley, inclusive of the brook that flows through it, on the traditional belief that the place was at some time abounding with wild hogs.

The parish church is dedicated to St Dogfan, also known as Doewan and Dogwan, said to have been a son of Brychan Brycheiniog, killed by the Saxons. The layout of the church is unusual with the north and south aisles standing alongside the chancel with only a single arch of the arcade overlapping the nave. The original site appears to have been a Celtic llan with monastic origins. The base of the tower is dated to the late 12th century with the church extended to the east in the 15th century. There was an extensive refurbishment in 1879-82 by the Oswestry architect W.H. Spaull which removed the 18th century west gallery and hearse house and the box pews, installing new windows and an entrance porch. The upper part of the tower had been rebuilt in the 18th century. The Cwgan stone, an early Celtic stone cross in memory of Gwgan son of Edelstan, a 10th century Welsh Prince stands against an arcade column. The tower has three bells installed to celebrate the coronation of George III. Among the incumbents was William

Morgan (1545-1604) who translated the Old Testament into Welsh and published this along with a revision of Salesbury's New Testament translation in 1588. He also revised Salesbury's version of the Prayer Book. He was appointed Bishop of Llandaff in 1595 and moved to St Asaph in 1601. William Worthington the vicar from 1747 to 1778 was responsible for building the road to the waterfall.

Bethesda Welsh Calvinistic Methodist Chapel on Back Chapel Street was built in 1828 and rebuilt in 1869 by W.H. Spaull. It is no longer in use as a chapel. The British School alongside was the Non-conformist school in the village and dates from the1860s. It too is now closed. The village also had a National (Church of England) School built in 1858 and now used as a hall. Salem Baptist Chapel on Waterfall Street was built in 1855 but closed in 1919 and is now the British Legion Hall.

The Wynnstay Arms was built in 1850 for the Wynnstay Estate. George Borrow stayed here in 1854, and described it as "*very large, but did not look very cheerful*". The Town Hall, described by Borrow as "*a strange little antique market-house, standing on pillars*". Has been demolished and the site is now a car park.

This attractive old village has a range of small shops but the HSBC bank closed in 2011.

A little under four miles north-west of the village is the Pistyll Rhaeadr at 240 feet it is one of the highest single drop waterfalls in Britain and heralded as one of the seven wonders of Wales. Borrow gave the following description: "*What shall I liken it to? I scarcely know, unless it is to an immense skein of silk agitated and disturbed by tempestuous blasts, or to the long tail of a grey courser at furious speed. I never saw water falling so gracefully, so much like thin, beautiful threads as here.*"

Llanrhaeadr-yng-nghinmeirch
The church of the waterfall in the commote of Cinmeirch

The beautiful small village of Llanrhaeadr lies two and a half miles south-east of Denbigh. It is the site of St Dyfnog's Well celebrated for the miraculous cures "*wrought upon those afflicted with diverse complaints that came in great numbers, from far and near, to bathe therein. The water owed its healing virtues to the saint, who, renouncing the world, had led an austere life here, doing penance by standing under the volume of cold water as it issued from the spout. He wore a thick garment of horse-hair, girded with an iron girdle, and his meat was bread and water."* (Baring-Gould) Little else is known of this 6th century saint to whom the local church is dedicated. An underground stream rushes out to form a waterfall beneath which is the holy well. It was in use into the 18th century when the bath was paved with marble and buildings bedecked with small human figures erected around it. The buildings have disappeared but the pool and waterfall remain.

The Grade I Listed church of St Dyfnog is double naved with a four bay arcade and is first mentioned in the Norwich *Taxatio* of 1254. It is celebrated for its Jesse Tree Window, which depicts the Virgin Mary as descended from Jesse, the father of King David. It is reputed to be the finest stained glass window in Wales and ranks among the best in Britain. It was installed in 1533. The glass in the west window is older and was found in a local farmhouse in 1830. During the English Civil War it was apparently takem down to avoid damage from Puritans and reinstalled in 1661. The ornate roofs date from a refurbishment circa 1500 and are a combination of hammerbeam and waggon. There was a further refurbishment by Arthur Baker in 1879-80. There are a number of fine monuments and near the Jesse window is a golden pelican copied from the stained glass depiction. It was believed that the pelican fed its young with its own blood, a symbol of the shedding of the Blood of Christ. The south-west four stage tower has a battlemented top while the porch has a carved wooden arch which once had a statue of St Dyfnog.

To the west of the church a group of eight single room almshouses were built in 1729 by Jane, widow of Maurice Jones of Ddol and Llanrhaeadr Hall, for the elderly poor of the parish. They were repaired in 1820 by William, second Baron Bagot of Blifthfield in Staffordshire, and Pool Park and Bachymbyd in Denbighshire, the great-great-nephew of the foundress. There was a further restoration in 1963 when the number of units was reduced to four.

Opposite the lychgate is the village smithy, now used as a pottery. The smithy dates from the 18th century and had a double forge and open shoeing bay. The King's Head dates from the 16th century. The National School was built in 1871.

Llanrhaeadr Hall, now separated from the village by the A525, dates from the 16th century and was home over the years to a number of High Sheriffs of the county, in the 18th century, including Maurice Jones of Ddol Esq., (1703) Richard Parry (1775) and Richard Wilding Esq., (1778). It was remodelled in the Jacobean style in 1841-2 by Thomas Penson the younger. It is now a care home while the stable block is now a spa and sports club.

Llanrhydd (see Llanbedr-Dyffryn-Clwyd)

Llansannan

Llansannan lies on the Afon Aled, a tributary of the Afon Elwy, seven miles west of Denbigh. There is some doubt as to the identity of St Sannan, Baring-Gould identifies him with the Irish St Senan, a friend of St David, but Robert of Shrewsbury identifies him as St Senan who was buried alongside St Winefred at Gwytherin though as Baring-Gould concedes the holding of the festival of the local patron saint was held in the village in June and points to an otherwise unknown saint.

The Grade II* listed church of St Sannan dates from the 13th century and was named in the Norwich *Taxatio* of 1254 as Llannsannan. A double naved church it stands on raised ground above the Afon Aled and the churchyard may originally have been circular. The church was partly rebuilt in 1778 and again in 1879 when the cost was £1,000 half of which was met by the Wynne Yorke family. John George Freeman in 1826 described it as "*a spacious room in the modern taste, neatly pewed*". The 1879 restoration replaced the roof, which early illustrations depicted as a single roof over the two naves with four sloping sides, otherwise known as a mansard roof, with the more common double gabled structure. Oak from the original roof was used in village housing, the new barrel roofs being of pitch pine. There is a five wooden column arcade between the naves. The furnishings are 19th century with the exception of the pulpit which was originally part of the triple decker pulpit of St Luke's church in Liverpool and donated by F. Frodsham in 1894 and the 17th century bench and chest at the west end. There are a number of memorial windows including that in the south chancel by Henry Gustave Hiller depicting the Light of the World, St Sannan and St David, given in 1910, by Mr Wynne Yorke of Bryn Aled in remembrance of Pierce and Lucy Penelope Wynne Yorke of Dyffryn Aled. Wall memorials are of the 18th and 19th centuries. Unusually the western bellcote stands between the two gables and is surmounted by a cross. The south porch has a low wall with an open timber frame supporting the slate roof. The lychgate is 18th century though the gates are modern.

The substantial Capel Coffa Henry Rees Welsh Calvinistic Methodist Chapel was built in 1811 and rebuilt in 1914. The 1875 map shows a smaller chapel nearer the road with a Gorsedd to the rear. Bethania Welsh Baptist Chapel on Ffordd Gogor was built in 1828, and rebuilt in 1884 and 1906. Welsh

Independent Capel Hiraethog near the bridge was built in 1903, replacing the 1829 Capel Aled on the northern side of the road.

Opposite the Red Lion is the statue of *The Girl* by Sir William Goscombe John R.A. Commissioned as a memorial to five Welsh writers born in the parish, Tudor Aled, 1480-1526, William Salesbury, 1520-c1584, Henry Rees, 1797-1867, William Rees, 1802-1883 (known by his Bardic name of Gwilym Hiraethog) and Edward Roberts 1819-1867 (known by his Bardic name of Iorwerth Glan Aled). The statue was unveiled by Thomas Ellis M.P. in 1899. Next to the statue is a row of early 19th century cottages with the village War Memorial outside the central cottage which was once the surgery but is now a snooker hall.

The village once had two inns, the Saracen's Head next to the Post Office, but now closed, and the Red Lion Inn. There is a community education centre, doctors' surgery and local store. The village has seen expansion but remains an attractive village set among the hills surrounding the Aled vale.

Dyffryn Aled was a mansion a mile north-east of the village built in the late 18th century for the Wynne family. Diana Wynne, the heiress of the estate married Philip Yorke of Erddig and the family adopted the name Wynne-Yorke. The estate was sold to Countess Dundonald of Gwrych Castle shortly before the outbreak of war in 1914. During the war it was used to house captured German officers. In 1915 there were two escapes from Dyffryn Aled, the first in April when two naval officers were captured near Harlech and the second in August when one army and two naval officers had arranged to meet a submarine off the Great Orme but after waiting for two days they decided to make for London and were captured. The house was demolished in 1920. Further east in woodland on the north side of the river are the remains of Dyffryn Aled Copper mine. In the vicinity are a number of barrows dating back to the Bronze Age.

In the 16th century John Leland reported *"There is in the paroch of Llansannan in the side of a strong hille a place, wher ther be 24 holes or places in a roundel for men to sit in, but sum lesse and sum bigge cutte oute of the mayne rok by mannes hand; and there childern and young men cumming to seke their cattelle use to sitte and play. Sum caulle it the Rounde Table".* The precise location of this feature is not known.

Llansanffraid Glan Conwy
St Bridget's Church on the Banks of the Conway

Llansanffraid Glan Conwy is located one mile south of Llandudno Junction. The name is usually shortened to Glan Conwy. The village stands on the A470, the main road from Cardiff to North West Wales, and on the Llandudno Junction to Blaenau Festiniog railway which opened in 1863. The station originally known as Llansaintffraid was renamed Glan Conway in 1865 and Glan Conwy in 1980. According to legend St Brigid of Kildare sailed across the Irish Sea on a patch of green turf in the 5th century but in accounts of her life there is no mention of this and evidence points to the land being granted for the church by Maelgwyn Gwynedd who before his death in 547 abandoned his former antagonism to Christianity.

The village developed with dry dock and ships chandlers before the building of the bridges at Conway and subsequently became a pleasant residential location. It has seen considerable development in recent years with apartments and housing along the river front as well as estates to the south. There is a primary school on Top Llan Road, replacing the National School which was on the A470. There is the Cross Keys public house, but the Wheatsheaf Hotel (later the Conwy Vale and the Estuary) and the Britannia have closed. There are a number of small shops and a garden centre together with sports pitches.

The church of St Ffraid was rebuilt in 1839-40 by John Welch, the Overton born architect. The old church was double naved and Samuel Lewis reported that at its demolition a coin of King Canute was discovered in the walls. The rebuilding in Romanesque style was financed by the Venerable Hugh Chambres Jones, formerly Archdeacon of Essex who had retired and was living in the 18th century Bryn Eisteddfod north east of the village. The church is wide and aisleless while the furnishings are by Hoare and Wheeler in a refurbishment of 1907. Some stained glass from the medieval church has been re-used and there are monuments from the old church. There is a fine chancel screen while the altar is set in a recess with a small east window with stained glass by Charles Clutterbuck. The window depicts the Adoration of the Magi and the face of one of the wise men is said to be that of Archdeacon Chambres Jones who commissioned the work while the mountains portrayed are a view of Snowdonia from Bryn Eisteddfod. There are two slim bell towers to the west. In 1594 the church was the scene of a Church Tribunal investigation into witchcraft by Gwen Ferch Elis. Gwen a weaver was also well versed in using medicinal herbs. She was accused of driving a child insane and killing a man through witchcraft with evidence provided by seven individuals. Found guilty she was passed to the civil authorities for trial at Denbigh and was hanged in the town square at Denbigh the same year, the first woman to be hanged for witchcraft in Wales.

Bryn Ebenezer Calvinistic Methodist Chapel on Bryn Eglwys was built in 1787, rebuilt in 1811 and in 1819. Tyn-y-Celyn Welsh Wesleyan Methodist Chapel on Top Llan Road was built in 1840 and subsequently used as a community centre. Peniel Independent Chapel in the Bryn Rhys area of the village had been built by 1875 but is no longer in use as a chapel.

Llansant Sior
Also Known as Llansansior but more commonly St George

This attractive estate village with its cottages lies two miles south-east of Abergele on rising ground giving views across to the coast. The old Welsh name for the village was Cegidog, 'cegid' meaning 'hemlock'.

The village owes its existence to Kinmel, an estate centred on the now named Kinmel Manor half a mile to the south-east of the village. The earliest known house was in the 13th century and from the 14th to the 16th century it was owned by the Lloyd family. It passed to Pyrs Holland of Faerdref on his marriage to Catherine Lloyd and their great-great-granddaughter married Sir John Carter, a colonel in the Parliamentary Army who had the distinction of being knighted by both Cromwell and Charles II. Carter sold Kinmel to Sir George Wynne. In 1786 it was purchased by Revd Edward Hughes, part owner of the Parys Mountain copper mine on Anglesey. The descendants of Edward Hughes continue to own the estate but ceased living at Kinmel Hall in 1929.

Kinmel was damaged by fire in 1841 and rebuilt for Colonel William Lewis Hughes M.P. who was created Baron Dinorben in 1831. It was rebuilt in 1871-76 on a grand scale by William Eden Nesfield for Hugh Robert Hughes, William's nephew, the title having died with the 2nd Baron. The new hall had 52 bedrooms and accommodation for 60 staff. In 1929 Kinmel School opened at the Hall but fire in 1934 caused its closure. It was then opened as a Rheuma Spa before being requisitioned as a military hospital in 1940. After the war it opened as a hotel before becoming the Clarendon School for Girls in 1948. Fire again caused extensive damage in 1975 and after a period of dereliction it reopened as a Christian Conference Centre but was sold in 2011 with plans to convert it into a hotel. The house, said to be the largest surviving country house in Wales is Grade I Listed.

In 1919 Kinmel Park was the scene of rioting by Canadian troops unaware that strike action had led to food shortages and delayed their journeys home. The Park is now run commercially with sporting rights, farms and a golf course.

The church of St George was built in 1887-94 by Charles Henry Money Mileham for Hugh Robert Hughes. It replaced the earlier double naved church on a site believed to have been used for worship since Celtic times. It is a single cell church with a south transept housing the organ. Of particular note is the upholstered Hughes family pew at the rear of the church. There are a number of monuments to members of the Hughes family and some earlier memorials from the old church. Entrance is via the south porch, the tall front of which forms the bellcote. In the churchyard is the Hughes family mausoleum, built in 1836 by Thomas Jones of Chester. The Hughes coat of arms is quartered with that of William's wife Charlotte Margaret Grey with a British warrior to the left and a dragon to the right with the inscription RHAD DUW A RHYDDID (God's Blessing and Freedom).

The Kinmel Arms was formerly known as the Dinorben Arms with the building to the east being the old post office. Cathrall in his *History of North Wales* recounts: "*In the Parish is a well, consecrated to St. George, who was the Tutelary Saint of horses; and when any of these animals were unwell they were brought here, in the times of Popery, to be blessed and sprinkled with the water, the priest at the same time pronouncing these words, "Rhud Duw a Said Sior", "The blessing of God and St. George be upon thee".*" The well which consists of a pool and spring lies in the field to the north-east of the entrance lodge. On Primrose Hill is the village school. Built in 1825 as an Independent chapel it became a National School in 1866 after the congregation moved to Bodoryn.

The Dinorben title was taken from the nearby hillfort which has largely been destroyed by the Parc-y-meich limestone quarry. Excavations documented its history from the late Bronze Age through to the Roman period and beyond. The Parc-y-meich (horse park) hoard discovered below the outer defences in the 19th century consisted of over 100 horse harness fittings.

Llansilin

Llansilin lies eight and a half miles south of Llangollen and is now part of Powys. It takes its name from the dedication of the church to St Silin. Silin has been identified with St Sulien and the 1888 Ordnance Survey map gives the dedication as St Sulien, but Baring-Gould identifies Silin with St Giles and in the Red Book of St Asaph of 1296, the church is recorded as "*ecclesia Si*

Egedii de Kynlleith", 'Egidii' being the Latin form of Giles. St Giles was a Greek, born in the 7th century who travelled to France. His cult was popular in England and Scotland in the 11th century.

Grade I Listed St Silin's church was originally a 'clas' or Welsh monastic church and there is evidence of the 13th century church although it was rebuilt in the early 16th century in an unequal double nave form. The north nave was the original and the southern nave was at one time dedicated to St Mary. The church was damaged during the English Civil War and a wooden framed spire was destroyed by fire in 1813. There were a number of restorations in the 18th and 19th centuries. The south porch was added in 1771 and box pews installed in 1782 some of which survive. The west tower was built in 1832 with the clock installed in 1848. In 1864 the west musicians' gallery was converted to an organ loft and the south porch removed. Major work was carried out in the 1890s when the architects were Arthur Baker of Kensington and Harold Hughes of Bangor. The box pews were replaced. The organ was resited and a new vestry added. The four bay nave roof has arch-braced collar beam trusses with cusped struts and windbraces of exceptional quality. The font is 17th century and the pulpit 18th century. Above the chancel steps is a beautiful brass chandelier, known as the Seren Silin, made by Richard Roberts of Birmingham, a native of the village, in 1824. Among the memorials is one to Sir William Williams of Glascoed, Speaker of the House of Commons from 21 October 1680 to 28 March 1681. Both his son Sir William Williams, 2nd Bt., and his grandson, Sir Watkin Williams Wynn, 3rd Bt. Were M.P.s. On the north aisle wall are the Royal Arms, in plaster, now painted white, of Queen Anne post 1707. The east window of the north aisle is in memory of the Royalist satirical poet, Huw Morris or Eos Ceiriog (Nightingale of the Ceiriog), who died in 1705 and is buried in the churchyard. Morris or Morys lived at Pont y Meibion, south of Glyn Ceiriog, where there is an obelisk in his memory. He was a churchwarden at Llansilin and is buried in the graveyard against the southern wall. During the English Civil War he wrote poetry supporting the Royalists and continued poking fun at the Roundheads throughout Cromwell's time though in the form of allegories giving his characters the names of animals. His poems could be sung to the popular tunes of the day and he enjoyed the patronage of leading families in the area. He supported James II until his attempt to overthrow the Church of England when he gave his support to William of Orange. He died in August 1709 at the age of 87. The east window of the chancel features the four

Evangelists and the Ascension by Powell and Sons now better known as the manufacturers of Whitefriars glass.

Salem Welsh Baptist Chapel was built in 1831. Capel Llansilin Welsh Wesleyan Methodist Chapel was built in 1858. Situated at the entrance to the school it is no longer in use. The house next door was previously the police station. Bethania Welsh Calvinistic Methodist Chapel to the north of the church was built in 1839 and is no longer in use. Bethesda Welsh Independent Chapel in what was the hamlet of Stent was built in 1815, rebuilt in 1832 and 1871.

The village has a pub, the 18th century Wynnstay Inn, formerly known as Tŷ Issa or the Cross Foxes (the crest of the Williams family of Glascoed) while the White Lion Inn on the road leading north from the church is now a private house. Opposite the church is The Malt House, an early 19th century maltings with kiln and two attached cottages. At the fork in the road north of the Malt House is a fountain erected in 1882 in memory of Walter Jones, surgeon, who was the son of the Revd Walter Jones, vicar 1827-1876. It was fed from the now filled in Ffynnon Silin.

A mile and a half south of the village, on the edge of Parc Sycharth wood is the motte and bailey Sycharth Castle. Not signposted and described simply as a motte and bailey castle on the map, this in 1400 was the home of Owain Glyndŵr, a fine moated mansion with tiled and chimneyed roofs, a deerpark, heronry, fishpond and mill. Glyndŵr, who held the lordships of Glyndyfrdwy and Cynllaith, was a member of the Welsh aristocracy, being descended from Madog ap Maredudd, the last King of Powys on his father's side and from the old royal family of Deheubarth (South West Wales) on his mother's. Owain studied law at the Inns of Court in London and served as a soldier for the Crown in campaigns against the Scots. He married the daughter of Sir David Hanmer, a justice of the king's bench, whose home was at Maelor Saesneg, the area centred on Bangor on Dee. In 1399 Owain was in dispute over common land with Reginald de Grey, Lord of Ruthin and, unable to obtain satisfaction from the new king, Henry IV or Parliament, he raised his standard and attacked Ruthin on 16th September 1400. The rebellion spread with Glyndŵr gaining prominent English allies, including the Percy and Mortimer families as well as alliances with France and Spain. Although there were early successes and large English armies tried to crush the rebellion, it continued for 10 years before petering out. Owain was never captured though did not accept a pardon offered by Henry V. He is thought to have received sanctuary at the home of his daughter Alice Scudamore at

Kentchurch on the Hereford side of the border. The bard Iolo Goch gave a detailed description of Sycharth with its nine rooms. The *"Well sheltered fishpond"* stocked *"With herrings and whiteheads as is seemly"*, is still nestling in the shelter of the wood. The house was destroyed but the moated motte remains. Borrow described his visit in 1854:

"Owen Glendower's hill or mount at Sycharth, unlike the one bearing his name on the banks of the Dee, is not an artificial hill, but the work of nature, save and except that to a certain extent it has been modified by the hand of man. It is somewhat conical and consists of two steps or gradations, where two fosses scooped out of the hill go round it, one above the other, the lower one embracing considerably the most space. Both these fosses are about six feet deep, and at one time doubtless were bricked, as stout large, red bricks are yet to be seen, here and there, in their sides. The top of the mount is just twenty-five feet across. When I visited it it was covered with grass, but had once been subjected to the plough as various furrows indicated. The monticle stands not far from the western extremity of the valley, nearly midway between two hills which confront each other north and south, the one to the south being the hill which I had descended, and the other a beautiful wooded height which is called in the parlance of the country Llwyn Sycharth or the grove of Sycharth, from which comes the little gush of water which I had crossed, and which now turns the wheel of the factory and once turned that of Owen Glendower's mill, and filled his two moats, part of the water by some mechanical means having been forced up the eminence. On the top of this hill or monticle in a timber house dwelt the great Welshman Owen Glendower, with his wife, a comely, kindly woman, and his progeny, consisting of stout boys and blooming girls, and there, though wonderfully cramped for want of room, he feasted bards who requited his hospitality with alliterative odes very difficult to compose, and which at the present day only a few book-worms understand. There he dwelt for many years, the virtual if not the nominal king of North Wales, occasionally no doubt looking down with self-complaisance from the top of his fastness on the parks and fish-ponds of which he had several; his mill, his pigeon tower, his ploughed lands, and the cottages of a thousand retainers, huddled round the lower part of the hill, or strewn about the valley; and there he might have lived and died had not events caused him to draw the sword and engage in a war, at the termination of which Sycharth was a fire-scathed ruin, and himself a broken-hearted old man in anchorite's weeds, living in a cave on the estate of Sir John Scudamore, the great Herefordshire proprietor, who married his daughter Elen, his only surviving child."

The factory referred to by Borrow was a woollen mill which was demolished and the site cleared in 1962. It is thought to have been the site of the medieval corn mill associated with Sycharth.

Llantysilio

Llantysilio is a scattered parish centred on its church a mile and a half northwest of Llangollen. The parish includes Valle Crucis Abbey and Rhewl (covered separately), Eglwyseg, Pentre-dwfr, Pentrefelin and Llandinam. It also includes the Horseshoe Pass on the A542.

The church is dedicated to St Tysilio, known as St Suliac in Brittany. He was the son of Brochwel, King of Powys but opted for the monastic life rather than that of a soldier and prince. Brochwel led the armies of the British against the armies of the Northumbrian Æthelfrith at the Battle of Chester in 616. Tysilio became Abbot of Meifod but left after the monastery was persecuted by his sister-in-law, Haiarnmed, acting as regent of Powys. Apparently Tysilio refused to marry her on the death of his brother, declining to give up his monastic life. Accompanied by many of his monks he established a monastery in Brittany on the estuary of the Rance, inland from St Malo, the town known today as St Suliac.

The Grade II* Listed church of St Tysilio dates from the 12th century and was recorded as *capellanum de Lantesiliau* in 1254. It was rebuilt in the early 15th century and enlarged with the addition of the north transept in 1718 before being refurbished in 1869 and 1919. Nave and chancel are of a single cell with a seven bay knee-braced collar trussed roof. The two eastern bays form the chancel with its barrel ceiling and raised floor. The chancel screen incorporating the pulpit, the altar and reredos all date from 1919 and are by R.T. Beckett. The font is 15th century as is the black oak eagle lectern. There are a number of memorials including one to Robert Browning who worshipped here while staying with Sir Theodore and Lady Martin, formerly the actress Helena Faucit, of Bryntysilio. The Martins are also remembered with a marble relief tablet. The windows are mainly 19th century though an early 14th century window has been reset in the transept and the east window has 15th century tracery. There is a western bellcote and south porch. In the churchyard is the chest tomb of Thomas Jones of Llantysilio Hall who died in 1761. The last of the line, another Thomas Jones died intestate with no direct descendants in 1821. It was thought that his will might have been buried with him and the tomb was disturbed on a number of occasions to try to find a will as the Thomas Jones who died in 1761 had claimed that he was heir to the Prichard estates which included valuable land in the centre of Liverpool. Nothing was found and the tomb raiders were arrested. Also buried here is Exuperious Pickering of Ruabon and Winnstay, agent for Sir Watkin Williams Wynn. He was the engineer and designer of the first chain bridge across the Dee in 1817. The lychgate was added in 1870.

Llantysilio Hall lies to the north-west of the church. The hall owned by the Jones family after the daughter of Thomas Cupper who built the hall in 1723 married Thomas Jones. After his purchase of the estate in 1867 Charles Frederick Beyer commissioned Pountney Smith of Shrewsbury to build a new hall, slightly to the north of the old hall, which was completed in 1874.

Carl Friedrich Beyer was born in Saxony, the son of a weaver. He attended the Dresden Polytechnic and was sent to Manchester by the government of Saxony to study weaving machine technology. On his return to Germany he was asked to manage the Saxony cotton mill but was determined to return to Manchester. Despite his lack of English, Beyer impressed his prospective employers Sharp Roberts & Co and worked under Richard Roberts in the design of locomotives. In 1852, he was admitted to the Institution of Civil Engineers, proposed by Richard Roberts and seconded by Robert Stephenson and Isambard Kingdom Brunel. He was co-founder of the Institution of Mechanical Engineers. He became a British citizen in 1852. In 1853 he resigned from Sharp Roberts and the following year joined Richard Peacock, formerly chief engineer of the Manchester, Sheffield and Lincolnshire Railway's locomotive works, to form Beyer Peacock and Company with Henry Robertson acting as a sleeping partner. Robertson was responsible for the northern lines of the Great Western Railway, as well as being a coal owner and head of the Brymbo iron and steel works ensuring the success of Beyer Peacock. The company exported railway engines across the world and manufactured the early steam engines for the Metropolitan Line of London Underground. Production continued until 1966. Beyer became a very wealthy man and provided the money for three churches in Gorton, Manchester near his works. The football team of St Mark's Church Gorton eventually became Manchester City F.C. He was also the largest benefactor of Manchester University which had started life as Owens College and later the Victoria University of Manchester. His bequest in his will provided the funds for the Beyer building in 1888, and for professorships in Engineering and Mathematics. After Beyer's death in 1876 Llantysilio Hall was bequeathed to his godson, Henry Beyer Robertson, the son of his close friend and business partner Henry Robertson. Sir Henry Beyer Robertson took over management of the Brymbo Steelworks from his father who died in 1888. The Robertson family remained at Llantysilio Hall until 1994 when it was sold to a private buyer. Built in Victorian Jacobean style the Hall is a three storey house with large cellars. It is Grade II* Listed.

Both Hall and church lie within a bend of the River Dee and a curved weir just below the church as the river diverts water to the Llangollen canal. The weir has become known as the Horseshoe Falls and stretches some 460 feet across the river. The Llangollen canal starts here but lack of space to turn around means that this section is not navigable by motorised canal boats. The tow path leads to Llangollen. As well as feeding the canal, water flows through to a reservoir north of Nantwich, a fact that aided the survival of the canal after much of the canal system was abandoned in the first half of the 20th century.

North-east of the falls is Bryntysilio, a Georgian gentleman's residence remodelled in the Italian villa style. It was the home of Sir Theodore Martin K.C.B,. K.C.V.O. a Scottish poet, author and translator. He was commissioned by Queen Victoria to write a biography of Prince Albert. Queen Victoria stayed at Bryntysilio. Sir Theodore married the celebrated Shakespearian actress Helena Faucit in 1851. Bryntysilio is now an Outdoor Education Centre for Walsall Education Authority.

Beneath the falls is the King's Bridge, built 1902-06 to commemorate the coronation of Edward VII. It carries the road across the canal and River Dee but passes under an arch of a viaduct on the 1862 Llangollen and Corwen Railway Viaduct. Henry Robertson was the chief civil engineer for the Llangollen and Corwen Railway. Below the King's Bridge is the Chain Bridge. A chain bridge was built here in 1817 by Exuperius Pickering to transport coal, lime and bar iron from the canal across the River Dee. It was rebuilt in the 1870s but required renewal after floods in 1928. Sir Henry Beyer Robertson decided that the replacement should be a version of the Menai Suspension Bridge and the old chains were re-used and the new bridge built by Brymbo Steelworks and opened in 1929. It was closed in 1984 on safety grounds and re-opened in 2015. It lays claims to be the oldest chain bridge in the world. Alongside the bridge is the Chainbridge Hotel and Riverside Restaurant.

A mile north-west of St Tysilio's Church in the tiny community of Llandynan is Horeb welsh Calvinistic Methodist Chapel, built around 1850 but now closed.

A mile and a half north of the church in the hamlet of Pentre-dwfr are Bethesda Welsh Calvinistic Methodist Chapel built in 1822 and rebuilt in 1903 and Siloh Welsh Wesleyan Methodist Chapel built in 1816 and rebuilt in 1844. Both chapels have been converted to residential use.

At Eglwyseg two miles north-east of St Tysilio's Church a school and chapel of ease was built in 1871, known as St Mary's Mission Church. This single cell building had a polygonal apse, east bellcote and north porch. It closed as a school in 1908 but continued as a church until 1985. It is now a private dwelling. Eglwyseg Calvinistic Methodist Chapel was built in 1848 and closed in 1901 and demolished.

The Eglwyseg River flows beneath the spectacular white cliffs of Eglwyseg Mountain. On the mountain are round barrows, cairns and standing stones while at the foot of the cliffs were lead mines and lime kilns.

The Horseshoe Pass on the A542 two miles north of St Tysilio's Church offers extensive views to the east as the road rises to 1368 feet. There are a number of deserted farmsteads and the Berwen Slate Quarry. Above the pass on Moel y Gamelin at a height of 1,893 feet is an undisturbed Bronze Age cairn some 100 feet in diameter and six feet high.

Llanychan

Lying a mile and a quarter south-west of Llangynhafal, Llanychan is barely a hamlet but possesses a beautiful, small secluded church. St Hychan was reputed to be one of the many sons of Brychan Brycheiniog, the 5th century king of Brecon. Hychan was slain by pagan Irish in a field near Llandybie in Carmarthenshire where the church is dedicated to his martyred sister St Tybie. Samuel Lewis in 1833 commented: "*This parish is pleasantly situated nearly in the centre of the fertile and picturesque Vale of Clwyd. It is only of inconsiderable extent, but in the beauty of its situation, and the richness and variety of the surrounding scenery, it is not inferior to any spot of the same extent in this part of the principality.*"

The Grade II* Listed church is set back off the road and surrounded by trees. The church was recorded in the Norwich *Taxatio* of 1254 but the present building dates from the 15th century and was renovated by Arthur Baker of Kensington in 1877-78 and financed by John Taber of Clwyd Hall. It is a single cell building with a south porch in the Arts and Crafts style, a small vestry to the north and a western bellcote. The braced collar beamed timber roof is 15th century, restored by Baker. There is a three panel window dated 1626 on the south side but other windows are 19th century, save for the east window of Christ in Majesty with Saints and Angels by J. Dudley Forsyth donated by Sir Crossland Graham of Clwyd Hall in 1925. The reading desk is dated 1730 and the reredos, thought to be constructed of wood from an early barrel roof is of 1846.

The Old School House next to the church was the former National School, built in 1866. Clwyd Hall, south of the church was built as Claremont in the 19th century. It later became a private school and more recently a care home known as Plas y Dyffryn.

Llanynys Island Church

Set on the small ridge between the valleys of the Clwyd and Clywedog, three miles south-east of Denbigh is the tiny village of Llanynys.

A Celtic Clas or monastery was established here in the 6th century by St Saeran, the son of Geraint Saer of Ireland. Saeran is said to be buried in the churchyard. Rice Rees in his Essay on the Welsh Saints (1836) suggests that the clas was founded by Mor ab Ceneu, but Baring-Gould dismisses this as a mistake. The church was of some importance with Edward Lhuyd writing around 1700 reporting it as being the mother church of a large neighbourhood. It was mentioned in a 9th century poem and in the Norwich *Taxatio* of 1254 as Ecclesiastica de Lanenys.

This Grade I Listed double naved church dates from the early 13th century with the north nave being the earliest part. Both naves were extended and heightened around 1500 and the roofs date from this time. The south porch was added later in the 16th century while in 1768 the stone columns supporting the eight bay arcade were replaced by fluted wooden columns, albeit on the original stone bases, and the nave windows were replaced. The ten bay roofs are particularly fine. The furnishings are mainly 19th century but the oak pulpit dating from the mid 17th century and the candelabra in the north nave were a gift of the Revd Mr. Rutter dated 1749. The chancel is in the north nave with the choir stalls formed from earlier box pews as evidenced by the remains of carved inscriptions. The reredos is 18th century and there is a section of carved oak panelling on the north wall. The southern nave contains a small chapel. There are a number of interesting monuments and memorials including the partial reconstruction of a 14th century effigy of a priest, a sepulchral stone cross of the same period and a Royal Arms tablet of 1661.On the north wall is a 15th century painting of St Christopher, the inscription in Welsh which was originally above the painting is now to the east. There is a large double bellcote at the western end of the south nave. In the churchyard there is a chest tomb of Elizabeth and John Simon, the children of John Simon of Glan Clwyd, who died in 1730 and 1738 respectively. There is a carving of a crown with crossed trumpets on the north side while the south side depicts a skull and cross-bones. There is also the poignant tiny chest tomb of two year old Martha, daughter of Charles Lloyd of Cwm Meyin, who died in March 1697. The church also has wooden dog tongs, used to keep fighting dogs in order during church services.

The Cerrigllywidion Arms has closed with planning permission granted for conversion into two houses.

Llay Welsh: Llai meaning Meadow

Llay is a 20th century model village three and a half miles north of Wrexham.

The oldest building in the village is Llai Hall, which in 1490 was the property of Thomas Hanmer. The Hanmers were the descendants of Sir Thomas de Macclesfield who married a Welsh heiress, acquiring lands in North Wales, a practice pursued by his successors who adopted the surname Hanmer after their estates in that parish in Flintshire. The property later passed through the Pulestone and Madocks families. The west wing was demolished in the 1930s and the Hall has now been divided into two residences.

Llai Place, another old building, disappeared under Acacia Court. South-east of the modern village under Gresford Road was the three storey Gresford Corn Mill with its enclosed water wheel powered by a 470 yard leat from a weir on the River Alyn.

Coal mining in the area began with the Llay Hall Colliery in 1878 though this colliery was situated three quarters of a mile to the south-west of the Hall in the village of Sydallt.

The new model village of Llay was established to provide accommodation for the new Llay Main Colliery, started in 1914 by Llay Main Collieries Ltd under Sir Arthur Markham, work was suspended in 1917 and recommenced in 1919, the colliery producing coal in 1921. It was to become the deepest mine in Wales at 3,000 feet and at its peak employed more than 3,000 men. Nine miners died in an explosion in 1924 but the colliery in later years had a good record for safety and productivity. It closed in 1966. The site is now occupied by the Llay Industrial Estate.

Originally Llay was envisaged to become a town of 30,000 inhabitants, part of the 'Garden Village' movement. But the recession of the inter war years resulted in the downgrading of plans and the resulting village of 4,800 inhabitants. The buildings in the village were of a high standard for the time and Llay continues to enjoy its parkland environment.

Llay Miners Welfare Institute was designed by the Mold architect F.A. Roberts in 1929, opening two years later. It is one of the largest institutes in Wales with sports facilities to the rear. The Hallé Orchestra under Sir John Barbirolli performed at the Institute during World War II. Like the sports pavilion to the rear the Welfare Institute is a Grade II Listed building. In addition to the Welfare there is the Royal British Legion and the Crown public house.

The first church services in Llay were held in a mission hut on 9th January 1916 and the church of St Martin of Tours was consecrated on 21st February 1925. The church was the first to be built after the disestablishment of the Church in Wales and was designed by the Chester architect R.T. Beckett. It is a red brick twin aisled church with timber arcading. There is a south transept and the aisles continue into the chancel with no arch but the final bay has a wagon ceiling. There is a fleche in line with the south transept and there are north and south porches.

Llay Main Presbyterian Chapel on School Road was built in 1922 but has subsequently been demolished, a fate which also met Llay Wesleyan Methodist Chapel on Second Avenue. Glanaber Calvinistic Methodist Chapel on Nant y Gaer Road was built in 1925 and has subsequently become Bethel Baptist Chapel, replacing the 1930 Bethel Baptist Chapel on Llay Court which has been demolished. The Nazarene Chapel on Nant y Gaer Road was built in the latter part of the 20th century. The Roman Catholic church of St Francis of Assisi lies on Llay Road.

The Park County Primary School provides education to children aged 3 to 11. There are a number of village shops and takeaway restaurants. The Alyn Waters Country Park adjoins the village offering a playground and forest walks with artworks littering the paths. There has been some modern development in this fine example of a garden village.

Llwynmawr (see Dolywern and Llwynmawr)

Llysfaen Stone Court
Llysfaen, three and a half miles west of Abergele sits on Mynydd Marian with views across the Irish Sea. It has grown considerably since Samuel Lewis recorded just five houses in the village in 1833.

Tradition suggests that St Cynfran established his church here in 777, but Cynfran was reputed to be the son of Brychan Brycheiniog who lived in the mid 5th century. The church at Llanddulas is dedicated to St Cynbryd, Cynfran's brother. The earliest surviving part of this double naved church is the 13th century north nave with the south nave added in the 14th century. The roofs date from the 15th century though until the 1860s they were thatched. There was a major restoration completed in 1870 by G.E. Street, financed by the local quarry owner J.W. Raynes and the Bamford-Hesketh family of Gwrych Castle. As a result of this work much of the medieval fabric was covered or replaced and a new porch and western bellcote installed. There is an arcade of four arches dividing the naves and a Memorial window of the First World War. The furnishings are Victorian, including the Gothic pulpit, font and rood screen. The church which was built on a Celtic llan enjoys a prominent position at the centre of the old village. In the churchyard, south of the church is a brass sundial of 1731 with an inscription in Welsh. It is mounted on a sandstone base.

To the east of the church is Church House, the church hall, opened in June 1930. The architect and Clerk of Works was Colwyn Foulkes. The tree on the traffic island nearby was planted in 1931.

Moriah Wesleyan Methodist Chapel was founded in 1820 and built on Pentregwyddel Road in the late 19th century but has been converted for residential use with little left to indicate its original purpose other than its name, Tŷ Capel. Mynydd Seion Wesleyan Methodist Chapel was founded in 1804 and built on Tan-y-Graig Road in the early years of the 20th century. It has now been converted to form three houses. Llysfaen Baptist Chapel on Dolwen Road was built in 1884. Bethel Welsh Calvinistic Methodist Chapel, also on Dolwen Road, was built in 1834 and rebuilt in 1891. It closed in 1981 and converted into three houses.

Mynydd Marian was the site of the Llysfaen Telegraph, part of the system developed by Jesse Hartley, Chief Engineer to the Mersey Docks and Harbour Board and opened in 1841. Originally built as a semaphore station in 1827, it had a single mast with three arms to denote the number of the registered vessel approaching Liverpool. In 1841 the single mast was replaced by two wrought iron towers each with two moveable arms allowing identification of up to four digits. The system was abandoned for an electric telegraph in 1861 and the station has now been converted to private accommodation.

South-east of the church along Ffordd-y-llan is the former National School built in 1870. Opposite is the entrance to Westwood Caravan Park and the Semaphore House inn.

There is a modern primary school, Ysgon Cynfran serving the much larger modern community that is Llysfaen today. There is a small shopping area on Gadlas Road and a small industrial estate to the west of the church on the former Tŷ Mawr estate which includes the Conwy Brewery. The Castle Inn on Tan-y-Graig Road has closed as has the Bod-hyfryd Inn on the same road.

Loggerheads

The hamlet of Loggerheads lies two and a half miles west of Mold on the A494. It takes its name from the We Three Loggerheads inn. The hamlet was unnamed on early Ordnance survey maps and later shown as Pentre. It has been surmised that the name comes from a dispute over boundaries. Carreg Carn March Arthur boundary stone east of the hamlet bears the inscription *"The stone underneath this Arch Carreg Carn March Arthur was Adjudged to be the Boundary of the Parish and Lordship of Mold in the county of Flint and of Llanverres in the County of Denbigh by the High Court of Exchequer at Westminster 10th November 1763".* The stone is said to bear the imprint of King Arthur's horse's hoof as it leapt from a cliff to escape the Saxons. The inn sign shows the heads of two men back to back. The original was by the Montgomeryshire born landscape artist Richard Wilson who frequented the inn when staying with his relative at Colomendy Hall where he passed his final years. The subjects were the local priest and a landowner who had fallen out while the third loggerhead is the viewer. A 'loggerhead' in the 18th century was a blockhead or fool. An article in the Somerset House Gazette and Literary Museum of 1824 gives the original village name as Llanverris, and attributes the Loggerheads name to the inn, though this is a confusion with the nearby village of Llanferres. The writer a Mr T. Wright suggests that the painting of the pub sign had been retouched several times since Wilson's day. A replacement sign now hangs outside the inn with the original valued at £30,000 according to an item of news on the BBC.

Loggerheads was a lead mining area and there are remains of the industry within Loggerheads Country Park where the Glanalyn and Penyfron mines stood on the banks of the River Alyn. Pentre Mill was built in the 19th century, on the site of a former mill. It was a saw mill in 1899 but later produced cattle food and continued in operation until 1942. It has been restored to full working order as a corn mill and is open to the public. Loggerheads Country

Park, which stretches across the border into Flintshire, offers walking trails and rock climbing, the Caffi Florence and an audio visual facility containing old films and other material.

Colomendy Hall lies south-east of the inn and was originally built in the 16th century. In the latter part of the 18th century it was the home of Mrs Catherine Jones, a relative of Richard Wilson. Wilson was a frequent visitor over the years and a number of his paintings are of the area. A prominent landscape painter he was a founding member of the Royal Academy. In later years however his heavy drinking saw him fall on hard times and he moved from London to live with his brother in Mold. On his brother's death he moved to Colomendy Hall, having lost his memory and in a state of childishness. He died in 1782. The house was rebuilt in 1810-11 in the Neo-classical style and was eventually purchased by Liverpool Corporation in 1956 as an educational establishment. It is now run as a schools' environmental studies centre.

Maeshafn

Maeshafn is a small hamlet on the Flintshire border, three miles south-west of Mold. The name is a corruption of Maes-y-safn translated as mouth or jaws field, the name of the local lead mine. The Maes-y-safn lead mine lay to the west of the hamlet and had been in operation since at least 1720 when Richard Richardson, a Chester gold and silversmith, took a stake in it. The mine had an underground incline used for haulage. It was taken over by John Taylor in 1861 and wound up in 1871. There was the Aberduna lead mine to the north of the village with the remains of the engine house near Aberduna limestone quarry now being reclaimed. The area around Maeshafn is littered with disused lead mining shafts.

The pleasant hamlet of Maeshafn has the Miners' Arms half hidden down a lane opposite the small village green. Formerly the mine pay office it has been a public house since before 1872. North of the green is the former Maeshafn Welsh Calvinistic Methodist Chapel, built in 1820, enlarged in 1843, rebuilt in 1863 and again in 1900 in the Arts and Crafts style and now a private house. There has been some modern building but Maeshafn remains small. There are attractive walks in the area which has nature reserves.

Marchwiel Welsh: Marchwiail

On the A525 less than two miles south-east of Wrexham, Marchwiel saw considerable expansion through the 20th century. The name is difficult. The literal translation is 'stallion rods', and Morgan suggests that it signified a boundary line of rods. Another suggestion is 'strong twigs'.

The church is dedicated to St Marcella and St Deiniol. Deiniol was the son of Abbot Dimawd Fwr of Bangor Maelor (Bangor Iscoed) and went on to found the monastery at Bangor in Gwynedd, later becoming Bishop of Bangor under the patronage of Maelgwn Gwynedd. The dedication to Marcellus is more difficult. Baring-Gould suggests that it has come about from the old name of the village, Plwyf y Marchwiail, meaning Parish of Marchwiel. There was a saint Marcella or Marchel, a nun at the nearby monastery at Bangor who is the patron the church at Whitchurch, but the Saint's day corresponds to an earlier Christian Martyr St Marcellus. Although recorded as 'Ecclesia de Marchocil' in 1254 the Grade II* Listed church of St Marcella and St Deiniol was rebuilt in 1778 in the Grecian style by the architect William Worral. The rebuilding was funded by public subscription started in 1774 and from a fund set up in 1626 by Sir Edward Broughton and four others when they purchased a 14 acre farm called Tyddyn Daniel from the Crown for the purpose of applying the proceeds to the repairs of the church. The tower was added in 1789 at the expense of Philip Yorke of Erddig and designed by James Wyatt. The north transept was added in 1829 when £200 was provided from the Tyddyn Daniel accumulated rents. The polygonal chancel was added in the mid 19th century. The furnishings are late 19th century while the restored organ in the west gallery was installed in the 20th century. The peal of bells was installed in 1930 replacing the former single bell while the 1892 clock with its faces to the south and west was made by Joyce & Co of Whitchurch. The church has connections with the Erddig estate and the Yorke family vault is in the churchyard and there are monuments within the church to members of the family. Of particular note is the 1788 Francis Eginton stained glass window of 21 panels with heraldry relating to the Edisbury, Yorke and Cust families of Erddig. Other later windows also contain heraldic links with the Yorke family. The tower has a balustrade with an urn topped with a weathercock at each corner.

The only other religious establishment in the village was a barn opposite Station Road which was used as a Wesleyan Methodist mission room and Sunday School from 1900. It was demolished in the 1960s.

Marchwiel Hall to the west of the village was rebuilt in the mid 19th century. It is unclear whether the original hall was on this site or at Old Hall Farm. In the 16th century Marchwiel Hall was in the possession of Henry Parry whose daughter Margaret married Morgan Broughton circa 1589. On the death of her stepfather in the 1620s she inherited Marchwiel Hall. Morgan Broughton was High Sheriff of Denbighshire in 1608 and his son Sir Edward Broughton was knighted in 1618 and pardoned for abetting a murder in 1639. Both Sir Edward and his son, also Edward fought on the Royalist side during the English Civil War. Edward was imprisoned at the Gatehouse Westminster but on his release married as his second wife the widow of the keeper, Mary Wyke. He died at sea in 1665 during the Dutch War having been created a baronet and was buried in Westminster Abbey. His son Sir Edward was High Sheriff in 1698 and when the Broughton line ended Marchwiel Hall passed to Aquila Wyke, grandson of Mary by her first husband. The Hall came into the ownership of the Mainwaring family and was rebuilt by Townshend Mainwaring, M.P. for Denbigh Boroughs 1841-68. The house was purchased in 1913 by Sir Alfred McAlpine who developed the cricket ground on the estate into one of the finest in the country. The Hall was held by his great-granddaughter before it was offered for sale in 2010.

Erddig Hall, two miles west of the village is one of the finest stately homes in Britain. It takes its name from the Welsh family who owned the estate in the 16th century. The Edisbury family had prospered under the patronage of Sir Thomas Myddelton and after the Restoration in 1660 John Edisbury acquired much of the Erddig estate though the old family retained Little Erddig. Joshua Edisbury began the building of Erddig Hall in 1684, but the lavish scale of building coupled with poor investment in Flintshire lead mines led to financial difficulties. His brother John Edisbury, M.P. for Oxford University (1678-9), and Master of the High Court of Chancery (1684-1708) misappropriated funds to try to help. Much of the family wealth was dissipated through the sale of other property and on Joshua's bankruptcy in 1714 Erddig was purchased by John Meller, the son of a London draper and a prominent London lawyer who had succeeded John Edisbury as Master of the High Court of Chancery. Meller added double wings to each side of the Hall but died childless in 1733. Erddig passed to his nephew Simon Yorke, the son of a Dover wholesale grocer and cousin of Philip Yorke, 1st Earl Hardwicke. Erddig remained in the Yorke family until 1973 when it was acquired by the National Trust. Simon's son Philip was responsible for refacing the brick front in stone in the 1770s, using James Wyatt as architect together with local architects, J. & W. Turner. Philip inherited further property in London and Hertfordshire from his uncle James Hutton and married Elizabeth Cust, the youngest daughter of the Speaker of the House of Commons, Sir James Cust.

Elizabeth died in 1779 when Philip was 36 and he married Diana, the widow of Ridgeway Owen Meyrick, a grandson of the Earl of Londonderry and a cousin of William Pitt. Philip was the author of the *Royal Tribes of Wales*, published in 1799. In 1804 Philip was succeeded by his son Simon, M.P. for Grantham 1793-1802. Simon's eldest son, also Simon, inherited the estate in 1834. The next to inherit was Philip Yorke (1849-1922), followed by his sons Simon (1903-1966) who died childless and Philip. Erddig required considerable maintenance due to mining subsidence and Philip conveyed ownership to the National Trust. In addition to the £120,000 received in compensation from the National Coal Board the Trust sold 63 acres of the park to pay for the restoration which was completed in 1977. Philip Yorke died in 1978. The hall and grounds are open to the public and Erddig Hall contains a collection of historical importance as the Yorke family with their interest in heritage had in the words of Philip Yorke *"foregone many luxuries and comforts over seven generations should now be dedicated to the enjoyment of all those who may come here and see a part of our national heritage preserved for all foreseeable time"*. Mains electricity was not installed at Erddig during the Yorkes' tenure, Philip using a portable generator to power his television set. The walled garden is a fine example of an 18th century formal garden while in the grounds a weir feeds a canal from which a hydraulic ram pumped water to the house and the fascinating cup and saucer pond which was installed in 1774 to prevent erosion of the Black Brook.

Marchwiel has a primary school and the Red Lion. There are some attractive older terraced cottages along the main road. The village had a railway station on the Wrexham and Oswestry Railway which opened in 1895 and closed in 1962.

Marford

Marford is a hamlet between Gresford and Rossett. Mentioned in the Domesday Book it was traditionally known as Merford a name that would appear to signify Ford of the Mere. It was once part of Cheshire. For hundreds of years the townships of Marford and Hoseley were part of Flintshire completely surrounded by Denbighshire, though this had ended before 1873. The hamlet of Marford was never part of this tiny enclave which extended to the south-east from the River Alyn south of Rossett but not as far as the estate village.

Rofft Castle, a motte and bailey castle on Springfield Lane consisted of an 18ft high mound with the bailey occupying part of an Iron Age promontory fort. It may have been the site of Osbern Fitztesso's court. It was damaged in 1140 but became the llys of Madog ap Maredudd and later Rofft Hall was built on the bailey in 1315. It has been identified as Bromhall Castle destroyed by the Welsh in 1140. In 1713, George Blackbourne, steward of Trevalyn Hall, known as a womaniser and drunk, murdered his wife, Madam Margaret at the Hall. Her body was found the next morning at the foot of the stairs with her neck broken. The inquest returned a verdict of misadventure and within six months George had remarried a younger woman. Madam Margaret did not rest easy in her grave however and each night her ghost ranged through Marford, tapping on windows, her dead eyes staring through as she travelled to Rofft Hall where she walked the corridors making a woeful wailing noise. When George moved with his new wife to take up residence at Trevalyn she followed him there. The archdeacon was summoned to lay the ghost to rest but villagers still heard the tapping on their windows and witnessed the ghostly face. When in the 19th century new houses were built crosses were incorporated in the walls to protect the inhabitants from the ghost now called Madam Blackbird.

In 1836-7 John Boydell, steward of the Trevalyn estate replaced the hall with Roft Castle House. The estate also built a number of houses in the distinctive Gothic style of the village with ogee and circular windows. The two storey stables also date from 1836-7 and are built in the style of the estate village. The first buildings of the estate village were built around 1805 and include Marford Hall and the remodelled three storey Trevor Arms. The inn dates from the 17th century and was a coaching inn on the Swansea to Manchester road. There was never a church in Marford, being initially in the parish of Gresford and later Rossett. There was a Methodist chapel in Turnpike Lane, covered under Gresford and the Cox Lane Baptist chapel built in 1809 but now a private house.

Marford grew dramatically in the 20th century with new houses built along Marford Hill towards Gresford, along Hoseley Lane and in the triangle formed by the right angled turn of Marford Hill and Marford Wood. Many of the houses are substantial properties. As well as the Trevor Arms there is the Red Lion Hotel on Marford Hill, the Rofft Primary School and the Marford Community Centre on Pant Lane.

Marford featured in an infamous trial for adultery in 1770. Mary Jones, wife of the landlord of the Toll House Inn on Marford Hill was called as a witness in the case of 'criminal conversation', i.e.adultery, between the Duke of

Cumberland and Strathearn and Lady Grosvenor. It appears that the Duke, the brother of King George III, had an affair with Lady Henrietta Grosvenor. The Duke together with a servant named John and an older man known as Farmer Tush travelled in disguise, staying at hostelries in the environs of the Grosvenor home, Eaton Hall, across the border in Cheshire for meetings with Lady Grosvenor. They stayed at Marford Hill in November 1769. Farmer Tush was in fact Robert Giddings, gentleman-porter to the Duke. The innkeeper was wary fearing that they were highwaymen but apparently the Duke met Lady Grosvenor who warned him that her husband was suspicious and they left hurriedly claiming the death of the father. The couple arranged trysts at the house of Lady Grosvenor's milliner in Pall Mall and she gave evidence that the two had engaged in 'carnal copulation'. On December 21st, 1769 the Duke and Lady Grosvenor were caught together in a room at the White Hart at St Albans. A book was published of the depositions which included the counter claims by Lady Grosvenor that Lord Grosvenor had for several years carried on a "criminal lewd and unchaste intercourse" with a Mrs Molesworth and employed her to procure and introduce young women "for his carnal use and knowledge". Lady Henrietta pleaded that the court should divorce her "from bed, board and mutual co-habitation from her husband". Divorce was however out of the question but the Duke of Cumberland paid £10,000 in damages to Lord Grosvenor. Not surprisingly the court case enthralled society in 1770.

Minera Welsh: Y Mwynglawdd

Minera is a small village four miles north-west of Wrexham. It was the centre of a lead mining industry and the name which is derived from the Latin for 'minerals' has been in use since 1339. The Welsh name meaning 'Mine' was not used until 1685.

Until 1865 Minera had been a chapelry of Wrexham. It was created a parish and St Mary's church was built replacing the 1700 chapel which had become too small and dilapidated. The new church was designed by the Bangor architects Henry Kennedy and John Mechelen Rogers and built at a cost of £2,000. It takes the form of an equal armed cross with the two storey 62 feet tall tower between the southern and western arms. The tower has a peal of 10 bells by Taylors of Loughborough installed in 1923. The main entrance is via the porch in the tower. Each arm has a three bay arch braced collar truss roof with an impressive structure to the crossing roof with a brass circular chandelier hung from the centre. There are a number of memorials and some fine stained glass, including the north window of 1867 by Alexander Gibbs to A. Reid, chairman of the Minera Mining Company which had donated £440 towards the cost of building. The 1935 pulpit in the crossing is given particular prominence.

A mile south of the village on the B5426 stands the 1892 Grade II Listed mission church, built to serve the district of Esclusham Above, otherwise known as New Brighton. The corrugated iron clad timber framed building has a spirelet with a single bell, a western porch and a small vestry at the south eastern corner. Apart from a new roof the church is largely unaltered and is one of the few remaining examples of this form of prefabricated church which proliferated between 1890 and the outbreak of war in 1914. The church is no longer in use.

Nearby in the New Brighton area is Hermon Wesleyan Methodist Chapel, another corrugated iron building built in 1890. Standing above the road to the west of St Mary's was Pen-y-bryn Wesleyan Methodist Chapel which was built in 1804, rebuilt in 1860 and 1902. It has now been converted to residential use. Opposite St Mary's is Tyn-y Capel inn dating from the 17th century. The 1872 map shows the spelling as Ty'n y capel meaning Chapel House. In 2013 the inn was purchased by 100 local residents aided by a grant from the National Lottery Village SOS Fund.

Minera Hall at the eastern entrance to the village was built around 1800 by Robert Burton who operated a number of lead mines in partnership with the Wilkinson brothers. The Burton family continued in ownership of mining interest until the late 19th century. In the 1950s the hall became a clubhouse for the Royal British Legion until 1998, after which it became derelict.

The National School was built in 1851, designed by Penson. It was later enlarged and is still in use as the Minera Aided Primary School.

Pen y Nant Home for the Elderly on Church Road was built as the William and John Jones Convalescent Home and opened in 1918 taking in 25 wounded soldiers and sailors. John Jones was a Wrexham brewer and the home was a bequest under his will. The architect, chosen by competition was Philip H. Lockwood. In 1951 the home was acquired by Denbighshire County Council, the name changed and it became an old people's home.

Minerals have been extracted from the Minera area since the time of the Romans but in the 18th and 19th centuries there was major expansion with the extraction of silica and limestone as well as lead and coal. There are the remains of numerous shafts, lime kilns and quarries across a wide area to the south of the village. The community of New Brighton was at the centre of the lead mining and processing in the 19th century and there is a museum and country park centred on the restored steam winder house off the B5426 half a mile south of the village. The hamlet of New Brighton was originally known as City and consists of two streets. On the northern side of the lead mines was the City Arms public house.

Mining ceased in the early 20th century though the population of Minera saw an increase in population post World War II with the building of estates to the north of the school.

Mochdre Pig Town

The village of Mochdre lies a mile and a half west of Colwyn Bay on the southern side of the A55 North Wales Expressway. According to legend, it owes its name to having been the place where a stolen herd of sacred pigs was stored. The story is told in *Math fab Mathonwy,* one of the stories of the *Mabinogion.*

In 1880 the village was very small, concentrated around the Mountain View Hotel, then known as the White Horse Inn, with a Post Office and the Welsh Calvinistic Methodist Chapel, Nasareth on Chapel Street having been built in 1780 and rebuilt in 1832 and 1880, with a Sunday School added in 1906. The chapel was put up for sale in 2009. The area to the north of the Mountain View was developed after the First World War, with Tanyrallt Avenue and Bryn Marl Road as well as housing on the old A55. The major development however was post 1945. The village now has a small shopping area as well as a primary school and a large commercial area of factories and offices.

The village was served by a station on the London and Scottish Railway which closed in 1931. Mochdre was the site of the first water trough for steam locomotives, built in 1860 it enabled engines to take on water without stopping, a system later adopted throughout the world.

To the north-east of the village on Conway Road in what was the hamlet of Bron-y-nant, the Wesleyan Methodist Chapel was built in 1809. In 2000 it was purchased by The Society of St Pius X and is now the Roman Catholic church of St David.

Moelfre Bare Hill (Abergele)

Moelfre is a scattered hamlet two miles south of Abergele. It takes its name from the 1,040 foot Moelfre Isaf to the south, where a hoard of Bronze Age axe heads was discovered. A Roman road runs east-west through the area. Ebenezer Welsh Independent Chapel was built in 1802 and rebuilt in 1891. Moelfre Wesleyan Methodist Chapel was built in 1836 and rebuilt in 1896. Tan-y-mynydd is a small holiday complex with fishing lakes and the North Wales Brewery nearby.

Moelfre Bare Hill (Llansilin)
The small hamlet of Moelfre lies in the community of Llansilin six and a half miles west of Oswestry. To the north is the 1,715 foot Gyrn Moelfre, while to the west is Llyn Moelfre, a small lake. The Baptist Capel Carmel was built in 1826 but is now used as a workshop. The village corn mill had been converted to a smithy by 1900, though the weirs for the mill race remain. Set in a well wooded valley this is an attractive area though the roads are very narrow. Moelfre Hall stands above the Llansilin road to the east of the village. A house has stood on this site from at least the 11th century and the Lloyd family built a late medieval house which was enlarged in the 17th century when it was regarded as one of the most important houses in the area and mentioned in the *Llyfr Silin*. The Lloyds continued in occupation until the 19th century but much of the house was demolished in the early years of the 20th century, with further demolition in 1950 leaving just a wing of the 17th century building.

Moss
Moss lies at the northern end of a group of villages that includes Brynteg and Pentre Broughton three miles north-east of Wrexham. The 1873 map shows Moss as including the areas of the other two villages and the hamlet of Cerney, though Brynteg is not named and Pentre Broughton is called simply Pentre.

This was a coal mining area and coal produced north-west of the village supplied Parys Mountain from the late 18th century. Bryn Mally Colliery was sunk in the 1830s and purchased in 1849 by Thomas Clayton. 13 men lost their lives due to flooding in 1856. In 1878 six men died in an explosion and in 1889 a further explosion caused the deaths of 20 miners. The colliery continued in operation until 1935 employing 482 men at its peak. The Westminster Colliery in the Moss Valley was started by Thomas Clayton in the 1850s but by 1869 was owned by the Westminster Brymbo Coal Company. It was worked in conjunction with Gwersyllt Colliery and employed over 1,000 men at its peak. Water ingress caused its closure in 1925. Thomas Clayton lived at Bryn Mally Hall, now known as Bryn Mally Farm which lies to the east of Clayton Road.

Zion Independent Methodist church, a mission hall, on Cerney Road was built in the early 20th century but has since been demolished. Zion Independent Methodist Chapel on Cerney Road was moved from Elizabeth Street, Liverpool in 1902. It was originally built in 1835. It closed in 1994 and has been demolished and replaced by housing. Cerni Welsh Calvinistic Methodist Chapel on Cerney Road was built in 1865-6 and rebuilt in 1891. After closure it was used as a sewing factory before being demolished and the site used for housing. Brake English Wesleyan Methodist Chapel on Brake Road was built in 1885 near the entrance of the Brymbo (Brake) Tunnel which was closed in 1862. Brake Chapel was demolished in 2009. Moss Congregational Chapel on Castletown Road was built in 1864 and replaced in 1907 by Westminster Road Independent Chapel which closed in 1970 and has since been converted to a private dwelling.

Moss Valley was the site of the Westminster Colliery and also a feeder reservoir for the Ellesmere Canal, built by Telford in 1796. The area was subject to reclamation and landscaping in the 1970s and now consists of a country park with two lakes and the Moss Valley Golf Club. Moss and Cerney are now residential areas with mainly modern housing taking advantage of the elevated position and lack of through traffic.

Nantglyn Vale Brook

A little under four miles south-west of Denbigh lies the little village of Nantglyn.

The 16th century bard Dafydd ab Llywelyn ab Madog wrote a cywydd or poem in praise of Modeyrn, an honoured saint in Nantglyn. Modeyrn was the son of Edeyrn and grandson of Cunedda, a warrior from Scotland who established the dynasty of Gwynedd in the 5th century. Edeyrn was granted the district of Edeyrnion in north-east Merionethshire. Baring Gould paraphrases the bard's words: *"Mordeyrn served God from his youth up. When many of his kin of the twenty thousand Saints went to Bardsey, a causeway rose out of the sea for their passage, but Mordeyrn crossed thither to them on his golden-maned steed without wetting so much as a hoof; hence his name, "the Sovereign of the Sea". This "leader and confessor of the Faith" afterwards returned to his home in the vale of Nantglyn, where he has "a befitting house (church), with ornate Sacrifice". Here, where he died, is his shrine, as well as his beautiful image, which* imparted health to all sick folk. His devotees he rid of every affliction, and such as resorted to him for their cattle had them preserved from disease for a whole year. They came laden with objects of fine wax and gold. "Might he ever defend his people from all harm and ill, and finally bring them all safe to heaven!"'

Capel Modeyrn was situated the east of the village opposite Glasmor Farm and was mentioned by Leland in the 16th century and by Edward Lhuyd in 1699 when the foundations only remained. Lhuyd records that turf from inside the chapel was sold as a cure for the diseases of cattle. The nearby bridge is Pont Rhyd Sant.

The church is dedicated to St James possibly because James and Modeyrn share the same festival day. The church was mentioned in the *Taxatio* of 1284 and was restored in 1777 when an additional sixth bay was added to the single cell building. A major restoration was carried out in 1860-62 by the prominent Denbigh architects Richard Lloyd-Williams and Martin Underwood, with further work undertaken in 1875 and 1879. The exterior appearance of the church is attributed to these restorations. The arched-braced collar truss roof is a combination of 18th century trusses and 19th century arched braces. There are a number of monuments and commemorative stained glass windows including the west rose window. There is a lean to vestry at the north-western corner and a south porch. The western bellcote is surmounted by a cross. In the churchyard are two ancient yews, one of which has stone steps and a seat inserted in the split. Local legend claims that this was a pulpit from which John Wesley preached a sermon. 250 yards north of the church was the site of St Modeyrn's well.

The National School was built in 1858 by the architect Richard Lloyd Williams but closed in the 1990s. Salem Independent Chapel to the south of the crossroads was built in 1820 but is now a private house as is the former Victoria Inn. At Waen to the west of the village, Soar Welsh Calvinistic Methodist Chapel was built in 1801 and rebuilt in 1862. Another Soar Welsh Calvinistic Methodist Chapel was built in the hamlet of Soar, a mile to the south of the village, in 1847 and rebuilt in 1888. It is now disused.

Plas Nantglyn lies half a mile to the south of the village. It is thought to have been built in 1573 by Robert Wynne ap Meredudd ap Tudor whose grandson Robert Wynne married Jane Llwyd in 1631. The house was restored and remodelled in the Arts and Crafts style in the first five years of the 20th century by the Wynne-Edwards family. The Plas is now run as a residential educational studies centre for schools.

In 1751 William Samwell vicar of Nantglyn had a son, David. In 1775 David Samwell qualified as a ship's surgeon and a year later joined Captain Cook's ship *HMS Resolution* as surgeon's 1st mate. He subsequently became surgeon on *HMS Discovery* and witnessed Cook's death in Hawaii in 1779, publishing an account of it in 1786. He continued as a navy surgeon until 1796 before acting as surgeon to British prisoners of war at Versailles. He returned to his London home in 1798 and died there the same year. He is buried at St Dunstan's church Fleet Street. A confirmed Welshman Samwell was a member of the London based Gwyneddigion Society, serving as secretary and in 1797 as president.

Nantglyn is set in a delightful rural area watered by a number of streams which powered corn mills at Waen and Soar. Slate was quarried on a small scale at Nantglyn Slate Quarry to the south-east and the community area includes the upper reaches of Llyn Brenig and the Bronze Age round Barrows on Cefn Brenig. The village has no amenities, the village shop and Victoria Inn having closed but the church hall serves as a village hall.

New Brighton (see Minera)

New Broughton

New Broughton, a mile and three quarters north-west of Wrexham was established in the 1890s on land south-west of Broughton Farm to house workers in the New Broughton Colliery. At first development was bounded on the south-west by the Wrexham and Minera Railway, completed in 1866 and to the north by the Brymbo branch of the Wrexham, Mold & Connah's Quay Railway, opened in the 1880s with passenger services from 1889. A terrace of workers' houses was built on the south side of Windsor Road, with Chapel Road, Bersham Road and Weston Road being the other streets in the early village.

The Broughton New Colliery was opened in 1883 by Thomas Clayton of Bryn Mally Hall. It was later owned by New Broughton Colliery Company, Wrexham but closed in 1910, having employed up to 328 men. It was situated on land now occupied by woods to the south-east of the bus garage on Southsea Road.

Soar Welsh Wesleyan Methodist Chapel was built on Bersham Road in 1894 and rebuilt in 1904. It has been demolished and a block of flats now occupies the site. An English Wesleyan Methodist Church was built in the 1900s on the corner of Windsor Road and Dale Road but had been demolished by 1983.

Cyssegr Welsh Calvinistic Methodist Chapel on Chapel Road was built in 1894 but has been demolished and replaced by houses.

East of the village is the three storey Gatewen Hall. The Hall was built in the late 18th century but enlarged between 1810 and 1830 for the then owner Thomas Hayes. It subsequently became a residential school which in 1982 was taken over by the Bryn Alyn Community Ltd and opened as a children's home in 1983 providing accommodation for 14 boys and girls aged 14-18. It became infamous for the abuse the children endured under the owners Roger Owen Griffiths and his then wife, now Anthea Beatrice Roberts between 1977 and 1982. The Bryn Alyn Community which owned three homes was also the subject of allegations of child abuse.

A new village development has taken place on the site of the old Gatewen Farm and Gatewen Colliery. The colliery was opened in 1877 by the Broughton Coal Company and employed up to 1,073 men before its closure in 1932. The headgear was later transferred to the Bersham Colliery where the wooden headgear was destroyed by fire in 1933.

The village, no longer constrained by the old rail lines has expanded and it is difficult to establish clear boundaries between the communities of Caego, Rhosrhedyn and Southsea. There are sports pitches and a few small businesses, including a Chinese takeaway and an off-licence but no public houses.

Pensarn Head of the Causeway

Pensarn lies on the north coast adjacent to Abergele from which it is separated by the North Wales Expressway. It is in effect the seaside resort of Abergele with a fine sandy beach, caravan parks, a promenade, amusements and cafés. The village developed in the mid 19th century with Marine Road and South Parade. More recently there have been developments of mainly bungalows. Marine Road has a selection of shops and takeaways together with The Park Hotel and the Yacht pub, originally the Railway Inn. The large Original Factory Shop was previously a Somerfield supermarket. The village has been the site of the Abergele and Pensarn railway station since 1848 when the Chester and Holyhead Railway opened. The line was taken over by the London and North Western Railway in 1858 and the station remodelled in 1883. The buildings are Grade II Listed.

The early Gothic styled English Presbyterian chapel on the corner of Marine Road and Benllan was built in 1878 by the Liverpool architect Richard Owens. Above the gable entry porch is an impressive wheel window. The chapel is no longer in use but the schoolroom to the rear which was added in 1890 is now the Pensarn Family Church. Pensarn Welsh Calvinistic Methodist Chapel at the end of Ger-y-mor was built 1858 but closed in 1956 and the site redeveloped for accommodation. St David's church on South Parade was built in 1886 as a temporary tin church. It was reclad in steel in 1982 but demolished and replaced by the Canolfan Dewi Sant Centre in 2008. The new centre contains a dedicated area for worship.

On 3rd October 1854 the 35 ton wooden sloop *Endeavour* carrying a cargo of cast iron was forced ashore at Pensarn and broke up the following day. The crew were rescued by the Rhyl lifeboat.

Pentre Broughton Broughton Village

Pentre Broughton lies some three miles north-east of Wrexham between Brynteg and Moss. Known in the 1870s as Pentre the name Pentre Broughton did not appear on maps until the second half of the 20th century. The village grew up in the late 19th century providing accommodation for workers in the nearby collieries and Brymbo Steelworks. There was also the Black Lane Colliery on a site now occupied by Broughton Heights. The colliery operated between 1879 and 1899 after the abandonment of the Moss Tunnel in the same area which carried the Brymbo and Minera Branch of the North Wales Mineral Railway.

St Paul's Church off Bryn-y-Gaer Road was built in 1888 to the designs of Howel Davies of Wrexham. There are north and south transepts off the chancel with the organ in the north transept. The pulpit is polygonal and the font is carved from Cefn stone. There is a double bellcote above the chancel arch. The graveyard has been extended to form a large cemetery.

Moriah Welsh Wesleyan Methodist Chapel on Gwalia Road was built in 1835 but has since been demolished. Caersalem Welsh Calvinistic Methodist Chapel on Bryn-y-Gaer Road was built in 1839 and rebuilt in 1878 but has been demolished. Black Lane Presbyterian Chapel on Long Lane opposite Black Lane Primary School was built in 1887 and a schoolroom added shortly after. Mining subsidence caused the closure of the chapel in 1994. Pisgah Welsh Wesleyan Methodist Chapel on Pisgah Hill was built in 1858 and enlarged in 1889. It closed in 1968 and council flats built on the site. The village consists of late 19th century industrial housing and 20th century developments. There is some light industry, local shops, a Chinese takeaway and the Cross Foxes inn. The White Hart closed in 2012 and plans were put forward in 2015 to convert it into a funeral parlour.

Pentrecelyn Holly Village
Lying three and a half miles south-east of Ruthin, Pentrecelyn is a small hamlet which has seen little development apart from a few bungalows and a house over the last 100 years.

Pentre-Celyn Welsh Calvinistic Methodist Chapel was built in 1820 and rebuilt in 1874, by the Liverpool architect Richard Owen. The chapel house was added in 1902. It is no longer in use.

Pentre-celyn Hall was built by the lead mine owning Lewis family in 1852, replacing a previous house on the site. The house became a hall of residence for Llysfasi College and then a restaurant before returning to its role as a private residence.

Pentrefoelas Village of the Green Bare Topped Hill
Situated on the A5 midway between Cerrigydrudion and Betws-y-coed, Pentrefoelas is an attractive village with its grey stone buildings. The older part of the village lies to the north of the main road and the river, the Afon Merddwr.

Above the village on top of Foel Las are the remains of a small motte said variously to have been constructed by Owain Gwynedd and Owain Glyndŵr. Beneath the hill was the site of the 1545 Wynne family mansion, Foelas, now called Old Foelas after it was demolished in 1819 and Voelas Hall built a mile and a half west of the village. In the grounds of Old Foelas is a replica of the Levelinus Stone commemorating the gift of land around 1230 by Llywelyn ap Iorwerth to Aberconwy Abbey. The original is in the National Museum of Wales.

The parish church was built in 1857-9 by Sir George Gilbert-Scott at the expense of Charles Griffith Wynne of Voelas Hall. It replaced the 1776 chapelry of Yspyty Ifan built by Watkin Wynne with its 1774 chapel housing monuments to the Wynne-Finch family. It is a single cell building with a south transept housing the organ and vestry. There is some fine stained glass by Clayton and Bell with the east triple lancets by F.W. Oliphant commemorating the death of Major Heneage Wynne of the Durham Light Infantry at the Battle of Inkerman in 1854 and a north window of 1932 by Sir Ninian Comper. This Grade II Listed church was for sale in 2016.

The present Voelas was built by Sir William Clough-Ellis for Colonel T.C. Wynne-Finch between 1957 and 61. It replaced the 1856-58 Voelas Hall of Charles Wynne-Finch which had in turn replaced the Regency Villa, known as Lima, of 1813-19 of the Hon Charles Finch (later known as Charles Wynne).

The Wynne family traced their ancestry back to Marchweithian, Lord of Is Aled in Rhufoniog. Cadwaladr Wynne was High Sheriff in 1548 and over the years the family was connected through marriage with the Myddeltons, Thelwalls and Salusburys. The male line died with Watkin Wynne (1717-1774) whose daughter Jane married the Hon Charles Finch. The house remains in the family. There is a memorial to Lt Col Charles Arthur Wynne-Finch (1841-1903) at the cross roads in the village, erected by tenants and neighbours.

Plas Iolyn lies a mile to the south-east of the village and was home to Sir Rhys Fawr ap Maredudd who led the men of central Wales at the Battle of Bosworth Field in 1485 and picked up the banner of Henry Tudor when the original bearer, Sir William Brandon was slain. One son, Maurice Gethin (father of Cadwaladr Wynne) lived at Foelas but a second son, Sir Robert ap Rhys, lived at Plas Iolyn and became chaplain to Cardinal Wolsey. He rebuilt Plas Iolyn as "a house fit for a duke, so high that its roof could be seen from Dublin". His son Dr Elis Prys D.C.L., known as Y Doctor Coch because of his red degree gown, was a friend of Robert Dudley, Earl of Leicester who was granted the Lordship of Denbigh in 1564. Prys became steward to Dudley and became the most hated man among the gentry of North Wales though he enjoyed a good reputation among the bardic community. He was M.P. for Merionethshire in 1558 and 1563. In 1566 he was put forward by Dudley to be appointed Bishop of Bangor but Archbishop Parker refused on the grounds that Prys was neither a priest nor possessed of "any priestly disposition". Elis Prys died in 1594 and was succeeded by his son Thomas Prys, a colourful character having been a soldier in the Low Countries and at Tilbury when Elizabeth I addressed the troops before the anticipated Armada invasion. Later he became a buccaneer and a poet, spending much time and money in London. He died in 1634. Plas Iolyn, which was described as having "walls were as good as the White Tower of London, his cellars holding a shipload of wine, the windows equal to those of Naples, the court like a street in Venice, and a hall like the palace at St David's" was left to his son Robert Price. Plas Iolyn was tenanted by Richard Myddelton in the 18th century when part of the house was destroyed by fire. The house remained in the Price family into the 20th century but is now a farmhouse and together with farm buildings is Grade II Listed.

The third major house in the area to the south-east of Plas Iolyn was Gilar (also spelt Giler), built for Robert Wynn in the latter part of the 16th century on the site of an earlier building and rebuilt in the 17th century. Robert Wynn was High Sheriff in 1658 when he called a rally at Gilar in support of Charles II.

The village of Pentrefoelas was an estate village, with a corn mill at the eastern entrance. The mill was rebuilt in 1815 and restored to working order in 1988. It has an overshot wheel and three pairs of millstones. To the rear is a virtually intact corn drying kiln. The mill pond was fed by a mill race running from the stream to the east. The Foelas Arms Hotel was first licensed in 1762 but was almost certainly trading long before that, being on the main route to Ireland. It was refronted and extended in 1839-40 by the Voelas Estate. The old school was built in 1852 at the top of the village. The new village Primary School lies to the south of the A5. There is a village store on the main road while to the south is the Riverside Chocolate House.

The area around the village has long been associated with the Tylwyth Teg or fairies. It is said that the lands of fairies and humans meet here. There is a Fairy Trail beginning in the car park to the south of the A5. The stories are similar to those told in other parts of Wales, for example the farmer's son who, enchanted by the fairies' music joins with them in a dance and returns home to find that he has been away for seven years. The story of the young man who lived at Hafod-y-Garreg in the village, who fell in love with a fairy and was granted her hand in marriage with her father's condition that if he ever struck her with iron she would immediately return to the fairy world has a striking resemblance to the legend of the Lady of the Lake who married the farmer from Myddfai whose sons became the first Physicians of Myddfai. In the story at Pentrefoelas the couple lived happily with their two children until one day the husband, in desperation, hurled a bridle at an escaping horse. It missed the horse and the metal struck his wife. Immediately her father appeared and took her away never to be seen again.

Penycae Head of the Field

Penycae lies a mile and a half north-west of Ruabon. The parish of Penycae was formed in 1879 and covered a wide area to the west and north, including Ruabon Mountain, Newtown Mountain, Eglwyseg Mountain and the southern part of Esclusham Mountain.The area was previously known as Cristionydd Fechan.

The church of St Thomas was built in 1877-8, designed by Sir Aston Webb, among whose works are the Victoria and Albert Museum, the façade of Buckingham Palace and the Victoria Memorial in front of the palace. The foundation stone laid by Lady Williams-Wynn. The nave and north aisle are separated by a four bay arcade with nave and aisle having a continuous roof

St Thomas Church designed by Sir Aston Webb

resulting in a series of small low windows to the north. The south wall has three sets of paired lancets and roundels with a single lancet at the western end. The west wall has two tall lancets, with cinquefoil above. There is a two tier pyramidal spire containing the bellcote above the east end of the nave. The chancel has the organ chamber to the north. Entrance is via the north porch. The pulpit is inscribed as a War Memorial, but the village's main War Memorial lies opposite Hill Street, a white marble statue of a soldier leaning on his rifle set on a square column above a stepped base.

A National School which predated the church stood to the west of the church and is now a private house. The next house to the west is the former vicarage, built on land donated by Lord Kenyon and Sir Watkin Williams-Wynn. It is in the style of the architect John Douglas.

Salem Welsh Baptist Chapel on Chapel Street was established in 1805. The present building dates from 1895 when it was rebuilt by architect Owen Morris of Porthmadog. Groes Welsh Calvinistic Methodist Chapel on Hill Street was built in 1863 but is no longer in use. Zion (Groes) English Baptist Chapel on Hall Street was built in 1899. Soar Welsh Wesleyan Methodist Chapel on Stryt-issa was built in 1838 and rebuilt in 1878 with a schoolroom to the rear added in 1899. Across the road is the modern Penycae Church of the Nazarene. The little Copperas English Primitive Methodist Chapel on Afonietha Road was built in 1890 in the vervacular style and has recently been converted to living accommodation. Carmel Welsh Wesleyan Methodist Chapel on Plas Bennion Road was built in the early 20th century but is now a private home.

At the junction of the B5097 Ruabon road and Plas Bennion Road, stands Grade II* Listed Wynn Hall. Built in 1647 for Captain William Wynn it passed to the Kenrick family, later known as Wynn Kenrick, in 1722 and remained in that family until 1970. It is a good example of a 17th century timber framed house extended in the early 19th century.

This pleasant village has seen expansion and retains its pub, the Black Horse, its village store and its primary school.

West of the village are two reservoirs of the Dee Valley Water Company while on the hills are prehistoric round barrows and cairns, numerous shafts and ruined buildings connected with the mining of coal, lead and silver as well as hunting lodges and shooting stands for grouse shoots.

Pen-y-lan Head of the Bank

The small hamlet of Pen-y-lan lies two miles south-east of Ruabon.

Pen-y-lan Hall was built in 1690 by Ellis Lloyd of Leighton Knole, Shropshire on the site of a previous farmhouse. In 1792 it was purchased by Roger Kenyon of Cefn Park Wrexham (brother of 1st Lord Kenyon) whose son changed his name to Edward Lloyd Williams. In 1854 it was purchased by James Hardcastle of Bolton, a partner in the law firm of Ormrod Hardcastle & Co. Hardcastle was succeeded by his brother-in-law James Ormrod and the house remains in the family, with the current owner being Emma Holloway nee Ormrod. The house was remodelled in Tudor-Gothic revival style in 1830. In 2011 it was the subject of the Channel 4 programme *Country House Rescue* and the Hall is now available for wedding receptions. It is also said to be haunted and there are paranormal events held at the Hall. Some have identified Ellis Lloyd with the father of Sampson Lloyd, the founder of Lloyds Bank but that branch of the Lloyds came from Dolobran Hall in Montgomeryshire and had no connection with Pen-y-lan Hall.

All Saints Church was built for James Ormrod in memory of his wife Cordelia in 1887-9 by the Bolton architect R. Knill Freeman. Constructed of red sandstone blocks the church has a bellcote with three bells over the chancel arch. The chancel is polygonal with stained glass by the Lancaster firm of Shrigley and Hunt. Both nave and chancel have barrel vaulted roofs, with that of the chancel being brightly decorated. There is an oak chancel screen. The crenellated churchyard wall is also of red sandstone with the upper part of the lychgate open timber framed under a tiled roof. Like Pen-y-lan Hall it is Grade II Listed.

The rest of Pen-y-lan is a mixture of farms and cottages interspersed by a few modern houses and bungalows.

Pen-y-Stryt Head of the Street
Pen-y-Stryt is a hamlet to the south of Llandegla, six miles south-east of Ruthin. Pisga Welsh Independent Chapel was built in 1817 and rebuilt in 1841. The Crown Hotel, formerly the Crown Inn, on the main crossroads is a 17th century coaching inn.

Pontfadog Madog's Bridge
The beautifully situated village of Pontfadog lies two miles east of Glyn Ceiriog in the Ceiriog valley. Much of the housing in the village is 20th century with older buildings clustered around the Swan Inn. The Glyn Valley Tramway ran alongside the road from the quarries at Glyn Ceiriog to Chirk.

The parish of Pontfadog was established in 1848, covering a large rural area. The church of St John the Baptist was consecrated in October 1847 and according to the *Chester Chronicle,* was built by Mr Vaughan, of Oswestry, after a design by Mr W. Ward. Coflein however suggests that the architect was F. Wehnert, on whose bankruptcy it was completed by R. Kyrke Penson. The church stands at the western end of the village on the bank of the Ceiriog. The three storey western tower is topped by a pyramidal spire. There is a small gallery beneath the tower. Pulpit, lectern and litany desk are of carved oak. The organ stands at the north-eastern end of the nave and there is a small chancel. The plum coloured wall of the chancel arch beneath the impressive roof contrasts with the white walls of the nave creating a dramatic visual effect.

A National School was established near the church. It was replaced by the council primary school and the old school building is now a private house, the first on the north side of the road after the Pontfadog sign entering from the west.

Pontfadog Bridge is a single arch bridge at the centre of the village and is believed to date from the early 19th century although Edward Lhuyd recorded a bridge here in the late 17th century. Near the bridge is the War Memorial in the form of a celtic cross with an inverted sword to the village side. Also nearby is the 1894 milestone erected by Denbighshire County Council.

The Pontfadog Oak which stood near the village was the oldest and largest oak tree in Britain before it blew down in a gale in 2013. The sessile oak had stood since 802 and had a girth of 42 feet 5 inches. Members of the North Wales and Borders branch of the British Woodcarvers Association used some of the wood to make 23 love spoons and 27 crosses which were donated to St John's Church.

Tabernacle was a Scottish Baptist Chapel built in 1892. It is now used as offices. Next door to the chapel is the waiting room of the Pontfadog station on the Glyn Valley Tramway, built in 1893 and now a small museum. The tiny Seion Welsh Wesleyan Methodist Chapel was built in 1812 and rebuilt in 1881.

The Swan Inn is an old drovers' inn and still offers accommodation. There is a village store which also serves as a post office.

Across the river and due south of the church is Glyn Mill (Felin Lyn), a flour mill which operated until 1936. The present buildings date from the end of the 18th century though a mill has stood on this site since medieval times. The small hamlet of Graig on the southern side of the river once had the Butchers' Arms and offers views across to Pontfadog.

Pwll-glas Blue Pool

Pwll-glas lies some two and a half miles south-east of Ruthin on the A494. This hamlet has seen considerable expansion with a relatively large development of bungalows and houses to the north of the main road and a smaller development to the south on the site of an old saw mill. Pwll-glas now has a village hall and community shop.

The Welsh Calvinistic Methodist Capel y Rhiw at the north-eastern end of the settlement was built in 1828 and rebuilt in 1865 and 1903. The chapel house dates from 1901. Salem Welsh Independent Chapel at the south-western end of Pwll-glas was built in 1806 and rebuilt in 1895. The Fox and Hounds lies at the south-western end of the hamlet. To the north-east of the village is the Ruthin-Pwllglas Golf Club with its 18 hole course.

Rhewl (Llantysilio)

Rhewl is a small scattered hamlet on the northern bank of the River Dee, two and a half miles north-west of Llangollen. The name is thought to be a corruption of 'Yr Heol' meaning 'The Street'. It once boasted a number of pubs serving the drovers. The Sun Inn remains but the Butcher's Arms, Bryn Ffynnon and Conquering Hero have disappeared. Hebron Welsh Wesleyan Methodist Chapel was built in 1826 and rebuilt in 1845 on a site some 600 yards south west of its second rebuilding in 1903. The red telephone box stands outside the old post office. The hamlet which lies in Llantysilio parish has attractive views over the River Dee.

Rhewl (Ruthin)

A mile and a half north-west of Ruthin on the A525 Rhewl was a small scattered hamlet with just a few houses in the 19th century. It saw considerable expansion in the second half of the 20th century and now has a primary school and playing fields.

Rhewl Welsh Calvinistic Methodist Chapel was built in 1844 and rebuilt in 1926. It incorporates the manse and schoolroom. The minister here until his death in 1906 was the celebrated bard and Methodist preacher Emrys ap Iwan. The Drovers' Arms dates from the 17th century and is noted for its food and real ales. Rhewl had a station on the Denbigh, Ruthin and Corwen Railway which opened in 1864 and closed in 1962. The old station is now a furniture showroom with the Sugar Plum tearoom attached.

The River Clywedog flows to the west of the village and is crossed by the 17th century Pont Rhyd-y-Cilgwyn, a double arched bridge with a central cutwater on both sides. The bridge leads to Lady Bagot's Drive, a private road built by Lord Bagot of Pool Park for his wife who was enamoured of the scenic route through the gorge of the Clywedog towards Pool Park (see Efenechtyd). The Drive is now part of a circular scenic walk. Rhyd-y-Cilgwyn is at the centre of a large farm complex. The house dates from the early 18th century and was remodelled in Tudorbethan style around 1830. It formed part of the Pool Park estate owned by Lord Bagot. Maps show that there was a flour mill and mill pond as part of the farming complex in 1900.

In 1118 the southern area of Rhewl was the site of the Battle of Maes Maen Cymro. Hywel ap Ithel, lord of Rhos and Rhufoniog, was joined by Maredydd ap Bleddyn and 400 men from Powys in an attack on the sons of Owain ap Edwin, the lords of the Dyffryn Clwyd cantref. After a bloody battle in which

Owain's son, Llywarch ab Owain was killed, Hywel was victorious but died some six weeks later from wounds he suffered in the fighting.

Rhosllanerchrugog Moor of the Heathery Glade
Three and a half miles south-east of Wrexham Rhosllanerchrugog is a large village founded on the mineral wealth of the area. There is some confusion as to the spelling with the village signs showing a double 'N' though maps use the single 'N' and the name derives from the Llanerchrugog Hall estate which dates back to 1551 when the owner was John ap Hugh ap John ap Ieuan ap Deicws, whose son adopted the surname Hughes. The village name is locally shortened to Rhos. Rhos has its own Welsh accent and dialect with those born in the village referred to as 'Jackos'. The parish of Rhosllanerchrugog was created by an Order in Council in December 1844. Previously the area was known as Morton Above or Morton Wallichorum. There were no collieries within the village by 1870 though there were numerous disused shafts in the area and brickworks on the outskirts. Rhos became a population and commercial centre for miners working at the large Ruabon, Bersham and Hafod collieries.

The chirch of St John the Evangelist is situated in a wooded churchyard to the south of the village with the entrance through the stone lych gate on Church Street or Stryt y Gof. Built in 1852-3 to designs by Thomas Penson the younger, the church is cruciform in shape with a bell tower topped by a pyramidal spire positioned east of the south transept. The Norman style of the exterior was matched by the interior. Grade II Listed the church was closed and put up for auction in 2013.

Built as a Welsh language church in 1892-3 by the Chester architects Douglas and Fordham, St David's church on Broad Street now conducts services in Welsh and English. A Ruabon red brick building, the chancel designed by J.H. Swainson was added in 1935-6. A planned steeple was never built. There is a south porch and western bellcote.

The Grade II Listed Bethlehem Welsh Independent Chapel on Hall Street was founded in 1812 but the impressive building which now stands was built with a Rundbogenstil (round headed) façade. The architect was Owen Morris of Porthmadoc. The wide central gable is flanked by a square clock tower to the south and a stair tower to the north, each topped by a spire. Another Grade II Listed chapel is Jerusalem Welsh Calvinistic Methodist Chapel on Brook Street, also known as Capel Mawr. First built in built in 1770, it was rebuilt in 1785, with alterations to enlarge the chapel in 1837 and further alterations in 1864. The schoolroom and vestry were added in 1894. Bethel Scottish Baptist Chapel on Campbell Street was built in 1847 but is no longer in use. Penuel Welsh Baptist Chapel on High Street is another Grade II Listed chapel in Rhos. The chapel was built in 1859 and was refronted and re-fitted in 1891, by Owain Morris Roberts, a local builder. The façade in red brick is particularly impressive. Horeb Welsh Wesleyan Methodist Chapel was built on Johnson Street in 1875. A chapel house added in 1904. Both have been demolished with new housing on the site. Salem Welsh Independent Chapel on Bank Street was built in 1896 in the Arts and Crafts style. Seion Welsh Baptist Chapel on Chapel Street was built in 1884 and rebuilt in 1901 when the architect was J.G. Owen of Liverpool. Seion is no longer in use. Opposite Seion on Johnson Street are two chapels, Capel Bethel now a schoolroom was built in 1859 as a Welsh Calvinistic Methodist chapel. The second, larger Capel Bethel was built in 1903 on the adjacent plot. Tabernacl Scottish Baptist Chapel on Chapel Street was built in 1883 replacing an earlier stone building. Soar Welsh Baptist Chapel on Aberderfyn Road was built in 1874 but has since been converted to residential use. Mynydd Seion Welsh Independent Chapel on Chapel Street was built in 1866 and rebuilt in 1891 in the Arts and Crafts style. It remains in use. Zion Primitive Methodist Chapel on Duke Street was built in the early twentieth century but has been demolished. Mount Pleasant English Baptist Chapel on Chapel Street was built in 1891 designed by the architect J.G. Owen of Liverpool. Ebenezer Independent Chapel on Queen Street was built in 1907. Hill Street English Presbytrian Chapel was built in 1872 in the Romanesque style. A manse was built in 1878 and a schoolroom in 1887.

The Grade II* Listed Miners' Institute known as the 'Stiwt' was built 1924-26, designed by John Owen of Wrexham and F.A. Roberts of Mold. An impressive building on Broad Street it contained a main auditorium, library, reading room, games room, billiard room and assembly hall. During the 1930s the auditorium became a cinema but the decline in the mining industry in the 1960s and 1970s saw the Stiwt close in 1977. It reopened as the Stiwt Theatre in 1999 with a 490 seat proscenium arch theatre and three function rooms.

Rhos has seen an increase in the population in the 20th century but has lost its railway line and the electric tram service to Wrexham. Gone too are a number of pubs and the Market Hall on Hall Street. There is a range of village shops and takeaway restaurants on Market Street and a number of pubs. There are both primary and secondary schools in the village and a small industrial estate.

Llanerchrugog Hall lies off Hall Lane to the north-west of the village. The present building dates from the mid 18th century and is Grade II Listed as an example of a mid 18th century gentleman's farmhouse. The three storey building has been used as a care home since the 1960s.

Rhos on Sea (see Llandrillo yn Rhos)

Rhostyllen

Morgan gives the following account for the name: *"The modern village has grown up between two farmhouses: the first of them was called 'y Rhos', and the other 'Bryn y pentre'. Perhaps the correct form is 'Rhos Astyllen', the Ribwort moor."* Rhostyllen lies a mile and a half to the south-west of Wrexham. Prior to 1879 the hamlet of Rhostyllen was very small, restricted to the area bounded by Hill Street, Mount Street, Poplar Road and High Street. The 1828 Tabernacle Chapel, the New Swan and the Black Horse public houses are shown on the 1872 map. Bersham Colliery was some 800 yards to the south-east. In 1879 the parish of Esclusham was created and Holy Trinity Church Rhostyllen was its centre. By 1900 there were houses along Wrexham Road which also carried a tramway but it was in the 20th century that Rhostyllen saw a major expansion in population.

The Bersham Coal Company sank the first shaft at Glan yr Afon Colliery in 1864 but it was not until 1874 that the first coal was produced under new owners at the renamed Bersham Colliery. At its peak Bersham employed 878 men. An explosion in 1880 caused the deaths of nine men including the manager. Bersham continued in production until 1986. The site is now the Bersham Enterprise Centre but the colliery buildings including the pithead baths opened in 1954, the lamp room and the winding gear remain.

Holy Trinity Church was built in 1876-7 to designs by J.E. Lash of Wrexham with the foundation stone laid by Simon and Victoria Yorke of Erddig. Cecil Hare designed the fittings which were added in 1916. The church is cruciform in shape with a blank bellcote over the eastern end of the nave. The flat roofed west porch supports a small bell frame. There are extensions on either side of the chancel. The four bay nave has a king post roof while the chancel has four narrow bays under an arch braced collar roof. The south transept forms a war memorial chapel with the window by Geoffrey Webb depicting St Michael. The north transept window by Herbert Bryans is particularly fine. The chancel screen is ornate with delicate tracery work.

Tabernacle Calvinistic Methodist Chapel on Mount Street was built in 1828. A new chapel, also known as Tabernacle, of the Presbyterian Church of Wales was built on Hill Street in 1897 but retains an internal date stone showing 1828. The old chapel is now used for industrial purposes with a garage door now providing the entrance. Salem Independent Chapel on Chapel Street appears to have had a short life in the last quarter of the 19th century. It was replaced by a new chapel built in 1897 at the junction of School Street and Henblas Road on a site now occupied by Trinity Close. Ainon Baptist Chapel on School Street was built at the end of the 19th century but has been demolished with a bungalow now occupying the site. Rhostyllen Primitive Methodist Chapel on Chapel Street was also built at the end of the 19th century but was not shown on the 1912 map and the site is now occupied by a bungalow.

The Parish Hall and Institute on Vicarage Hill was built in 1924 with recreation ground to the rear.

As well as the colliery there was a foundry started in the early years of the 20th century and located between Mount Street and the railway. Rhostyllen had a station on the Rhos Branch of the G.W.R. which opened to passengers in 1902 but closed to passengers in 1931. Freight trains continued until 1963.

The village, which today is largely a commuter area for Wrexham, has a primary school and local stores. The New Swan Inn and the Black Horse (now known as The Old Black Horse) are still open but the Black Lion on Wrexham Road is now the China Star. At the western end of Wrexham Road is a Travelodge together with Starbucks and Subway, together with a number of large motor dealers and builders merchants.

Rhos-y-madoc Madoc's Moor

Rhos-y-madoc is a small hamlet at the south-eastern end of Wynnstay Park, a mile and a half south-east of Ruabon. To the west of the hamlet is Belan Place, the three storey 18th century house built as the dower house of the Wynnstay estate. It was for a time used by the Williams-Wynn family after the sale of Wynnstay Hall. There are terrier kennels, stables and a coach house in the grounds.

Rhosymedre Meadow at the end of the Town (Source Morgan)

The name Rhosymedre is associated with the Welsh hymn tune used by Vaughan Williams in his *Three Preludes on Welsh Hymn Tunes*. The hymn was composed by John David Edwards, the vicar from 1843 to 1885. In 1847 Edwards commented on the "the prevalence of drunkenness, foul language, fighting and bestialities of a worse description". The village lies between Ruabon and Cefn Mawr and the parish of Rhosymedre established in 1844 included the industrialised Cefn Mawr with its brickworks, iron and coal mines and later chemical works.

The church of St John the Evangelist was built in 1836-7 and largely financed by Sir Watkin Williams-Wynn. The architect was Edward Welch. There was a restoration in 1888 by J.C. Spaull of Oswestry partly funded by J.C. Edwards the owner of the Penybont tile works in Cefn Mawr. These works were pioneers in the production of terracotta. The tiled reredos is particularly fine. The church is cruciform in shape with nave, chancel, north and south transepts, west porch and a tall bellcote topped by a saddleback roof. The short sanctuary is narrower than the chancel. The appearance of the church is austere but relieved by the later tilework. The reredos was made by local parishioners at the Trefynant Tileworks, in July 1906, and there is an inscription to the memory of J.C. Edwards.

Rhosymedre English Primitive Methodist Chapel was built in 1832. Bethel Welsh Independent Chapel was built in 1836 and rebuilt in 1858 and 1883. It closed in the 1980s and is currently used as an upholstery workshop.

Much of the housing in the village is post 1870 and post dates the railway which dissects the village. There are two pubs, the Plough Inn and the Jolly Masons. The new stadium of Welsh Premiership football club, Cefn Druids is now located west of Rock Road.

Rhydlydan Broad Ford

The hamlet of Rhydlydan lies just off the A5 between Cerrigydrudion and Betws-y-coed. There is an inn, the Giler Arms named after Giler, the Wynn mansion at Pentrefoelas, a fishing lake and a caravan park. On the A5 is the Rhydlydan Welsh Calvinistic Methodist Chapel which was built in 1824 and rebuilt in 1872. It is no longer in use.

Rhydycroesau The Ford that Crosses

Rhydycroesau straddles what is now the Powys Shropshire border three miles west of Oswestry. The main part of the village lies on the English side of the Nant Penygwely with just a row of cottages, a bungalow, outbuildings and the church on the Welsh side.

Christ Church was built in 1838 on land gifted by Sir Watkin Williams-Wynn. The rectory, now a hotel, was built across the border. The church was refurbished in 1886 by the architect W.H. Spaull when the chancel was enlarged, a new vestry built and the windows replaced. The church is entered through the base of the short three storey battlemented tower. The west gallery now houses the organ. The three bay nave leads to the chancel with its large east window and sigle lights to the side. The tower has clock faces to the west and north. When the Church in Wales was disestablished in 1920 the parishioners voted to remain with the Church of England. The first rector of Christ Church was Revd Robert Williams, an eminent Celtic scholar who produced the first dictionary of the Cornish language. He also wrote *Enwogion Cymru: A Biographical Dictionary of Eminent Welshmen* which was subsequently translated into Welsh by the Cymmrodorion Society.

Half a mile to the north-west in the small community of Cefn Canol is Cefncanol Welsh Calvinistic Methodist Chapel which was built in 1820 and rebuilt in 1882.

Rhyd-y-foel Bare Ford
Rhyd-y-foel is a small leafy village a mile to the south-east of Llanddulas on the north coast. The main road passes above the attractive valley of the Dulas which once had the Cwymp Corn Mill near the ford which gives the village its name though a bridge now crosses the Dulas. The main part of the village lies to the east of the valley along the narrow main road. Much of the village is 19th century except for the late 20th century houses on Tan-y-foel. Salem Wesleyan Methodist Chapel was originally built to the east of the main road in 1825. It underwent a number of enlargements until it was rebuilt on the western side of the road in 1894 by Richard Davies of Bangor.

Rossett
Welsh: yr Orsedd or yr Orsedd Goch meaning The Red Throne
Rossett lies a little under five miles north-east of Wrexham, to the east of the A483 dual carriageway. Morgan in the *Placenames of Wales* suggests the name is a corruption of 'Rhosydd', meaning 'meadows'.

Historically Rossett was part of Gresford parish and is not mentioned in the early 19th century topographical dictionaries. A chapel existed in the 16th century to the north of the village. This was originally the private chapel of the lord of the commote of Marford and dedicated to St Peter. In 1620 it was leased to the Crown to form a chapel of ease to Gresford parish church. Baptisms and marriages were carried out until 1703 but the chapel was demolished at the end of the 18th century and its bell transferred to Trevalyn Hall. St Peter's Spring was situated some 450 yards north-west of the chapel and is the source of the Lavister Brook. Its waters were reputed to be effective in the treatment of sore eyes and sprained limbs. The first church was built in 1841 and Rossett Station on the Chester to Wrexham line of the Chester and Shrewsbury Railway opened on the 4th November 1846 (closed 1964). By 1872 the village stretched from Rossett Mill to the Golden Lion together with Gun Street and Station Road. The Rossett, now the Rossett Hall hotel was outside the built up area. The latter part of the 20th century has seen a major expansion in housing with the village now meeting Lavister on the Chester Road.

Christ Church was built in 1891-2 to the design of the Chester firm of Douglas and Fordham. In a late Victorian Gothic revival style the church is cruciform with the south transept containing the vestry and the north transept a chapel, opening on to the north aisle. The substantial crossing tower has a clock to the east face inserted in 1902. The furniture was designed by Douglas and Fordham while the stained glass is early 20th century. The font from the 1841 church now rests in the graveyard.

John Douglas was also the architect of Rossett English Presbyterian Chapel on Station Road which was built in 1877 and remains in use. The foundation stone was laid by Mr D.L. Moody of Chicago. It replaced the oldest place of worship in the village, the Gun Street Calvinistic Methodist Chapel at the south-western end of the street. Built in 1811 it has been converted into two houses.

The Roman Catholic church of Christ the King on Holt Road is a modern prefabricated building. A National School was built in the 1860s on Station Road. Its site next to the village hall is now a car park.

The River Alyn played an important part in the development of the village, supplying the power for the mills. The earliest known mill was the Old Marford Mill, now demolished. It stood to the east of the Gresford Road and was recorded in the Domesday Book. It was a King's Mill and also known as Crown Mill. It was destroyed by fire in 1791 with the large Marford Mill to the north replacing it in the early 19th century. It was powered by an undershot wheel which is still in situ at the southern end of the building. This large mill is now the headquarters for the British Association for Shooting and Conservation. The chocolate box Rossett Mill stands across the road. The first mill on the site was built in 1544 as a 'free' mill to compete with the royal Marford Mill.

Rossett Mill

The present timber framed building dates from 1588 with further extensions. It was sketched by J.W.M. Turner in 1795. It was operational until 1959 and the undershot wheel and machinery remain. Both the Marford and Rossett mills came under the ownership of Sir John Trevor of Trevalyn Hall in 1661. The 1872 maps combine the two mills as Rossett Mills.

Records show that on May 21st, 1777 John Thomas was executed for highway robbery and his body hanged in chains at Rossett Green near Marford Mill.

Rossett has two inns, The Alyn, formerly the Alyn Hotel, and the Golden Lion. The Golden Lion played an important part in the life of the village, serving as court house and cattle market with auctions held behind the inn. Gun Street is named after a third pub, The Gun, later called the Pig and Whistle. Until 1589, when the first bridge was built, Gun Street was the main route through the village, crossing the River Alyn by a ford.

The village now has two schools, a village hall and some local shops.

Rossett Hall Hotel was built in 1750 by John Boydell as Rossett Hall though known as The Rossett. Boydell was born in Shropshire but the family moved to Hawarden in Flintshire when he was 11. He trained as an engraver in London and set up his own business on the Strand in 1746. He married his long time sweetheart Elizabeth Lloyd in 1748. In 1751 he became a member of the Stationers Company and in 1760 became a member of the Royal Society. He was Lord Mayor of London in 1790. He died childless in 1804 and is attributed as having established the printing of engravings as a viable industry in Britain. In 1789 The Times paid the following tribute: *"Historical painting and engraving are almost exclusively indebted to Mr. Boydell for their present advancement".* Rossett Hall remained in the family until the 1970s when it was converted to a hotel. The red brick and stone three storey building retains some early features, including a fireplace and the early 19th century staircase. It is rumoured that Lord Nelson courted Lady Hamilton at the Hall while in more recent times it was the venue for the wedding of footballer Paul Scholes, with the Beckhams among the guests.

The old name for the area was Allington or in Welsh, Trefalun, the township on the Alun. Trevalyn Hall to the south of the village was built in 1576 for John Trevor, great-grandson of Sir Richard Trevor who had acquired the estate in 1476 through marriage with Matilda the heiress of Jenkyn ap David ap Griffith of Allington. Sir Richard was the 4th son of John Trevor of Brynkynallt, Chirk. John Trevor had made a fortune in London through the patronage of his wife's cousin Thomas Sackville, Lord Buckhurst (later 1st Earl of Dorset). He died in 1589 and is buried at Gresford church. He was succeeded by his son Sir Richard Trevor, who served as a soldier in Ireland, commanding the Denbighshire levies. He was knighted for his services and enjoyed the patronage of Lord Admiral Howard of Effingham who made him vice admiral of North Wales in 1596. It was through Howard's influence that he became M.P. for Bletchingley in 1597. Failing to win the election for Denbighshire in 1601 when the election was postponed because of armed affrays between the opposing parties in Wrexham, Sir Richard returned to Ireland to command the Newry garrison, returning in 1606 to act as deputy lieutenant of Denbighshire and subsequently High Sheriff in 1610 and High Sheriff of Flintshire in 1613. He died in 1638 and is buried at Gresford. Having no male heir the estate passed to his nephew Sir John Trevor II. Sir John was a parliamentarian, representing Denbighshire in 1621 and later Flintshire and other constituencies under the control of Howard and the Earl of Pembroke. He continued in Parliament during Cromwell's rule. He was pardoned by

Charles II and died in London in 1673. He never lived at Trevalyn which was occupied by agents of the estate until 1835. Sir John II's son Sir John Trevor III was also a Parliamentarian, entering Parliament for Flintshire in 1646 but retired from public life after the King's execution in 1648, returning during the Protectorate and later in the Cavalier Parliament. He was knighted by Charles II and became a junior secretary of state before his death in 1672. His son, also John Trevor inherited Glynde Place in Sussex which became the family home. On the death of his grandson John in 1743 the male line came to an end and Trevalyn passed to the Griffith-Boscawen family who took up residence in 1835. Another branch, the Trevor-Ropers took the Plas Teg estate in Flintshire that had been built by Sir John Trevor I, brother of Sir Richard in 1610. Among other members of the family, Thomas Trevor (1658-1750), 2nd son of Sir John Trevor III was a judge and 1st Baron Trevor of Bromham. He acted as solicitor-general in 1692, attorney-general in 1695, chief justice of Common Pleas in 1701 and became a privy councillor in 1702. He was made lord privy seal in 1726 and lord president of the council in 1730. His second son Richard Trevor (1701-1771) was appointed Bishop of St David's in 1744 and Bishop of Durham in 1752. He inherited Glynde Place in 1743 and bequeathed it to his brother Robert Hampden-Trevor, 1st Viscount Hampden. Glynde Place is today owned by the 8th Viscount Hampden. The Griffiths-Boscawen family remodelled the interior of Trevalyn and created the topiary garden. The house was sold in the 1980s and converted into two apartments. Regarded as one of the most important Elizabethan houses in North Wales Trevalyn Hall is Grade II* Listed.

Trevalyn Hospital lies to the south of Trevalyn Hall. It was known as Trevalyn House or simply Trevalyn. This estate came into the ownership of John Langford of Ruthin at the end of the 15th century through his marriage to Catherine, the daughter and heir of William ap David ap Gruffydd ap David of Trefalyn and Burton. John Langford's father and grandfather were constables of Ruthin Castle. Trevalyn remained in the Langford family until 1747 when it was sold to William Travers. Travers' father John had trained for the law but married the daughter of Edward Mainwaring, a prosperous Wrexham draper and inherited the business before his wife's death. His second marriage was to Anne the daughter of Simon Thelwall Esq. of Llanbedr and William, born in 1721, was their eldest son. By 1739 John Travers was the agent of the Trevor estate and lived at Trevalyn Hall. He was succeeded in that role by William who rebuilt Trevalyn. William died in 1765 and was succeeded by his brother

Edward, a lawyer, who died in 1777. Both are buried at Gresford. Trevalyn in the next 20 years passed through various connected family members before being sold in 1810 to John Stanislaus Townshend a descendent of Sir Robert Agborough alias Townshend. Sir Robert's father died when he was three months old and his mother married Aurelian Townshend. Sir Robert was the first man to be knighted by Charles II in 1660 at the restitution of the monarchy. He married first Anne Spencer a daughter of Lord Spencer, an ancestor of Princess Diana, and secondly Mary Askew by whom he inherited Hem House a little under two miles south-east of Rossett. Sir Robert formally changed his name to Townshend by a grant made in 1663 and adopted the title Knight of the Manor of Hem. John Stanislaus Townshend who is said to have been the godson of King Stanislaus II of Poland had interests in Chester including the Royal Theatre. Trevalyn was extended by the Townshends over the course of the 19th century. During World War II it was used by the army and in 1947 it was opened as a maternity hospital by Aneurin Bevan. It is now an old people's hospital and the formal gardens are retained.

Hem House to the east of Rossett Road was never home to the Townshends. It is an 18th century red brick farmhouse set in open countryside.

Ruabon Welsh: Rhiwabon St Mabon's Path

Ruabon is located four miles south-west of Wrexham to the west of the A483. The area has been occupied since the Bronze Age with finds in Cleveland Street dating to 1400BC. West of the village is Y Gardden a hilltop enclosure which has been dated to 400BC. Both Offa's Dyke and Wat's Dyke pass nearby. Until the mid 19th century, Ruabon was at the centre of a much larger parish containing coal mines, iron and chemical works and brickworks. The village of Ruabon itself was relatively small with three brick and tile works, Ruabon Brick and Terra Cotta Works, Tatham Brick and Tile Works and Terra Cotta Brick and Tile Works (later Monk and Newall) all situated to the north of the village and all now closed.

A mile to the north of the church was the Vauxhall Colliery, opened in the 1850s as the Kenyon Colliery. It employed up to 420 men and operated until 1928. The Wynnstay Colliery 1,100 yards south-west of the church on a site now occupied by Clwyd Caravans was sunk by the New British Iron Company in 1856. Originally known as the Green Colliery it changed ownership over the years and employed over 1,400 men at its peak before closing in 1927. Explosions in 1863, 1868 and 1873 resulted in the deaths of 29 men.

Much of the land around Ruabon formed part of the Wynnstay Estate. Madog ap Gruffydd Maehr, the founder of Valle Crucis Abbey, had a fortified house here, called Rhiwabon. The estate was originally known as Watstay after Wat's Dyke which runs through the parkland. The Wynn family had its roots in Anglesey where Hugh Williams was rector of Llantrisant and Llanrhyddlad in the 17th century. His son was Sir William Williams, a lawyer who as an M.P. became Speaker of the House of Commons and subsequently Solicitor General. He was knighted in 1687 and created a baronet. He purchased the Llanforda Estate near Oswestry from Edward Lloyd in 1665. Sir William's grandson was Sir Watkin Williams who in 1740 inherited not only his father's share of the Williams estates but also through his mother the Wynnstay Estate. Sir William Williams II had married Jane Thelwall, great-granddaughter of Sir John Wynn of Gwydr. The Watstay Estate had come into the hands of Sir John Wynn, the last baronet of that line, through his marriage to the daughter of Eyton Evans, owner of Watstay and changed the name of the estate to Wynnstay. Sir Watkin Williams adopted the additional surname Wynn and added to his fortune through his marriage to Ann, daughter and heiress of Edward Vaughan of Llwydiarth and Llangedwyn. The family continued to own the Wynnstay Estate until 1948. The 7th baronet Sir Herbert Williams-Wynn inherited Bodelwyddan Castle in 1880 and made this his main seat. Costs of upkeep and death duties took their toll in the 20th century and the 8th baronet, Sir Watkin sold Bodelwyddan in 1925 and Wynnstay in 1948 as well as the Llwydiarth Estate in Montgomeryshire while the Glan-llyn Estate in Merionethshire was given to the government in lieu of death duties. The 11th baronet, Sir Watkin Williams-Wynn now lives in St Asaph. Born in 1940 he is a direct descendant of Owain Gwynedd and head of the only surviving branch of the royal house of Gwynedd.

The Grade II* Listed Wynnstay Hall, which lies to the south-east of the village, was rebuilt in 1858 by Benjamin Ferrey in French Renaissance style after the old building was destroyed by fire. Following its sale in 1948 it was aquired by Lindisfarne College and used as a school until the college's bankruptcy. The hall was subsequently converted into apartments. Ferrey converted the orangery into a French Renaissance style chapel, replacing the earlier chapel which had been converted from a dairy. The extensive grounds are landscaped with a lake and cascade designed by Capability Brown (his last commission before his death) and a number of listed buildings including the 18th century rustic boat house, the 19th century ice house, the late 18th century bath house and the Wynnstay Column. The column was erected in 1789 by Dame Francis Williams-Wynn in memory of her son Sir Watkin who died in 1788. Designed by James Wyatt it stands 115 feet high and a spiral staircase leads to a railed platform. Many of the outbuildings on the estate have been converted to living accommodation. From Ruabon the park was entered through the gates and arch at the end of Park Street which is lined with estate houses. The drive from this arch has been blocked by modern roads.

At the head of Park Street is the Wynnstay Arms, an 18th century coaching inn enlarged in 1841.

The Grade I Listed church of St Mary stands opposite the Wynnstay Arms. It is suggested that the original dedication was to St Mabon, a Cornish saint, and the raised circular churchyard points to a Celtic origin. The first mention of the church was in 1253 when the dedication was to St Collen the monk who founded the church at Llangollen. The tower dates from the 14th century while the south-east chapel and the north-east chapel date from 1755 and 1769 repectively. The church was remodelled by the Shrewsbury architect T.F. Pritchard between 1769 and 70 before being largely rebuilt by Benjamin

Wynnstay Hall

Ferrey for Sir Watkin Williams-Wynn in 1879-72. The nave, clerestory, aisles and the majority of the windows date from this refurbishment. The nave has a five bay arcade while the short chancel has the two 18th century chapels alongside. The font consists of a small marble bowl mounted on a wooden tripod by Robert Adam, a gift of the Williams-Wynn family. There are a number of monuments and memorials to the Wynn and Williams-Wynn families and a 1526 chest tomb with two recumbent alabaster figures representing John Ap Ellis Eyton and his wife Elizabeth. In the south chapel the tomb of Sir Watkin Williams-Wynn has a reclining effigy by Rysbrack, while the wall medallion in memory of William Watkin Williams-Wynn is attributed to Robert Adam. The buttressed four storey tower is to the west while the porch is to the north.

South of the church is the Round House, the old village lock-up. The house next to the church in Church Street was the former grammar school, established by a bequest of Thomas Nevitt in 1632. The school was in use in 1837 but the house was later converted to a shop before being in turn converted to a private house. The small garage-like building to the east was the Hearse House. The five single storey almshouses set back from Church Street were built in 1711 by Vicar Richard Davis from a bequest by Vicar John Robinson. Originally designed around a courtyard with arms coming towards the road, three sides were demolished. The five houses were refurbished in 1979 by the trustees of Ruabon United Charities.

The English Congregational Chapel on Pont Adam was built in 1858, and designed by the Liverpool architect William Ithell Mason in the Gothic Revival style. The red brick English Primitive Methodist Chapel on High Street was built in 1892. Ruabon Presbyterian Chapel on Bryn Street was built in 1900 to the design of architect George Dickens Lewis of Shrewsbury. The chapel has been demolished and replaced by two pairs of semi-detached houses. Bethania Welsh Baptist Chapel on Cleveland Street was built in the late 19th century but has been demolished.

Ruabon saw considerable expansion in the 20th century with council and private estates built to the north. Modern roads have also had a major effect on the village though the heart of the village is largely unaltered with High Street offering a small range of shops and a bank. The Ruabon Grammar School survived until 1967 when it merged with the 1922 Girls' Grammar School to form Ysgol Rhiwabon Comprehensive School. A National School was built in 1848 on Overton Road and having been rebuilt on the same site in

1976 is now known as St Mary's Church in Wales School. Another primary school Ysgol Maes-y-llan opened in 1912.

Ruabon railway station is a Grade II Listed building. Built originally by T.M. Penson when the Shrewsbury and Chester line was opened to Ruabon in 1846, the station was rebuilt in the 1860s to a design by Henry Robertson in Tudor Gothic style. Although the station is still in use, part is now used for offices and the platform canopy has been removed.

In the 18th century Ruabon was home to John Roberts, nicknamed Mochyn y Nant (Pig of the Brook). Roberts was said to have studied the occult and made a living from consultations on missing cattle, money or jewels. He claimed to have the powers of a fortune teller and in the event of an unidentified thief was able to cast a spell on the thief, inflicting infirmity or disease according to the wishes of the victim. He died in 1806 at the age of 90.

St George (see Llansant Sior)

Southsea Welsh: Glan-yr-afon Riverside

Southsea is a compact former mining village two and a half miles north-west of Wrexham and lying across the Afon Gwenfro from New Broughton. The name derives from the South Sea Inn which once stood opposite the Broughton Hall Ironworks which closed in 1881.

Plas Power Colliery to the west of the village was sunk in 1875-7 by the Old Broughton Coal Company. By 1880 its owners were the Plas Power Coal Company. At its peak in 1918 it employed over 1,000 men. In 1885 riots by local miners forced immigrant Irish to leave the colliery. Plas Power closed in 1938. The site is now used for Plas Power Adventure offering a climbing wall, karting, archery, zip wire and orienteering. A number of the colliery buildings still stand, including the workshop and power house while the two winding houses are roofless.

All Saints Church was converted from the church hall in 1984. Two former churches stood across the road in the graveyard. The first was built in 1884 but replaced by a larger church in 1926. The second church is said to have been built around the old church which was then demolished. By the 1980s the second church had become unsafe and it was deconsecrated and demolished in 1984.

Seion Welsh Calvinistic Methodist Chapel on High Street was built in 1879. The 1873 map shows a Calvinistic Methodist Chapel on Church Road and it is thought that Seion replaced that chapel. Seion is now a private dwelling. Glanrafon English Presbyterian Chapel was built in 1877 and rebuilt in 1905, by the architect George Dickens Lewis of Shrewsbury. It has since been demolished and replaced by the stepped terrace of five houses on Church Road. Salem Methodist Chapel on High Street was built in 1877 with a schoolroom added in 1891. It has been demolished with houses built on the site.

The village has a pub, the Rollers Arms. It was closed in December 2015 and reopened in February 2016.

Sydallt

Sydallt is a 20th century community lying to the west of the A541 Wtexham Mold Road between Gwersyllt and Cefn-y-bedd.

The Llay Hall Colliery was sited to the east of the A541. The colliery operated between 1877 and 1947 employing up to 530 men. Two men and ten horses were killed in an explosion in 1881 while in 1947 five men were injured in an explosion. The site is now occupied by the Riverside Business Park and the Alyn Industrial Estate.

Oak Alyn Hall at the southern entrance to Sydallt is now a residential care home. It was the home of London born Edwin Stanley Clark, a civil mining engineer, whose family had funded the initial survey work for the colliery. In 1885 he purchased the colliery out of bankruptcy. He died in 1900 and was succeeded by his son Edward Stuart Clark.

The Wrexham Mold rail line divides the community with the post First World War council estate and community hall to the west and later private housing to the east.

Tafarn-y-Gelyn Holly Tavern

Situated half a mile south-west of Loggerheads, Tafarn-y-Gelyn is a hamlet that was once the starting point for the old coach road, Bwlch Penbarras across the Clwydian range, now replaced by the A494. To the west lies Moel Famau the highest point of the Clwydian hills, a country park and an area of outstanding beauty. Offa's Dyke crosses the summit where the Jubilee Tower was commenced in 1810 but never completed. It was designed by Thomas Harrison of Chester who also designed Glan-yr-afon, a villa to the east of Tafarn-y-Gelyn on the Afon Alun.

Bethania Wesleyan Methodist Chapel was built in 1866 and rebuilt in 1896 with Tŷ Capel attached. Across the road is a small wildlife pond.

Tal-y-cafn Head of the Trough

The hamlet of Tal-y-cafn is situated four miles south of Conway on the A470. The Roman road from Chester to Caernarvon crossed the river here and it was the site of a ferry across the River Conway from the 14th century until a bridge was built in 1897. The present bridge was built in 1977-8. The railway station was opened in 1863 on the Conway and Llanrwst Railway. The Tal-y-cafn Hotel on the main road was a coaching inn closed in 2011 and re-opened in 2016.

There were wharfs on both sides of the river and a cattle market was established to the south of the hotel which operated until the 2001 foot and mouth outbreak. A new house now occupies part of the site. Across the river was the Ferry Hotel the site of which is now occupied by a development of new houses, some with river frontage.

Penrhyd Hall is now a centre for equestrianism. The house is not listed but the lodge on the A470 was built in 1927 to a design by the Arts and Crafts architect Herbert Luck North of Llanfairfechan. It is Grade II Listed.

Tanyfron Beneath the Breast Shaped Hill

Tanyfron is a former mining/industrial village a mile south of Brymbo. It began as a place of housing for the miners at the Vron Colliery in the hamlet of Fron to the west and the Plas Power Colliery at Southsea to the south-east. Later the Brymbo Steelworks extended to the northern edge of the village.

St Alban's Church was built as a chapel of ease to All Saints Southsea in 1896-7. The architect was Howel Davies of Wrexham. Set in a square plot it is constructed of red brick with an apse under a slate roof with terracotta ridge tiles. The tall western bellcote is topped by a cross and there is a south porch. St Alban's closed in 2010.

Mynydd Seion Welsh Wesleyan Methodist Chapel was built in 1896 on Park Road but has been demolished. Cana Welsh Independent Chapel on St Alban's Road was built in 1841 and rebuilt in 1860. It is now used as a performing arts studio.

In recent years the village has seen a massive expansion with new housing estates built on the reclaimed site of the Brymbo Steelworks. The village retains its primary school though its playing field was sold off for housing. There is a convenience store, community centre and the Brymbo Sports and social club with its extensive playing fields..

Towyn Welsh: Tywyn

Towyn sits on the North Wales coast in what is now an urban conurbation with the adjoining Kinmel Bay and Pensarn. The name is thought to be a corruption of 'Tywodyn' meaning 'sand' though another suggestion is that it derives from 'Twyn' meaning 'hillock'.

The parish of Towyn was created in 1873 when the Grade II* Listed St Mary's church was built to the designs of George Edward Street at the expense of Robert Bamford Hesketh of Gwrych Castle. Street also designed the vicarage and church school which were built at the same time. The church has a north aisle with clerestory, separated from the nave by an arcade of four arches. Furnishings are by Street. The choir is beneath the tower with the raised sanctuary with its sedilia and piscina beyond. The floor tiles in the nave were replaced after the storm of 1990 when the sea entered the building. Street designed the east window which depicts Christ with Saints and Martyrs in Heaven. There are War Memorials and a memorial to Winifred Countess of Dundonald of Gwrych Castle. The external roof is decorated with blue and green slates. The three storey tower has a saddleback roof again highly decorated. There is a south porch and a north vestry which once connected with the vicarage.

The Vicarage to the north of the church is now Ty'n Llan Nursing Home. To the east of the church St Mary's School is now home to the Towyn and Kinmel Bay Youth Club. Along with the church and old vicarage it has the decorated green and blue slate roof. The schoolmaster's house formed the east wing. Originally there were tall octagonal chimneys but these have been removed. Slightly offset above the main entrance is a bellcote in the form of a slender fleche with weathervane above. Both nursing home and school are Grade II* Listed.

St John's Wesleyan Methodist Chapel on Wendover Avenue was built in 1932. Salem Welsh Calvinistic Methodist Chapel on Gors Road was built in 1818 and rebuilt in 1838. Also on Gors Road are the modern Maranatha Hall, Church of God, the North Coast Church affiliated to the Assemblies of God and the Roman Catholic Church of Christ the King.

Towyn remained a scattered collection of farms until World War II but expansion since has seen a large amount of building and the establishment of camping and caravan parks. Catering for the holidaymaker are numerous takeaway restaurants, pubs and clubs within the holiday parks. There is a small funfair near the beach which is bordered by the North Wales main railway line.

Trefnant Brook Town

The village of Trefnant, three miles north of Denbigh on the A525, is a relatively modern village, constituted in 1855 as a chapelry under Henllan. It has since grown with a population in 2011 of 1,581.

The Grade II* Listed church of the Holy Trinity was designed by Sir George Gilbert Scott and built 1853-55 as a memorial to Colonel John Lloyd Salusbury of Galltfaenan Hall, commissioned by his daughters Mrs Townsend Mainwaring and Mrs Charles Mainwaring. Little expense was spared with arcade columns and capitals of polished Mona marble and foliate carving completed by the Denbigh stonemason J. Blinstone who was taken to London for training by Gilbert Scott. The vestry was added in 1907 by Scott's son Sir Giles at the expense of Colonel Charles Salusbury Mainwaring of Galltfaenan Hall. There is a four bay arcade to the nave which has a fine tall scissor truss roof. The font is of Llaniestyn red-stone as is the pulpit. The tall tracery windows of the aisles extend above the eaves. The chancel has a richly gilded pointed waggon roof. The east window is a memorial to Colonel Salusbury and his wife. It depicts the Passion and was designed by William Wailes. Other stained glass is by James Powell of Whitefriars while other windows are memorials to the families of Llanerch Hall and Galltyfaenan Hall. The oak choir stalls commemorate W.C. Jones of Llanerch Hall while the sanctuary panelling was removed from Kinmel Park in 1936. The Great War commemorative marble tablet is by Sir Giles Gilbert Scott who was later to design Liverpool Cathedral, the red telephone box and Battersea Power Station. There is a south porch and a double bellcote above the eastern end of the nave. The lychgate was in place by 1856 and formed part of Sir George Gilbert Scott's original commission.

The National School and Rectory were built at the same time as the church and both designed by Sir George Gilbert Scott.

Capel Trefnant or Green Methodist Chapel on the A541 north-east of the crossroads in the village was built 1824 and rebuilt in 1840.

At the centre of the village the Trefnant Inn dates from the early 19th century. The building near the pedestrian crossing was the Stag's Head. There are a number of village shops and a village hall. There are small estates to the north-east of the village and the Clwydian Park development to the north-west. Until 1955 Trefnant had a station on the Vale of Clwyd Branch of the London and North Western Railway which connected Denbigh and Rhyl. The bus depot and garage on Bodfari Road was previously the site of a small brick and tile works.

Galltfaenan Hall is today a residential care home situated a mile and a half west of Trefnant. Originally known as Alltvaynan it was owned by the Ravenscrofts of Bretton in Flintshire. It was purchased by a branch of the Salusbury family of Lleweni (Flintshire) in the early 16th century and continued in the male line until 1731 when Edward Salusbury died and bequeathed the estate to his niece, Elizabeth Welshman. She married Dr John Jones of Penyfed, Llangwm and their daughter Margaret dying childless bequeathed Galltfaenan to Colonel John Lloyd, her cousin's son, on condition that he adopted the Salusbury name. His eldest daughter, Anna Maria, to whom the estate passed, married Townshend Mainwaring of Marchwiel Hall, in 1837. Their heir was Charles Salusbury Mainwaring whose son sold Galltfaenan to Sir Ernest Tate who, in 1918, had instigated the merger of Tate's Sugar with the Lyle Company which produced golden syrup and treacle. Sir Ernest died in 1939. The house was remodelled in 1810 by Colonel Salusbury and again by his son-in-law in the 1860s. Sir Ernest Tate added a wing designed by F.C. Saxon while interior work was carried out by Waring and Gillow.

Llanerch Hall is Grade II* Listed and lies a mile north of the village. Known in the later medieval period as Lleweni Vechan, it was described by its 1523 owner, the poet Gryffydd ap Ieuan as *"a high-crested, too long sided, loose-eaved, short-raftered, rambling, soot-accumulating old ornament of ancient workmanship"*. The hall was renamed in the early 17th century and rebuilt in the Jacobean style by its then owner Sir Peter Mutton. Sir Peter was a lawyer and subsequently a judge. He served as M.P. for Denbighshire representing the Salusbury interests and later M.P. for Caernarvonshire representing the Wynns of Gwydr. His son-in-law Mutton Davies laid out elaborate terraced gardens in the 1660s said to have been one of the most important in Wales. One description was *"in the foreign taste, with images and water tricks. Among the rest you were led to a sun-dial, which as you approached spouted in your face"*. Another description was *"The gardens were formerly laid out by Mutton Davies, Esq. on his return from visiting Italy, in the foreign outrageously unnatural style, with formal walks, dipt trees, and hydraulic statues"*. They were however destroyed in the 19th century. Llanerch Hall itself was remodelled in 1772 and again in 1862 by Whitehall Dod, Deputy Lieutenant of Denbighshire and High Sheriff of Flintshire. Dod was a descendant of Mutton Davies. Today the Hall is divided into 13 apartments and the grounds form the North Wales Golf Course.

Tregeiriog Settlement on the Ceiriog

Situated a mile and a half north-east of Llanarmon Duffryn Ceiriog on the B4500, is the small hamlet of Tregeieriog. According to local tradition this was once a sizeable town with a church. Ploughing has uncovered considerable amounts of stone and paving. The substantial farmhouse north of the crossroads known as Pen-y-Rhewl or Pen yr Hewl (Head of the Street) also suggests a larger settlement.

Gwynfa Welsh Wesleyan Methodist Chapel on the main road was built in 1861 but has now been converted to residential use. On the side road to the north is Tregeiriog Welsh Calvinistic Methodist Chapel which was built in 1804 and rebuilt in 1878, when the architect was Richard Owen of Liverpool.

South of the crossroads is the 18th century single arched Pont y Felin across the Ceiriog. Tregeiriog Mill produced flour and was fed by a mill race which ran 633 yards from the river. Borrow described the scene thus: "*The bridge was small and presented nothing remarkable in itself: I obtained, however, as I looked over its parapet towards the west a view of a scene, not of wild grandeur, but of something which I like better, which richly compensated me for the slight trouble I had taken in stepping aside to visit the little bridge. About a hundred yards distant was a small water-mill, built over the rivulet, the wheel going slowly, slowly round; large quantities of pigs, the generality of them brindled, were either browsing on the banks or lying close to the sides half immersed in the water; one immense white hog, the monarch seemingly of the herd, was standing in the middle of the current. Such was the scene which I saw from the bridge, a scene of quiet rural life well suited to the brushes of two or three of the old Dutch painters, or to those of men scarcely inferior to them in their own style, Gainsborough, Moreland, and Crome.*"

Trevor Welsh: Trefor meaning Large Village (a corruption of Tref Fawr)

Trevor lies between Llangollen and Ruabon and stands on the Llangollen canal to the north of the Pontcysyllte Aqueduct (see Froncysyllte). The village is relatively modern. In 1801 the parish of Llangollen consisted of three portions, one of which was the Traian Trevor which contained the townships of Trevor Uchaf and Trevor Isaf. It is unclear whether the Trevor family gave their name to the area or vice versa. The village is not shown on the 1875 Ordnance Survey map other than Trevor Station. The area north of the aqueduct is shown as Pont Cysyllte. The Trevor family claim descent from

Tudur Trevor, the son-in-law of Hywel Dda. The surname was said to have been fixed in the 15th century, but John Trevor was appointed Bishop of St Asaph in 1346 when his uncle Griffin de Trevor refused the appointment. Bishop John Trevor is claimed to have resided at Trevor Hall and to have built a stone bridge at Llangollen though the present bridge dates from the time of Elizabeth I.

The Grade I Listed early Georgian brick built Trevor Hall is situated in 150 acres of garden and woodland, three quarters of a mile west of the village of Trevor. The male line of this branch of the Trevor family ended in the 18th century and the heiress Mary Trevor married John Lloyd of Glanhavon, Montgomeryshire in 1715. They rebuilt the hall in 1742-3 to designs thought to be of Richard Trubshaw of Staffordshire. The house was extended in 1800 with alterations in 1870 when the tenant was James Coster Edwards the founder of the J.C. Edwards Ruabon Brick and Tile Company. The house remained with the Edwards family until 1956 when the lease was surrendered and the estate sold to a local timber merchant. He felled many of the trees but failed in his attempt to demolish the hall and build four houses on the site and a preservation order was placed on the house. In 1961 it was purchased by the Dudley branch of the W.R.V.S. for use as a children's home but fire partly destroyed the hall in 1963. A local farmer purchased the hall, installed a flat roof and used it for his cattle. In 1987 it was purchased by chartered surveyor Michael Tree who set about renovation, installing a modern hipped roof. In 1998 Tree sold the Hall to the Parker family who now operate Trevor Hall as 'A Luxury Private Hire Stately Home', available for holidays and weddings.

Trevor church was built by the Lloyd family in 1717 as their private chapel. It is thought to have been built on the site of an earlier chapel used by the Trevor family with links to Valle Crucis Abbey. The chapel was consecrated as a chapel of ease to Llangollen in 1777, serving the hamlets of Trevor Uchaf and Trevor Isaf. The east window was replaced in 1841, having been blown out by a gale during a service in 1837. The box pews were added at this time, as was a gallery which has since been removed. A simple single cell building there is a western bellcote above the west door. A small vestry was added in the late 19th century.

1200 yards north of Trevor Hall in Tower Wood stands Trevor Tower, also known as King William's Tower. It was built in 1827 as a hunting lodge with a gamekeeper's house attached with an underground passage between the two. Some sources suggest that it was built by George Hammond Whalley, but he was only born in 1813 and was brought up in Gloucestershire. He succeeded to the Plas Madoc estate at Ruabon on the death of his mother in 1838. Whalley was prominent in North Wales. A barrister, he was High Sheriff of Caernarvonshire in 1852 and subsequently Deputy Lieutenant of Denbighshire, Merionethshire and Montgomeryshire. He was chairman of the Llanidloes & Newtown Railway and the Mid Wales Railway and owner and founder of the Cefn and Rhosymedre Water Co. An Anglican, he was a staunch adversary of Roman Catholicism. His ancestor Edward Whalley was a cousin of Oliver Cromwell and one of the judges at the trial of Charles I. George Hammond Whalley stood unsuccessfully for the Montgomeryshire seat for Parliament in 1852. He was eventually elected as member for Peterborough in 1859 and remained an M.P. until his death in 1878 despite having been jailed for contempt of court. He died insolvent at King William's Tower in 1878 and was buried at Ruabon. The origin of the name of the tower is also in dispute. It is suggested that it occupies the site of a castle built by William II, but a more likely explanation given his anti Roman Catholic views is that it was named by Whalley after William III. The three storey castellated tower has 16 pane tracery windows to each floor. The lead from the roof was stolen in the 1950s and the tower has been allowed to deteriorate. In addition to the cottage there were dog kennels and a pheasant breeding ground.

The area around the village of Trevor was important as the junction of the Llangollen and Ellesmere Canals. The Ellesmere Canal terminates north of the aqueduct with what was an early transfer dock between canal and railway. The earliest part of the village was just north of the River Dee. Between the B5434 and the river was Yr Hen Gapel a Welsh Calvinistic Methodist chapel built in 1824. It was demolished in 1905 after the building of Bryn Seion on Station Road in 1903. The red brick Bryn Seion ,which is Grade II Listed, was converted to an antiques centre in 1994. The Telford Inn was formerly known as Scotch Hall and was built to house the site manager for the building of the canal and aqueduct.

Trevor Uchaf (Higher Trevor)

Trevor Uchaf is located on the hillside above the A539 a mile west of Trevor Hall. Until the opening of the canal this was an agricultural area but in the early 19th century intensive limestone quarrying and lime production began. The housing which accommodated quarrymen and limekiln workers has now been modernised and offer superb views across the Dee. There are the remains of lime kilns and traces of the tracks which conveyed the limestone and lime to the wharf on the canal. The Sun Inn, now known as the Sun Trevor, marks the entrance to the scattered hamlet where Soar Welsh Independent Chapel was built in 1840 though is now a private house. The industry declined at the start of the 20th century and gave way to tourism with the popular Panorama Walk, a track following the contours below the quarries. To the east of Sun Trevor is Plas Ifa, a 17th century farmhouse altered in 1865. It was a Quaker Meeting House and alleged to be the one time home of John ap John, known as the Apostle of Quakers in Wales.

Trevor Isaf, Garth and Garth Trevor
(Lower Trevor, Mountain Ridge and Trevor Mountain Ridge)

Trevor Isaf, Garth and Garth Trevor lie along Garth Road which rises from the A539 at the Aussie Rooster, formerly the Australian Arms public house. The former agricultural area developed in the early 19th century with lime kilns and a small coal mine. From the mid 19th century employment also included the Garth Brickworks. Garth had an early Government School. Brynhyfryd Calvinistic Methodist chapel was rebuilt in 1847 and altered in 1885 when a schoolroom was added. It is now converted to private accommodation. Noddfa Welsh Baptist Chapel at the junction with Trevor Hall Road was built in 1834 but has also been converted for residential use. Just behind the Aussie Rooster, Seion English Presbyterian Chapel was built in 1905 to the design of architect Trefor Hall of Trevor. It too is now a private house.

The Oaks development near the Aussie Rooster occupies the site of the former brickworks. Moses Evans left the area in 1851 for Australia where he made his fortune in the gold fields. He returned some 10 years later and built the Australian Arms and also rented the brickworks which he renamed the Australia Brickworks. (They were also known as the Garth Brickworks.) Producing a silica brick, the silica was brought from Garth Mountain by an aerial ropeway. The brickworks had a chequered history following the bankruptcy of Moses Evans in 1866 and had numerous owners until closure in 1979. Following his bankruptcy Moses Evans continued his quest for gold and in 1888 discovered gold in Flintshire. He was granted the rights by the Crown to mine 100 acres for gold and silver.

Trofarth

Trofarth, four and a half miles south of Colwyn Bay, is a scattered agricultural community created a parish in 1873 when the church of St John was built to the designs of Sir George Gilbert Scott. A vestry was added in 1899 as part of a restoration in memory of Major General E.W.L. Wynne of Coed Coch who had served at the siege of Sebastopol in 1855. This small church was declared redundant and permission given for conversion to private accommodation in 2009. Externally there is a bellcote beneath a spirelet at the western end, with a south porch and a slate roof with Westmoreland slate forming decorative bands.

A National School was established 500 yards to the south, now a private dwelling. A mile to the south-west of the church on the B5113 is The Holland Arms.

Valle Crucis (see Llanegwestl)

Ysbyty Ifan Hospital of St John

Ysbyty Ifan is an attractive village of mainly stone built terraced cottages on the River Conwy seven miles west of Cerrigydrudion. Now incorporated in the county of Conwy, the river formed the boundary between Denbighshire and Caernarvonshire with the village divided between the two old counties. Prior to 1190 the village was known as Dôl Gynwal (Welsh for Gynwal's Meadow) and was on an ancient pilgrims' road to Bardsey. The Knights Hospitallers of St John established a commandery and hospice for pilgrims that was endowed by Llewelyn the Great in 1221-4. The commandery owned the lordship and manor of Ysbyty, the chapel and mill of Penmachno, the manor and church of Carno, the church of Tregynon (Montgomeryshire) and the granges of Gwanas and Llanwddyn. After the dissolution of the moasteries under Henry VIII the church of St John became the parish church and in 1600 the Hospital was replaced by the foundation of some alms-houses by Richard Vaughan.

It is claimed that the Red Bandits of Mawddwy, a group of red headed men used Ysbyty Ifan as a hideout, taking advantage of its privilege of sanctuary. They murdered the Sheriff of Meirionethshire, Baron Lewis ap Owen, on 12th October 1555.

The church of St John the Baptist was repaired and partially rebuilt in 1790 before being demolished in 1858 and rebuilt in Victorian Early English style by local architect George Benmore, re-opening in 1861. It contains a number of tombs and effigies from the old church including Marared ferch Hywel, who married Hywel ap Cynwrig of Plas Iolyn. His grandfather Cynwrig ap Llywarch is remembered by another slab with a sword and shield as 'Kynwricus Filius Lywarch'. Marared and Hywel's great-grandson was Rhys ap Maredudd of Foelas whose alabaster effigy and those of his wife and son Robert are at the western end of the church. In the summer of 1485 Rhys led a local army in support of Henry Tudor and carried the banner of the Red Dragon of Cadwaladr on the battlefield at Bosworth. It is claimed that Rhys dealt the fatal blow to Richard III although the same claim is made for Rhys ap Thomas who led an army from Dyfed. Robert ap Rhys was chaplain to Cardinal Wolsey and it is conjectured that he commissioned the effigies in London. Robert's grandson Tomos Prys is buried at Ysbyty Ifan. Tomos was a poet adventurer and buccaneer who built a residence from the ruins of the monastery on Bardsey Island. Having sailed with Raleigh and Drake, Tomos claimed to be along with Captain William Myddelton and Captain Thomas Koet the first to smoke tobacco publicly on the streets of London. (Details of Foelas and Plas Iolyn are given under Pentrefoelas.) The old church had transepts containing the Pant Glas and Foelas chapels. The Victorian church has a five bay nave with arched-braced collar trusses, the braces resting on moulded corbels set against the walls. There are commemorative windows to the Pierce family of Plas Uchaf and memorial brasses to the Gethin family. The chancel has two bays with a roof of similar structure to the nave. There is a south porch and a western double bellcote. The old boiler room to the north-east now forms the vestry with its own entry door.

Seion Welsh Calvinistic Methodist Chapel on Chapel Street was built in 1803, rebuilt in 1855, and 1893 but is no longer in use. The chapel overlooks the village rugby pitch.

The village school and the old corn mill with wheel intact lie on the Caernarvonshire side of the river as does the former Penrhyn Arms.

The area around the village was part of the Penrhyn Estate which has been in the hands of the National Trust since 1951. At 20,316 acres it is one of the Trust's largest agricultural estates with 51 farms and 30 houses. Abraham Lincoln's great-grandmother Ellen Morris was born within the parish at the now derelict farmhouse Bryngwyn.

Bibliography

Baring-Gould, Sabine and Fisher, John 1913, 2005 reprint. *The Lives of the British Saints:The Saints of Wales, Cornwall and Irish Saints.* Kessinger Publishing 2005
Borrow, George 1862 *Wild Wales: Its People, Language and Scenery*
Burke, Bernard Sir 1879 *Genealogical and Heraldic History of the Landed Gentry*
Burke, Bernard Sir 1869 *Genealogical and Heraldic Dictionary of the Peerage and Baronetage of the British Empire*
Cliffe, Charles Frederick 1851 *The Book of North Wales*
Evans, Rev. J. 1812 *The Beauties of England and Wales or Original Deliniations, Topographical Descriptive and Historical of Each County Vol XVII Part 1*
Henry, Gastineau 1830 *Wales Illustrated in a Series of Views*
Hicklin, John 1853 *The Illustrated Handbook of North Wales*
Hubbard, Edward 1986 *Clwyd, Debighshire and Flintshire* Yale University Press
Jones 1810 *Wales Illustrated in a Series of Views*
Lewis, Samuel 1848 *A Topographical Dictionary of Wales*
Nicholas, Thomas 1872 *Annals and Antiquities of the Counties and County Families of Wales* Republished 2000 by Genealogical Publishing Com.
Palmer, Alfred Neobard 1903 *History of the Thirteen Country Townships of the Old Parish of Wrexham, and of the Townships of Burras Riffri, Erlas, & Erddig: Being the Fifth and Last Part of "A History of the Town and Parish of Wrexham".*
Pennant, Thomas 1810 *Tours in Wales with Notes*
Sykes, Wirt 1880 *British Goblins: Welsh folk-lore, fairy mythology, legends and traditions*

Online Resources:
Archaeologia Cambrensis
National Library of Wales Dictionary of Welsh Biography
www.map.coflein.gov.uk
www.britishlistedbuildings.co.uk
http://welshjournals.llgc.org.uk/

Also from Sigma Leisure:

Monmouthshire Villages
Geoffrey Davies
The villages of the old county of Monmouthshire reflect the history of this border county. As well as highlighting the well known beauty spots in villages along the River Wye and the many castles and Roman remains, some hidden gems are revealed like the roodscreen and loft in St Jerome's church at Llangwm and the isolated church at Kilgwrrwg along with legends of fairies in Abertysswg and Bassaleg being the birthplace of the Arthurian Merlin.
£8.99

Vale of Glamorgan Villages
Geoffrey Davies
Through the ages the wealthy have chosen to live in the Vale, from the Norman conquerors who built the castles and the coal and iron magnates of the 19th century who constructed luxurious mansions, to the pop stars, footballers, businessmen and politicians of today who see the area as an attractive peaceful haven. The villages of the Vale are rich in history and legend and this book gives a brief description of each, their attractions and a little of their history.
£8.99

All of our books are all available on-line at **www.sigmapress.co.uk** or through booksellers. For a free catalogue, please contact:

Sigma Leisure, Stobart House, Pontyclerc, Penybanc Road, Ammanford, Carmarthenshire SA18 3HP
Tel: 01269 593100   Fax: 01269 596116

info@sigmapress.co.uk   www.sigmapress.co.uk